AF471072

How to Produce
Concert Versions
of
GILBERT & SULLIVAN

by

IAN TAYLOR

ROBERT HALE & COMPANY
63, Old Brompton Road, London S.W.7

PRINTED IN GREAT BRITAIN BY
BRISTOL TYPESETTING CO. LTD.
BARTON MANOR - ST. PHILIPS
BRISTOL

To

JOY

whose companionship in Gilbert and Sullivan
study and performance is a constant delight;
and with gratitude for her advice on costuming

ACKNOWLEDGEMENTS

My thanks to Messrs. Macmillan and Co., Ltd., for permission to quote extracts from *The Savoy Operas* by Sir W. S. Gilbert; Messrs. G. Bell and Sons, Ltd., for permission to quote from *The Pinafore Picture Book* by W. S. Gilbert.

Ian Taylor

St. John's College, York.
1972.

CONTENTS

1

THE ISSUES

Reasons for Presenting Concert Versions

The operas of Gilbert and Sullivan are masterpieces of construction for full stage performance. There is a consistency of standard in music, libretto, lyrics and dramatic situation which is frequently lacking in other light operas or musicals, where either music or libretto is inferior to the other. The very fact that these operas are referred to as 'G and S' proves the point — equal status is given to librettist and composer. Of how many other works can the same be said? Can one, for instance, name off-hand, the librettists of *Merrie England* or *The Merry Widow*?

Yet, having said this, one admits the distinct feasibility and desirability of presenting concert versions of the Savoy Operas. Obviously such presentations are far less costly — an important issue where amateur societies are concerned. But other reasons can be advanced, giving justification on artistic as well as financial grounds

1. Very useful means for a newly established society to raise funds for future stage productions.
2. For fund raising between stage productions.
3. Less time is required for rehearsal. Two stage productions a year might well tax the time commitments of members of amateur societies. To present one stage production annually means either protracted, and so boring, nine-month rehearsal time, or a lively six-month effort with the consequence of a fallow and interest-sapping half year of nothingness. Therefore — to present one stage and one concert version per annum keeps society enthusiasm high.
4. Allows lesser known works to be studied — and presented to a public possibly unaware of them.

   Finance enters into this argument again. A society must watch box-office appeal. To stage *The Sorcerer* might be a grave financial loss in that smallish audiences for a week would in no way compensate for hire of theatre, costumes and orchestra. But the attendance figures for a three-night-stand concert version would more than offset the limited cost of that presentation. An opera such as *Utopia Limited* requires superb scenery and magnificent costuming, as well as a large company for stage production. Even assuming packed houses, which is unlikely, financial loss could be incurred. The concert version obviates these difficulties.

5. Allows works to be presented which may stretch vocal and acting resources of a company if staged. For example, *The Yeomen of the Guard* and *The Pirates of Penzance* have split male chorus. A company with, say, a male chorus of a dozen, may well cope musically; but visually, four 'crowd' men and eight yeomen is barely acceptable, while a fight between these numbers of pirates and police is hardly convincing!

6. Gives opportunity for good solo singers who, on account of being poor speakers, never attain principal parts.

7. For schools and colleges examination time-tabling frequently prevents sufficient rehearsal time for a full stage production. Yet a static 'music only' performance holds a limited appeal to youth, who prefer the freedom that movement and dance bring, and enjoy the mingling with partners and fellows that acting allows. These concert version presentations will fulfil in a large measure youthful extrovert desires, while not being over-consuming as to time.

The Problems of Presenting Concert Versions

THE APPROACH

There are three basic approaches to presenting concert versions of light opera.

1. As a concert — using scores.
   Narration — by a speaker.
   This method is completely static, oratorio-like and entirely alien to the spirit of the 'G and S' works.

2. As a concert — using scores.
   Narration — by a principal player, as link-man.
   Still too staid, although the principal keeping in character to unfold the story, makes a communication bridge between audience and players.

3. Without scores.
   Narration — by a principal player, as link-man.

The abandoning of scores lends an air of much greater emotional involvement in the actual situations emerging as the plot proceeds, and makes the link-man's task much easier as he can make reference to the players as participants in the drama, rather than, as in 1. and 2., mere commentators.

It is with method 3. this book is concerned; and, as will be seen, this approach can be made remarkably life-like.

STAGING

Assumptions

Concert versions are unlikely to be given in a real theatre. The probable place would be a public or school hall, or art gallery. One expects, therefore:

Only some form of platform or stage,
No proscenium arch,
No curtains,
No stage lighting,
Probably only *one* entrance.

Rostra, however, can usually be borrowed or manufactured cheaply.
Accompaniment — one or two pianos.
All Productions provided are based on these minimum provisions.

Seating Plans

   1. Basic.

      4 rows (dependent on numbers), 3 raised.

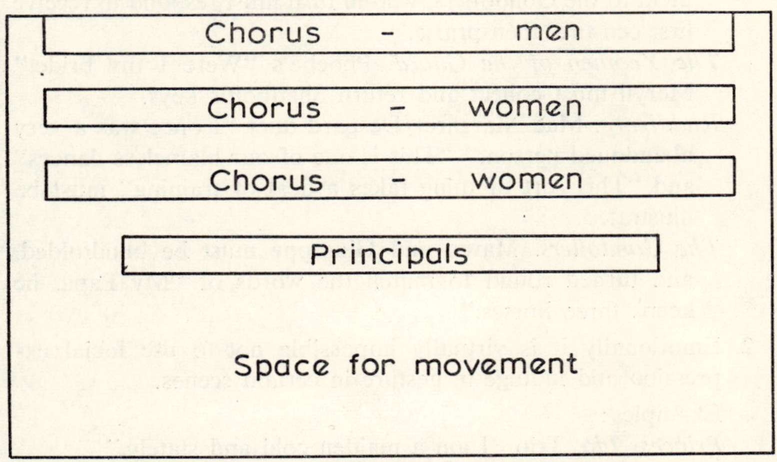

(See *Princess Ida* for illustration of this plan)

2. Alternatives.

Dependent on — size and shape of platform, balance in numbers of vocal parts (chorus), musical director's requirements for tonal balance, time for rehearsal.

The great variation possible from the Basic 1. , but still using only rostra, chairs and stools, can be seen by studying the complete range of Seating Plans.

3. Scenic Design.

Where a company possesses a scenic designer of talent and a team of enthusiastic workers, for a relatively small additional cost such furnishing as arches or draped screens can add tremendously to the total impact. (See *The Yeomen of the Guard*.) But as these items must be designed with a specific hall in mind and adapted to suit its dimensions and background, for this reason particularly — quite apart from that of cost — this aspect is not developed herein.

ACTING

A decision not to use scores brings the immediate question, "Is action necessary?" The answer must be "Yes" for the following reasons.

1. Specific cases where action is imperative.

Some examples prove the point:

The Gondoliers. "Gavotte". The Duke must illustrate deportment to the Gondoliers, who in turn must respond to receive first censure, then praise.

The Yeomen of the Guard. Phoebe's "Were I thy bride." Meryll must collect and return Shadbolt's keys.

Ruddigore. Mad Margaret/Despard duet "I once was a very abandoned person." "This is one of our blameless dances" and "This sort of thing takes a deal of training" must be illustrated.

The Gondoliers. Marco and Giuseppe must be blindfolded, and turned round to match the words of "My Papa, he keeps three horses."

2. Emotionally it is virtually impossible not to use facial expression and indulge in gesture in certain scenes.

Examples:

Princess Ida. Trio "I am a maiden cold and stately."

The Gondoliers. Quartet "Now Marco, dear". Could any

actor/actress play this moving farewell 'dead-pan' and motionless?

H.M.S. Pinafore. Trio "Never mind the why and wherefore."

Can Sir Joseph be restrained from ringing different 'bells'?

Accepting that there must be some action, the next problem is, in the context of a concert version, how much? Experienced actors (principals and chorus) *will* act; the inexperienced will be uncertain. Result — a mixture of over-acting (in the circumstances) and tentative, unconvincing, embarrassing attempts.

It is *essential* to have a producer (often neglected in concert performances). In a sense his task may be even harder than for a stage version, as he must suggest characterisation, without full opportunity to attain his desires; and he must modify and restrain actors who try to give a full characterisation relevant only to the staged version.

Suggestions for Production
Chorus — stylised gesture with limited movement.
Principals — full action within the limits of planned stylisation.

COSTUME

1. A unity of style is most desirable.
2. An untidy, unformalised hotch-potch of attire ruins the total standard of performance, and lowers the status of the company in the eyes of the audience.
3. Nothing is more distracting to the eye than a miscellany of lounge suits and different ties for gentlemen; and, even more, different styles, colours and textures of ladies' dresses, ranging from mini to maxi through blouse and skirt and cocktail dresses.
4. Principals must be in some way distinctive, or they will be absorbed within the chorus, with consequent underplaying of their roles.

It is, of course, one thing to raise objections, another to overcome the practical difficulties. A general statement of advice cannot be given. Each opera must be 'costumed' to suit its needs, and suggestions will be made for each — taking as a first principle, the necessity of keeping expense to a minimum.

It is *essential* to have a costume advisor/wardrobe mistress.

Summary of Essentials for Concert Version Presentation

Music	Abandon scores.
Narrative	By a principal as link-man.
Acting	Limited stylised gesture.
	Producer essential.
	Stage-manager essential.
Costume	Unity of a style a prerequisite.
	Wardrobe-mistress essential.

2

NOTES ON THE TEXTS

In the following pages eleven of the fourteen operas of Gilbert and Sullivan are considered. They are taken in chronological order of writing. Each is provided with a narrative script for a principal as link-man, and followed by a production plot (in the case of *The Yeomen of the Guard* and *Utopia Limited* these are supplied side by side as most fitting to the smooth linkage of narrative and action) and suggestions for costuming.

The operas omitted are *Thespis*, *Trial by Jury* and *The Grand Duke*. Nothing can be done for *Thespis*, as virtually all the music is lost; *Trial by Jury* is already in suitable form for concert version performance. Justification however, must be made for the exclusion of *The Grand Duke*. The last opera written jointly by the partners, it was considered a failure at the time, and it is doubtful if many stage productions of it have been seen since 1896. The contemporary criticism of the work suggested the partners' creative muse was played out—and time has done little to change that opinion. Largely the music is pedestrian; the plot laborious. It is this last which is one reason for not considering a concert version presentation. The story being unknown, the narrator(s) would be faced with a most unenviable task of revealing its tedious complexities. To maintain sparkling linkage between music would be well-nigh impossible, and the audience would look in vain for relief from a dull script in the compensation of bright musical numbers. Even accepting these facts, a concert version of the type designed here is impossible. In Act II of *The Grand Duke*, Gilbert calls specifically for the theatrical company to be dressed in the costumes of *Troilus and Cressida*. No 'mock-up' for these is possible. They would have to be hired. Were this done, the admixture with the modern-style dress of the other players would be incongruous. Thus the entire work would require authentic costuming. Since it has been taken throughout this book that expense must be kept to a minimum — so envisaging no costume hire — Gilbert's direction on dress is the over-riding factor which precludes the inclusion of *The Grand Duke* here.

Narrative

Where necessary, short notes are given to account for the choice of principal(s) as narrator(s). (For *The Gondoliers* an alternative is supplied.) While the selection has been made with the greatest care to provide the most appropriate characters to tell the story — taking into account the necessity to be informative without being 'wordy', to maintain flow, to provide characterisation — it is recognised that within a specific company an outstanding individual — called upon to play a role other than the narrator's character herein provided — may be the most suitable choice as narrator. In this situation another script could be written, taking the examples here as models. And it will be noted how wide is the range of possibilities for narration — sometimes male, sometimes female; couples or groups; on occasion going straight to a page of libretto; with approaches using past tense, or present tense, and anticipation by future tense. In some instances it is admissible, in order to establish continuity, to transpose the order of musical numbers — but great caution must be exercised as Gilbert and his partner were masters in the ordering of items in balanced fashion.

Notation

The notation used is: X — male
O — female
(number ringed) ④ — principal's seat

An individual notation for principals is given.

Technical terms are kept to a minimum and confined to:

L — stage left, i.e. left facing audience
R — stage right
(Stage) centre is written in full except for L.C., R.C. — left centre, right centre.

Seating

The basic seating plan is shown first, then amplified. It is important to observe the following points:

Rostra should be broad enough to take chairs and allow for easy walking movement in front of them.

Unless otherwise stated, rostra should be 15 to 18 inches high — which necessitates a double step to reach each level.

To show the steps on a two-dimensional sketch, without using perspective, means that the area of floor occupied by the rostra appears greater than it is. Thus:

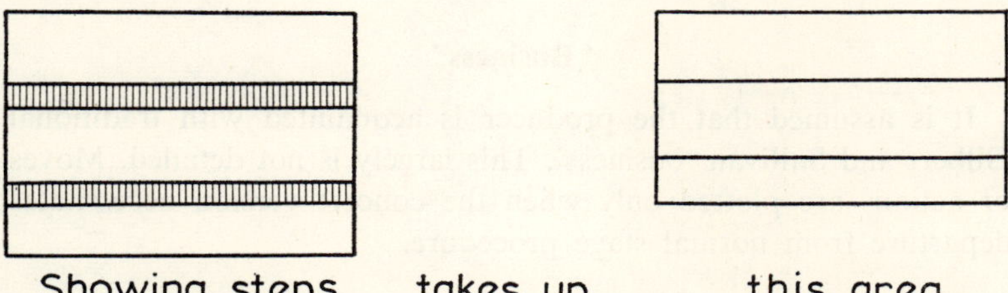

Unless otherwise stated X, O, ④ on Basic Seating Plan have chairs provided.

On large diagrams positions are plotted to scale, but inset sketches showing positions of two or three players at one instance, are not necessarily to scale.

Size of Company

In general, plotting is for a chorus of approximately twenty women and twelve men. (A *Ruddigore* option offers a total company of twenty-two.) It is impossible to lay down numbers exactly — even within two years the strength of a society can change radically, particularly in the balance for vocal division. Where the inevitable small alterations must be made, the producer, having satisfied the musical director's requirements, should bear in mind the necessity of balanced 'picture' groupings.

References

LIBRETTI

There are so many editions of libretti, some bound and page numbered straight through, that it is impossible to quote page references.

VOCAL SCORES

The items are listed as V.S. No. 5, etc., but a word of warning is necessary here. The numbers may alter depending on the date of publication of the score. Pre-World War I scores (and there are many in existence and worthy of study for subtle variations) list the numbers consecutively from Act I through Act II. Most modern scores recommence at No. 1 from Act II.

' Business '

It is assumed that the producer is acquainted with traditional Gilbert and Sullivan 'business'. This largely is not detailed. Moves or actions are plotted only when the concert version necessitates departure from normal stage procedure.

Costuming

Costume suggestions are provided to convey the essence of a style of 'costuming' rather than as models to be copied slavishly. In individual cases, where a player's physique or acting ability is of particular note, a radical change would be in order. (See *The Pirates of Penzance* — alternative costume for Ruth. The wearing of such a costume is dependent on having an actress of shapely physique, capable of playing a 'mannish' woman.) Thus the framework of costuming is provided, leaving the alert producer the chance to seize upon practical opportunties as various circumstances permit.

List of Narrators for the Operas

The Sorcerer	Dr. Daly
H.M.S. Pinafore	Dick Deadeye
The Pirates of Penzance	Samuel
Patience	Patience, Angela, Saphir
Iolanthe	Celia, Leila
Princess Ida	Hilarion, Cyril, Florian *et al*
The Mikado	Pooh-Bah
Ruddigore	Dame Hannah
The Yeomen of the Guard	Narrator
The Gondoliers	Don Alhambra or Giuseppe
Utopia Limited	King Paramount

3

THE SORCERER

Note on Dr. Daly as Narrator

One might argue that Alexis, Sir Marmaduke or the Sorcerer could act as narrator, but each choice would have shortcomings. It would be difficult for Alexis to confess his gradual disillusionment with his own scheme; it would be incongruous for Marmaduke to be seen in love with Mrs. Partlet yet have to comment on the ludicrous situation of their pairing; while Wells would have to return from Hades to narrate!

From the negative, therefore, all points to Dr. Daly as narrator. When the positive aspects of having him in this role are examined, the choice becomes inevitable. His regret at his continued bachelordom, particularly when all are coupled bar himself, stresses the main theme of love matches — and Dr. Daly up to this point appears almost as a fore-runner of Bunthorne in being left brideless. As he has hinted in the script that he is now married, when Aline and he fall in love, the effect is dramatic, in that the audience will wonder if this is to be the final pairing. It is for this reason of stressing the love element that Dr. Daly's solo is transposed to start the performance.

The final justification for his being selected as narrator is that, as a churchman, he would be accustomed to addressing gatherings; and he should thus appear, in his mannered clerical way, to be regaling the audience with the daily news of his parish.

Script for Dr. Daly as Narrator

ACT I

Overture.
V.S. No. 3. *Recit*. "The air is charged."
V.S. No. 3a. *Ballad*. "Time was when love and I." (Stop after solo.)
DR. DALY My dear friends and brethren, Time spares no man, and I am no exception to his ruling. I am getting on in years —

some would say I am an old fogey — and I always felt that a help-mate would cheer my declining days. My little ballad which always proved so popular on my rendition of it at the Women's Guild Social Evenings, was in very deed my own story. I felt that I had left things too late — that I should live and die a solitary old bachelor. Still, Love cometh to all who yearn for it, 'tis said. So it proved for me. But Cupid wounded more than me with his darts — his shafts touched every one of my parishioners. As I recall, he began the busy bending of his bow at a celebration in the grounds of Sir Marmaduke Pointdextre's mansion.

V.S. No. 1. *Chorus*. "Ring forth, ye bells."

V.S. No. 2. *Recit*. "Constance, my daughter."

V.S. No. 3. *Song*. "When he is here."

DR. DALY Ah! The good widow Mrs. Partlet, my honest pew opener, and her daughter Constance. Poor girl, she appeared to have conceived some romantic affection for my humble self. A comely maiden indeed — but I felt, at this time, that the differences in our ages would militate against our union. With some fluttering at my heart, I watched her depart disconsolate — and turned to find the vigorous Alexis and his father, my old friend, at my side.

V.S. No. 3a. (continued). *Recit*. "Sir Marmaduke — my dear young friend, Alexis."

DR. DALY (Speaking through music)

May fortune bless you! may the middle distance
Of your young life be as pleasant as the foreground —
The joyous foreground! and, when you have reached it,
May that which is now the far-off horizon
(But that which will then become the middle distance),
In fruitful promise be exceeded only
By that which will have opened, in the meantime,
Into a new and glorious horizon!

V.S. No. 5. *Chorus*. "With heart and with voice."

V.S. No. 6. *Recit/Song*. "My kindly friends" / "Oh happy young heart."

V.S. No. 7. *Recit*. "My child."

V.S. No. 8. *Chorus*. "With heart and with voice."

V.S. No. 9. *Duet*. "Welcome, joy."

V.S. No. 10. *Ensemble*. "All is prepared."

V.S. No. 11. *Ballad*. "For love alone."

DR. DALY Yes, indeed, Alexis held noble principles. So happy was he with his beloved Aline, that he wished all to share the joy that Love can bring. But he was no idle visionary. Determined to implement his theories, he had engaged the services of J. W. Wells and Co., the old established family sorcerers of St. Mary Axe. By the art of the alchemist, they had discovered a philtre, a love-potion, reputed to be infallible. Despite Aline's misgivings. Alexis was insistent that all the villagers should partake of it, and so learn the secret of pure and lasting happiness.

V.S. No. 12. *Song.* "My name is John Wellington Wells."

DR. DALY Alexis, assuring Mr. Wells of his purely philanthropical motives for distributing the philtre, learnt that it would prove efficacious within half an hour of its being partaken, and that, after losing consciousness for a period, the imbibers would fall in love with the first person of the opposite sex on whom their eyes fell. Accordingly, he ordered a tea-pot to be fetched so that Mr. Wells could prepare sufficient proportion of the potion to suffice the whole village population.

V.S. No. 13. *Incantation.* "Sprites of earth and air."

V.S. No. 14. *Finale Act I.*

ACT II

V.S. No. 15. *Trio/Chorus.* "'Tis twelve, I think" / "If you'll marry me."

V.S. No. 16. *Ensemble.* "Dear friends."

DR. DALY With the whole village paired, Alexis waxed eloquent to Aline on the success of his ploy, and asked her to observe the good that would become of these ill-assorted unions — how the miserly wife would check the reckless expenditure of her too frivolous consort; how the wealthy husband would shower innumerable bonnets on his penniless bride; and how the young lively spouse would cheer the declining days of her aged partner with comic songs unceasing. But one thing remained to be done to make his happiness complete. He desired of Aline to partake of the potion that he might be assured of her love for ever. Alas for him, the minds of womankind are ever contrary. Aline took some umbrage at the suggestion with its inference that he doubted her love. She refused, thereby bruising her lover's feelings rather badly.

V.S. No. 17. *Ballad.* "It is not love."

DR. DALY You will realise my friends, that at this time I had no inkling of these machinations. Knowing from experience that the village had not been addicted to marrying and giving in marriage, I was distinctly surprised when the whole body of the village implored me to join them in matrimony with the least possible delay. I said as much to Alexis and Aline, adding that his father had hinted that he, too, was like to be married 'ere long. The young couple were delighted, feeling that the union between Sir Marmaduke and Lady Sangazure would be a most happy circumstance.

I confess that melancholia overtook me when I realised that I alone of the entire village would be unmated. But my reverie was rudely disturbed by the arrival of Sir Marmaduke with his bride-to-be — not the expected Lady Sangazure — but humble Mrs. Partlet. Alexis was considerably taken aback at the difference of social status of the pair — and perhaps at this stage began to query the wisdom of his use of the philtre. Nevertheless, he wished his father every happiness with the choice of his heart.

V.S. No. 18. *Quintet*. "I rejoice that it's decided."

V.S. No. 19. *Recit and Duet*. "Oh I have wrought much evil."

V.S. No. 20. *Recit and Air*. "Alexis, doubt me not."

V.S. No. 21. *Song*. "Engaged to so-and-so."

V.S. No. 22. *Ensemble*. "Oh joyous boon."

V.S. No. 23. *Recit*. "Prepare for sad surprises."

DR. DALY I had no option but to interpose. I reasoned with Alexis that his fiancée had drunk the philtre at his insistence, and having met me instead of him, we both being under its influence, the result was inevitable. Then Mr. Wells, arriving with Lady Sangazure in hot pursuit, offered a solution to the dilemma. The entire spell could be removed by either him or Alexis yielding up their lives to Ahrimanes. With nobility of spirit, he left the decision to the company.

V.S. No. 24. *Finale Act II*.

Basic Seating Plan

NOTES

The 'set' (see facing figure) should suggest a garden fete. Thus:

1. The rostra for chorus suggest a tiered stand. There are no seats on it. Chorus sit on each step — and when standing are on step below.

2. N.B. Height of each step at least 15 inches.
   There is no need to have these steps broken by additional steps to allow for gracious movement. All chorus are villagers, accustomed to scrambling. For ladies to be assisted by men up the high steps adds to the rustic atmosphere.

3. Seating for principals — while satisfactory to have chairs, it
   is better for maintaining garden party atmosphere if ① ②,
   ③ ④, ⑤ ⑥ can be double garden seats.

4. The large table should be light-weight. A long trestle table is
   admirable. It need not be covered with a cloth. On it are
   placed trays of cups and saucers, plates of buns and sandwiches. Beneath it: two kettles, two tea-pots, tea caddy,
   cosy and small tray.

5. The two small tables should be more solid. The circular,
   tripod-legged Victorian type is ideal. Table L, to be covered
   with an antimacassar.

6. The chorus is positioned as shown so that pairings can be
   achieved without re-arrangement. Within the lay-out, the
   disposition of soprano, alto, tenor, bass is left to the musical
   director.

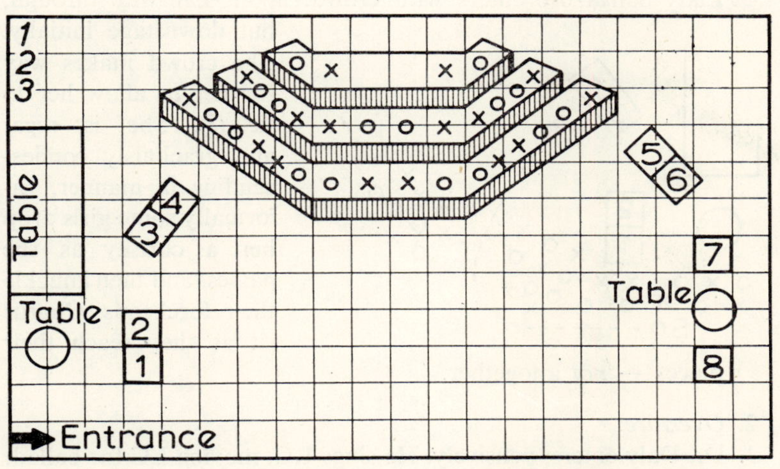

ROW 1 (Raised 3 steps) ROW 2 (Raised 2 steps)
ROW 3 (Raised 1 step)

PROPS

(apart from those listed above)

Act I.   Contract, fireworks.

Act II.   Lantern, ear trumpet, wine-glass.

M — Sir Marmaduke   S — Lady Sangazure
As — Alexis   A — Aline
D — Dr. Daly   P — Mrs. Partlet
N — Notary   C — Constance
W — John Wellington Wells

Production for Script with Dr. Daly as Narrator

ACT I

1. Chorus enter, paired, but not in formal lines. They should be in groups together, laughing and chatting. While basically they would be in order Row 1, 2, 3, a deliberate wrong placing or two, resulting in a scrambling for position, would be in keeping with the atmosphere of rural festivity.

   Places for the four ladies Row 3, centre, to be left vacant. Lady Sangazure enters with crowd, about half-way through, but downstage initially. The crowd makes way for her to allow her to sit ④. She is regal and graciously condescending in manner. Informally some girls drop her a curtsey as she passes, and men knuckle their foreheads. Chorus sit as they reach their places — *not* altogether.

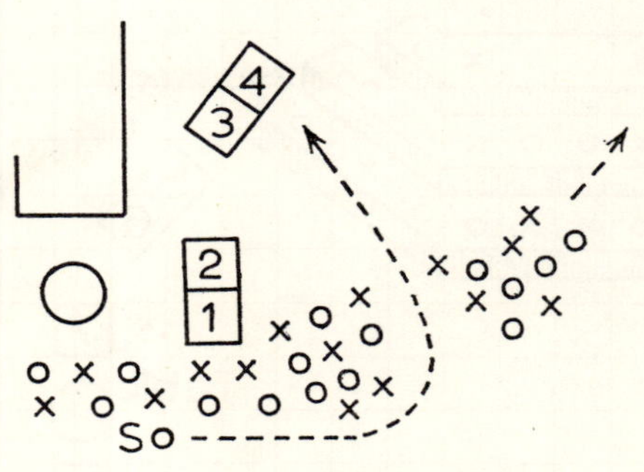

2. *Overture.*
3. Dr. Daly enters, pensively. He sings RC, moving LC for ballad. He delivers narrative from there, then sits ⑧.
4. *Opening chorus.* Chorus rise. In this and in all their singing, they should act with vivacity and carefree abandon, turning to each other, holding their partners, etc.

   At final "Ring forth, ye bells", Constance and Mrs. Partlet enter to RC and, sideways to audience, observe the gay scene. On last few bars, Constance turns away (i.e. to audience) with bowed head. Chorus sits.

5. "When he is here" (*Postlude*). Constance is led, disconsolate, by her mother to sit R, Constance ①, Mrs. Partlet ②.
As they turn away, Dr. Daly rises and comes LC.

6. *Narrative*. Dr. Daly delivers first sentence looking **R**, then faces audience. Marmaduke and Alexis enter as he is concluding, in time to be advancing RC as he ends.

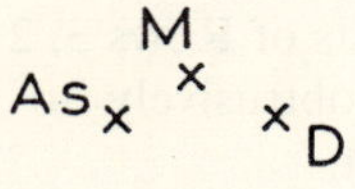

7. *Recit*. All meet centre, where Dr. Daly shakes hands as he sings. Dr. Daly's speech should conclude as the music is still being played, to allow him to depart to sit ⑧, Marmaduke and Alexis to sit ⑤, ⑥.

8. "With heart and with voice" (*Female Chorus*). Ladies, Constance and Mrs. Partlet stand.

At "Comes the loving young heart', Aline enters, attended by four ladies. She moves to centre, middle stage.

After second "Heaven bless our Aline", the four ladies dance, in couples on either side of Aline. Dance should conclude at end of postlude with dancers in a semi-circle round Aline.

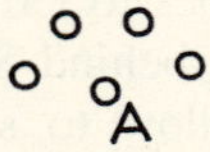

9. "My kindly friends." Aline sings to four ladies. As recit. finishes, dancers curtsey to her and take their places on front row. All ladies sit.

10. "Oh happy young heart." Sung centre, middle stage, to audience.

11. Lady Sangazure comes forward in stately fashion to stand right of Aline for her *Recit*.

12. "With heart and with voice" (*Male Chorus*). Men rise. At "Comes Alexis the brave" Alexis and Marmaduke come slowly to centre — Alexis acknowledging the greetings, Marmaduke proud.

"To the maid of his choice." Alexis should now have reached Aline. They meet with outstretched arms, then embrace as chorus is ending. Sangazure and Marmaduke, standing back the while, watch the couple proudly.

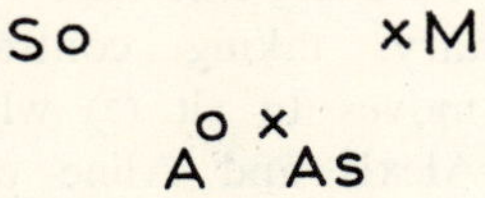

Postlude. Alexis leads Aline to sit ④, ③.

End of music. Men sit.

13. "Welcome, joy." Marmaduke and Sangazure, who have been watching their offspring attentively, now become fully aware of each other's presence.

Postlude. Couple dance and separate, Sangazure to RC middle stage, Marmaduke LC, to exchange courtly bows on penultimate bar. They then rise and remain in position.

14. *Ensemble.* Company rises. Notary enters to RC front. As he does so, two men at ends of Rows 3, 2 move unobtrusively to Table left.

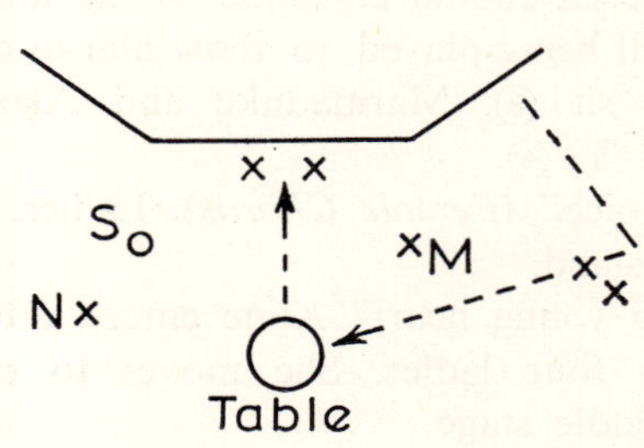

As chorus sing "All is prepared," they bring table to centre front, then move quickly between Sangazure and Marmaduke to stand centre, just in front of chorus.

"Approach the table" (*Notary*). Notary goes to left of table. Alexis and Aline come down centre, passing behind Sangazure to table ⓐ. Sangazure and Marmaduke follow to stand just behind them ⓑ.

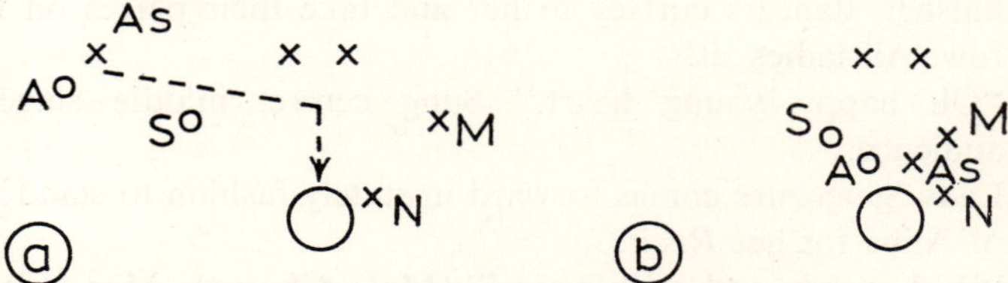

"Approach the table" (*Chorus*). Ladies in front (as always anxious to view a wedding or engagement) step forward to make a semi-circle round the main participants.

During *Interlude* Notary, taking contract, moves to sit ⑦ while Alexis and Aline embrace.

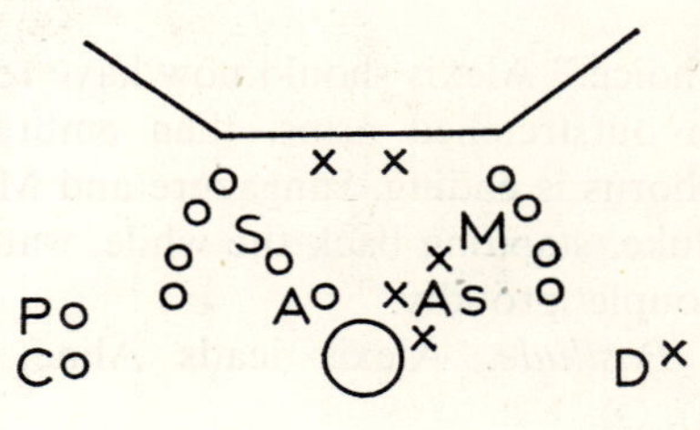

During "With heart and with voice" the following business takes place — without haste: Alexis steps back a pace and, taking Aline's hand, directs her to Marmaduke. (He does not go with her). Alexis then crosses to Sangazure. Both couples embrace. Aline then crosses back to Alexis, RC, and kisses her mother. Sangazure crosses to Marmaduke and embraces him, to be led to sit ⑤, ⑥. Men come forward to remove table to original position, then return to their seats, passing behind ⑤, ⑥.

Postlude. Eight ladies, with curtsies to the couple, return to their places.

Company sits, leaving Aline and Alexis standing centre.

15. After "Love feeds on many kinds of food" Alexis leads Aline away and they sit respectively ③, ④.

16. *Narrative.* Dr. Daly stands at ⑧, sits on conclusion.

17. Wells enters and sings centre, using stage as he pleases.

18. *Narrative.* Dr. Daly stands at ⑧ talking to audience, not looking at players. As he does so, Alexis brings Aline to introduce her to Wells (who is most deferential). They 'talk', RC middle. Alexis breaks from them to speak to Constance and her mother. They rise, Constance fetching table right and placing it RC front. Her mother brings tea-pot and paraphernalia for Wells' Incantation, and places them on the table. Both curtsey to Alexis and return to their seats. Dr. Daly sits.

19. *Incantation.* (If possible, all lights should be extinguished save that illuminating RC). Chorus now sit formally, upright. They sing sitting absolutely motionless, without facial expression. Wells busies himself (traditional 'business'), basic position on right of table, but using stage as he pleases. Alexis and Aline, rather fearful, stand holding each other, left of table, slightly back.

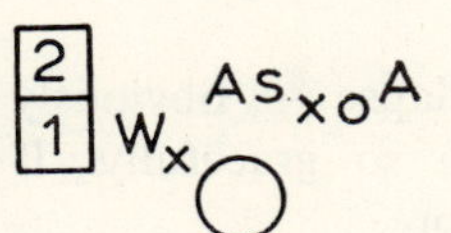

20. *Finale Act I.*
Lights up.

Chorus resume carefree pose. As introductory music starts, some rise, others remain seated, grouped carefully by producer.

Constance removes table, then helps Mrs. Partlet and Wells to distribute cups of tea (poured at large table) and sandwiches to chorus.

Couples from front row dance during the singing.

First postlude. Marmaduke advances centre, with Sangazure on his arm, and sings from there.

"None so knowing as he." Constance takes tray with teapot, kettle, caddy, cups and saucers over to Dr. Daly, who brings forward his table.

End of chorus. All movement stops as Aline, Alexis and Wells, RC, sing "See, see, they drink."

All chorus drink together. Mrs. Partlet at large table, also has a cup of tea.

Dr. Daly, during his verse, prepares tea with precision. He pours some for Sangazure and Marmaduke, and Constance takes it to them. As she does so, Dr. Daly gives a cup to the Notary. Constance returns to Dr. Daly, and he gives her a cup and takes one himself. Positions:

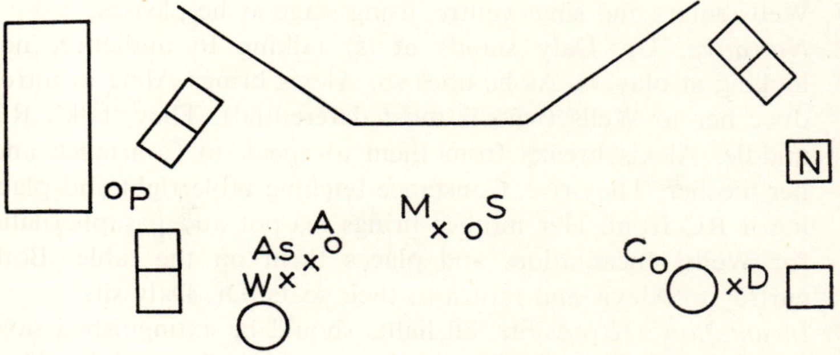

"Oh marvellous illusion." Gradually effects of potion show, affecting some before others. Actions should be varied, individual, in no way stylised, e.g. holding head, staggering, sitting down, clutching partner.

End of chorus. Those still standing, collapse — obviously Marmaduke, Sangazure and Dr. Daly do so gracefully. If possible, lighting should be dimmed as before.

Wells, Alexis and Aline, still standing RC, are aghast at the effect. They hold pose for a moment, then exit quickly, Aline, holding her hands to her face, led by Alexis, Wells following.

Still in dim light, all rise and exeunt in this order: Marmaduke and Sangazure, Dr. Daly, Notary, Mrs. Partlet; Chorus in groups — supporting each other but in no way amorous!

Basic seating plan as for Act I except that all tables and seat ⑦ are removed.

Lighting. If possible, dim as before.

1. Chorus walk on in couples, very sluggish in movement. Move in groups. Rows 1, 2 on rostra. Row 3 — some on rostra, some on floor in front of it. Constance and Notary to ⑤, ⑥. On reaching their places, all flop immediately, half-seated, half-lying in pairs or fours.

2. *Introductory music.* Wells, Alexis, Aline enter single file in that order, Wells with lantern. They move furtively, tip-toeing.

Crossing stage, starting L, they peer at all 'bodies' on floor, sometimes rolling one over to identify it. Return to RC (lit area) in time to sing.

After *trio* Wells exits, Alexis and Aline tip-toe to sit ①, ②, there to watch unobserved.

"Why where be oi." Lights up.

Chorus sit up, bewildered, rubbing eyes, ruffling hair.

"Eh what a nose." All still sitting. Men start to notice partners, make amorous advances.

"Oi tell you true." Women respond.

Blank bar before "Eh but I du loike you." All lean forward to kiss partner.

Allegro — ten bar introduction. All rise — not together, and with individual actions.

Chorus. Now full of animation and vivacity — much flirtation.

Last five bars of chorus. Movement still, couples clasp each other, women leaning heads on men's shoulders. Then front row dance, finishing in arcs just in front of rostra.

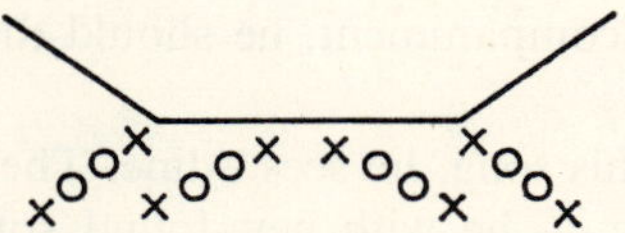

3. Constance leads Notary into arc.

"You very plain old man" (*Chorus*). Alexis and Aline rise.

Postlude. Front row return, still joyous, to their seats; Constance and Notary to sit again ⑤, ⑥, Aline and Alexis, watching, move to sit ③, ④. All sit.

4. *Narrative.* Dr. Daly enters to RC, pauses and crosses LC for "But one thing remained to be done," then sits ⑧.

5. "It is not love." Alexis comes forward to sing centre.

6. *Narrative.* Aline joins Alexis. Dr. Daly stands at ⑧ initially, moving towards centre at "I was distinctly surprised."

   "I said as much." Aline and Alexis show pleasure. He breaks away from couple to deliver "I confess that melancholia" to the audience.

   "But my reverie." Marmaduke, with Mrs. Partlet on his left arm, enters. Alexis is dumbfounded as his father presents her. He pulls himself together to smile graciously upon her.

```
          As      A
       Po   x   o
   Mx              xD
```

7. "I rejoice that it's decided." At the end, Marmaduke proudly leads Mrs. Partlet to sit ①, ②. Alexis and Aline move after them to sit ③, ④, respectively. Dr. Daly remains for a moment shaking his head wistfully, then slowly, despondently, crosses to sit ⑧.

8. Wells enters, full of remorse, paces up and down as he sings. He sees Sangazure approaching as he is centre, and remains there. Sangazure, melancholy, does not lift her eyes as she enters, singing. As she reaches RC, she catches sight of Wells.

   After *Duet*, both exit, walking quickly and wrangling.

9. Aline walks RC slowly, just in front of chorus, singing *Recit*; drinks from a wine glass. Stands to sing *Air*. As it ends, Dr. Daly rises for his song. Aline sees him and steps back further to be unobserved. (When audience's attention is devoted to Dr. Daly, she can slip her glass to a chorus member.)

10. "Oh my voice is sad and low." Dr. Daly walks slowly, pensively to LC. (N.B. If only piano accompaniment, he should dispense with flageolet.)

11. *Ensemble.* As Dr. Daly ends his song, he sees Aline. They rush into each other's arms, centre — he with new-found sprightliness.

12. "Aline, my love." Alexis approaches the couple quite happily initially.

    "Come one, come all." Company rises, wondering what is happening.

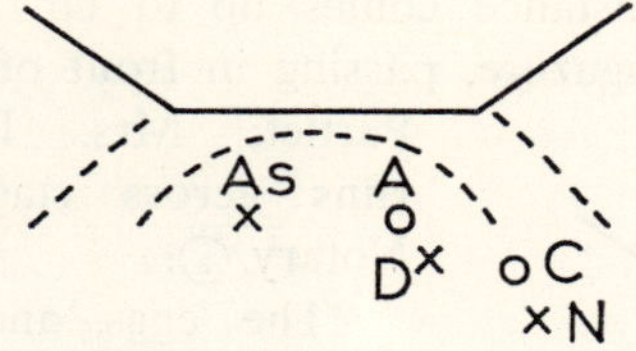

Two bar introduction. Front row gather in arcs round trio, as before. Constance and Notary join on the left. 13. "A lover's curse." Alexis raises his left hand to pronounce curse. Dr. Daly takes a pace forward, raising an admonishing hand. All *freeze* as Dr. Daly continues narrative, speaking to audience. As he is speaking, Wells runs in, followed by Sangazure, a little behind him. Wells takes Alexis's right hand, whereupon Alexis drops his pose and turns to him. Sangazure remains on diagonal ⓐ.

14. *Finale Act II.*

Wells goes centre, pointing dramatically to Alexis ⓑ.

"Die thou" (*Marmaduke*). Wells shrinks back melodramatically to stand on first step of rostrum. Chorus parts for him.

"Die thou" (*Dr. Daly*). Wells to second step.

"Die thou" (*Chorus*). Wells to third step, arms up to shield his face.

As he sings, he drops his arms and sings resignedly. Having sung "Oh where," he steps back off top rostrum, dropping out of sight behind it. As this is approximately a four-foot drop, he must be prepared to bend his knees immediately his feet touch the ground to avoid a 'two-part' disappearance. The four chorus members on top rostrum can help cover up by running forward to the gap he has left, with gasps of "Oh!". (If any firework or smoke devices are available and permissible, these would heighten the effect.)

Wells remains hidden behind rostrum till end of opera. "Oh my adored one." Chorus hug their partners enthusiastically — closing gap in centre of steps. Principals swap partners thus:

Aline moves to Alexis; Constance comes up to Dr. Daly;
Marmaduke advances to Sangazure, passing in front of Mrs.
Partlet; Mrs. Partlet runs across stage to Notary ⓐ.

"The eggs and the ham." Chorus on floor split into four groups to dance — two groups L and R, front; two groups behind principals ⓑ.

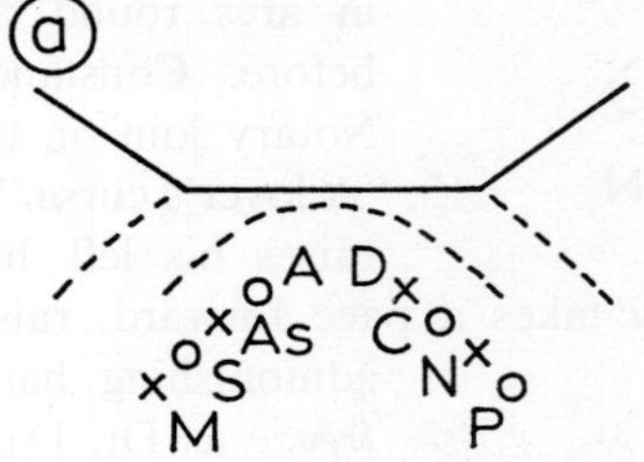

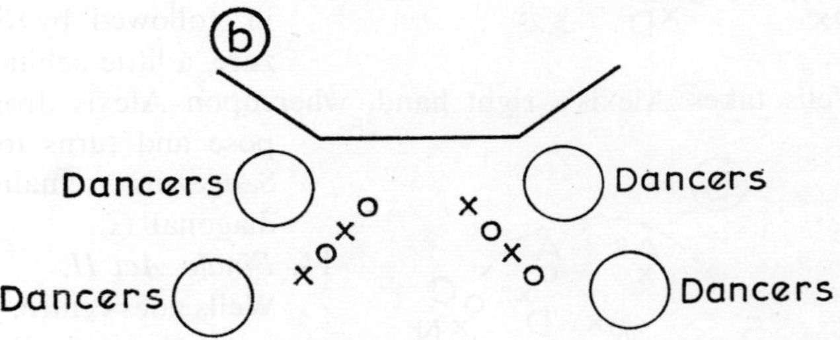

Postlude. Principals join in dance.

15. *End of opera.* Wells is hoisted on to top rostrum.

All take one bow.

Then exeunt: Marmaduke and Sangazure, Alexis and Aline,
Dr. Daly and Constance, Notary and Mrs. Partlet, Wells (who
has come down steps. Dancers, R, in twos; dancers, L, in twos;
chorus in twos.

Suggestions for Costuming

SIR MARMADUKE POINTDEXTRE	Morning tails, with grey topper
ALEXIS	Well-cut sports suit
DR. DALY	Dark clerical-grey suit; clerical collar
NOTARY	Black jacket, pin-strip trousers; or dark, three-piece suit with white shirt
JOHN WELLINGTON WELLS	Rather common, but pretentious shop-keeper's attire. Linen jacket, dark slacks, white shirt, club tie, flower in button-hole
LADY SANGAZURE	Garden party ensemble. Dress/coat, large hat, elegant gloves. Darkish colours.
ALINE	Garden party ensemble as for Lady Sangazure, but more youthful. Light colours.
MRS. PARTLET	Drab blouse and skirt, with apron.
CONSTANCE	A modern miss. Fashionable dress (maxi, midi or mini).

CHORUS	ACTS I, II
	For once, motley attire is in order. The country yokel is depicted with absence of taste. Colour clash is acceptable. No elaborate garments.
MALE	Sports jackets, polo-neck sweaters, short-sleeved shirts, open-necked or with cravats.
FEMALE	Dresses (any length), blouse and skirt, sweaters, slacks. (No trouser suits.)

4

H.M.S. PINAFORE

Script for Dick Deadeye as Narrator

ACT I

Overture
V.S. No. 1. *Chorus*. "We sail the ocean blue."
V.S. No. 2. *Recit/Song*. "Hail! Men-o'-wars-men" / "I'm called little Buttercup."
V.S. No. 2a. *Recit*. "But tell me who's the youth."
V.S. No. 3. *Scena*. "The nightingale sighed."
V.S. No. 4. *Recit/Song*. "My gallant crew" / "I am the captain of the *Pinafore*."
DICK   Here we go again. Spit and polish, spit and polish. 'And for what?' sez you. 'To cover up the faults of the British Navy,' sez I. We're to have an inspection today from the Rt. Hon. Sir Joseph Porter, K.C.B., First Lord of the Admiralty. (*Sneering*) So it's out with the holystone, me lads, polish, sweep and clean. Tchah! (*He spits*) As if Sir Joseph will look at us. He's aiming to get himself hitched to the captain's daughter, Josephine, and he's coming to inspect her, if you asks me.

And we've this here romantic simpleton, Rafe Rackstraw, a-pining his heart out for the self-same gel. (*In bitter derision*) An able-seaman. As if our captain, (*cynical*) for all his noble sentiments and fine phrases would stand for it. And the little lady herself? Well who knows what females think?
V.S. No. 4a.   *Recit*. "Sir, you are sad."
V.S. No. 5. *Song*. "Sorry her lot."
DICK   So ho! The little miss has some spunk in her. But her father won't stand for it. No. I thought not. He's shocked. He aims higher for his daughter than a humble foremast lad. See, he gives her a photograph of Sir Joseph and urges her to reconsider. Perhaps he should have given her this book I've just been areading. It's a bi-hography of Sir Joseph himself. (*He reads*)

'You would naturally think that the person who commanded the entire Navy would be the most accomplished sailor who could be found, but that is not the way in which such things are managed in England. Sir Joseph Porter, who had risen from a very humble position to be a lawyer and then a Member of Parliament, was, it is believed, the only man in England who knew nothing whatever about ships. Now as England is a great maritime country, it is very important that all Englishmen should understand something about men-of-war. So as soon as it was discovered that his ignorance of a ship was so complete that he didn't know one end of it from another, some important person said, "Let us set this poor ignorant gentleman to command the British Fleet, and by that means give him an opportunity of ascertaining what a ship really is." This was considered to be a wise and sensible suggestion, and so Sir Joseph Porter was at once appointed First Lord of the Admiralty of Great Britain and Ireland.'* What is the country coming to? (*shaking his head sadly*)

V.S. No. 6. *Chorus.* "Over the bright blue sea."

V.S. No. 7. *Chorus.* "Sir Joseph's barge is seen."

V.S. No. 8. *Solos and chorus.* "Now give three cheers."

V.S. No. 9. *Song.* "When I was a lad."

DICK   So we're to have an inspection after all. (*Sir Joseph looks at him.*) Very well, thank you, me Lord. (*Sir Joseph continues his inspection.*) 'Remarkably fine crew,' sez he. His party piece all prepared beforehand. 'And here's a song I've composed to sing at your leisure' — whenever that may be! And — oh my! (*Sir Joseph speaks to the Captain*) A reprimand to the Captain — don't be patronising to the men, but remember, always say please and thank you.

V.S. No. 9a. *Solo and chorus.* "For I hold that on the seas."

V.S. No. 10. *Trio and chorus.* "A British tar."

DICK   Sir Joseph's song having encouraged independence of thought and action, our splendid seaman is left alone — to try his luck with the lady.

V.S. No. 11. *Duet.* "Refrain audacious tar."

V.S. No. 12. *Finale Act I.*

ACT II

Entracte

V.S. No. 13. *Song.* "Fair moon, to thee I sing."

V.S. No. 14. *Duet.* "Things are seldom what they seem."

* From *The Pinafore Picture Book*, by W. S. Gilbert.

V.S. No. 15. *Scena.* "The hours creep on apace."

DICK It's a queer world. Josephine can't make up her mind which side her bread's buttered on. Her father, for all his learning couldn't make head nor tail of what Buttercup was talking about. Now Sir Joseph tells him he's disappointed in Josephine. He don't think she will do. That really upsets Papa. He says perhaps Sir Joseph's exalted rank (*Dick spits*) has terrified her. Would Sir Joseph be kind enough to inform her that there is a standing rule at the Admiralty that love levels all ranks? Poor chap, he doesn't realize how this will strengthen the lass's hand.

V.S. No. 16. *Trio.* "Never mind the why and wherefore."

V.S. No. 17. *Duet.* "Kind Captain."

DICK Ha, ha! They are foiled, foiled, foiled.

V.S. No. 18. *Chorus.* "Carefully on tip-toe stealing."

DICK Well, well. Captain in disgrace and Sir Joseph in a fine tizzy. 'What's the reason for the Captain's behaviour?' sez he. Rafe tells him. And at that Sir Joseph blows his top. No equality for foremast hands — that's reserved only for him and his likes. (*Dick now mimes Sir Joseph*) 'Insolent sailor, you shall repent of this outrage. I will teach this presumptuous mariner to discipline his affection. To the dungeons with him and load him with chains.'

V.S. No. 19. *Octet.* "Farewell, my own."

V.S. No. 20. *Song.* "A many years ago."

DICK Here's a fine turn up for the book. Josephine is to marry above her station. The lowly Captain can now marry Buttercup — he always had a fancy for her. But what about Sir Joseph? Ah ha, Cousin Hebe can't see him — or his money—left alone.

V.S. No. 21. *Finale Act II.*

Basic Seating Plan — Act I

NOTES (see figure overleaf)

Rostrum taken as Poop-deck
Principals seated ⑦ to ⑩ are on floor level, behind rostrum,
backs to audience. 'Off stage', they should remain motionless:
the reasonable temptation for Ralph to sit with his arm around
Josephine should be avoided on account of the proximity to her
father and Sir Joseph.

PROPS

Act I.   Old book, photograph, pistol.
Act II.   Cloak and 'cat-o'-nine-tails', concealed behind rostrum.

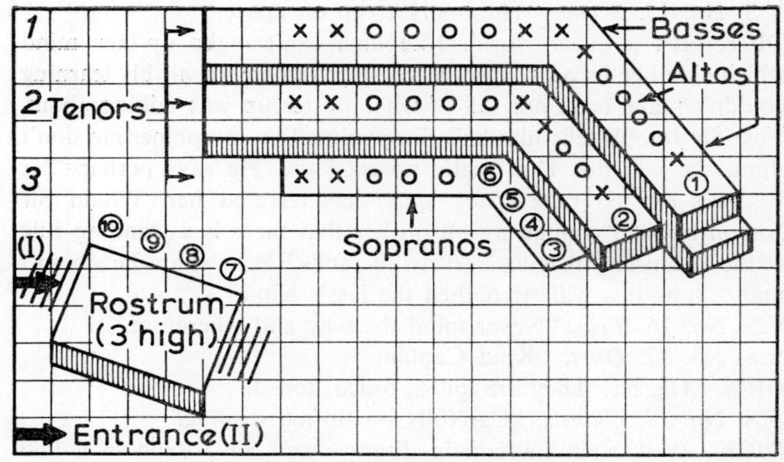

ROW 1 (Raised 2 single steps) ROW 2 (Raised 1 single step)
ROW 3 (Seated floor level)

NOTATION

P — Sir Joseph	D — Dick	J — Josephine
C — Captain	Bn — Bo'sun	H — Hebe
R — Ralph	Ca — Carpenter	B — Buttercup

Production for Script with Dick Deadeye as Narrator

ACT I

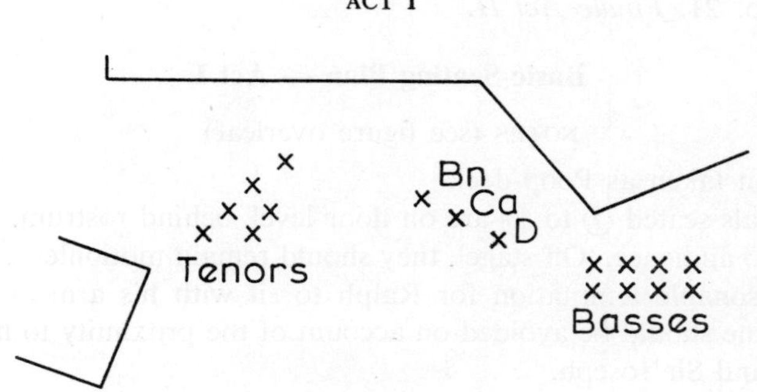

1. *Overture.*
2. *Opening chorus.* Men enter (II) in this order: Basses, in twos;
   Dick, Bo'sun, Carpenter; tenors in twos. While in reasonable

38

order, they should not march military style. Groupings as shown above.

3. Buttercup enters (II) to RC. Tenors cluster round her, buying articles at introduction to song, then go back to their original positions while she sings RC. She then joins Bo'sun.

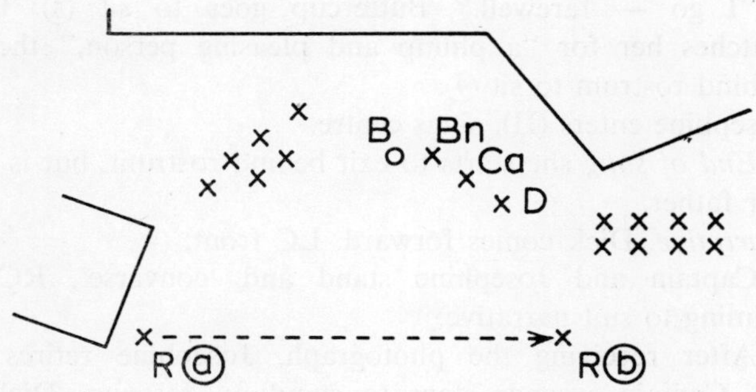

At postlude to her song, Ralph enters (II), slowly, to lean at rostrum, R, and sings his *scena* from there. ⓐ

4. At "I know the value of a kindly chorus," Ralph starts to cross L, slowly, arriving LC front for "A maiden fair to see." ⓑ

End of song, Buttercup sits ⑤.

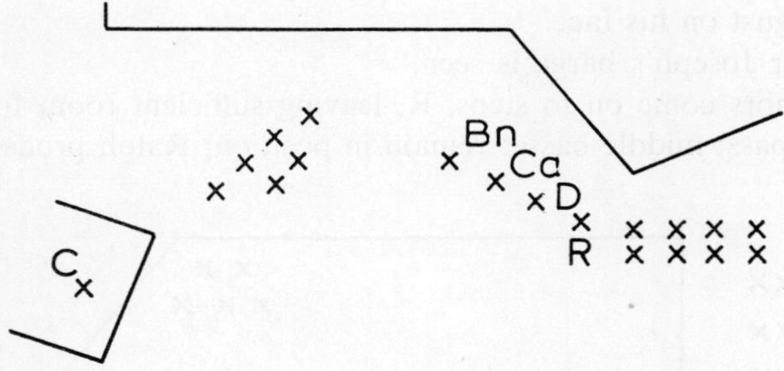

5. Captain enters up steps (I) and stands to sing on rostrum. At introductory music, chorus stands to attention in straight lines.

6. End of Captain's song, Captain remains on rostrum, tenors go to their seats R, basses to seats middle and L, and Bo'sun and Carpenter to ② and ①, Ralph to ④. All sit.

Dick steps forward for Narrative.

7. *Narrative.* "Well, who knows what females think?" — A throw-away line, spoken as Dick moves to sit ③.

8. Buttercup moves to RC and sings to Captain, who is still standing on rostrum.

"Yes, little Buttercup." Captain comes down steps, near to her.

"I go — farewell." Buttercup goes to sit ⑤. Captain watches her for "a plump and pleasing person," then goes behind rostrum to sit ⑨.

9. Josephine enters (II), sings centre.

End of song she starts to exit behind rostrum, but is met by her father.

10. *Narrative.* Dick comes forward, LC front.

Captain and Josephine stand and 'converse', RC back, miming to suit narrative.

After receiving the photograph, Josephine retires to sit ⑧. Captain ascends steps to stand on rostrum. Dick reads from an old battered volume. After quoting, he closes book meditatively, shaking his head to deliver "What is the country coming to?", then sits ③.

11. "Over the bright blue sea." Sung off-stage, R.

Captain turns in direction of singing. Men, including principals except Dick, start to rise, showing interest and excitement.

Dick sits with his back turned to singing, an expression of disgust on his face.

12. "Sir Joseph's barge is seen."

Tenors come on to steps, R, leaving sufficient room for ladies to pass; middle basses remain in position; Ralph prods Dick to

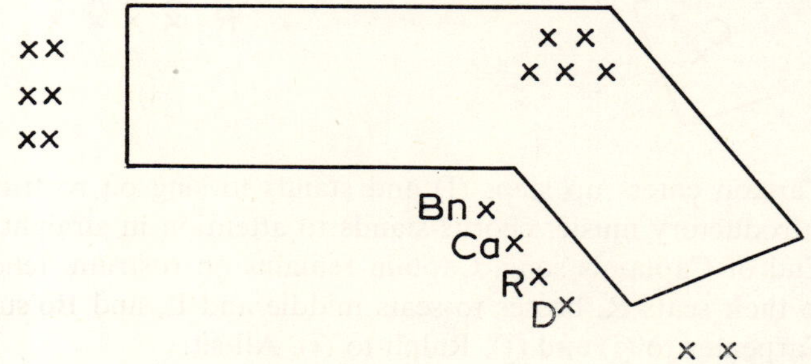

his feet and Bo'sun and Carpenter, coming forward, push him into some semblance of uprightness before taking their places in line; two basses on R step out (as for tenors).

All men stand to attention on "None are so smart as we are." Ladies enter (II), dancing, single file; order:

ⓐ six altos, ⓑ three front-row sopranos, ⓒ second row sopranos, ⓓ first row sopranos.

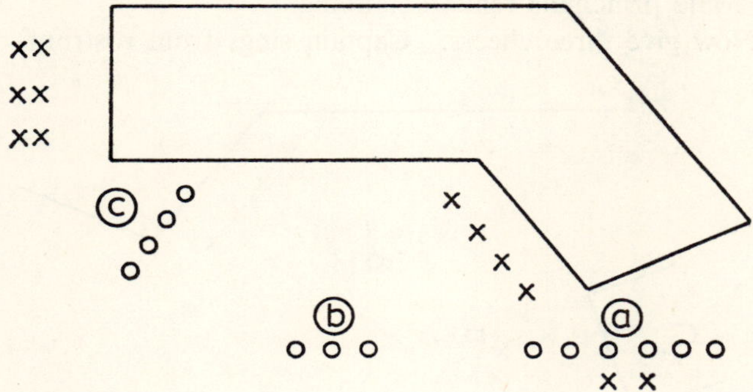

ⓐ cross to stand behind the two basses, L.

ⓑ centre front.

ⓒ diagonal RC, to match four male principals.

This should take introductory music and ladies' first line of singing.

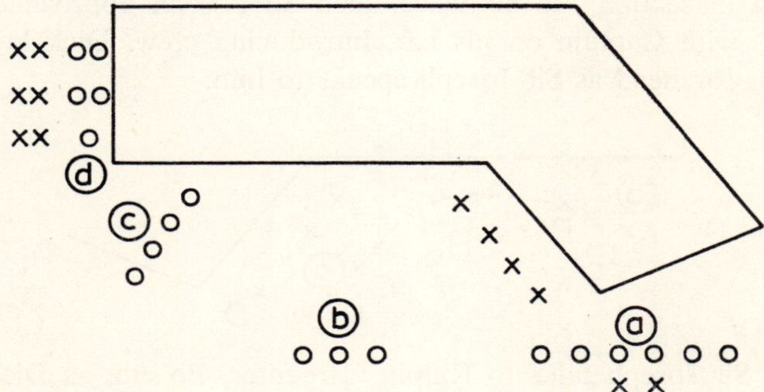

As men start "Flags and guns" ⓓ should be arriving to go up steps R — two to Row 1, two to Row 2, one to Row 3. They should be in position before ladies sing "Sailors sprightly." They stand in these positions for remainder of chorus.

At *Postlude* ⓓ they file into Row 1.

ⓑ follow and file into Row 2.

ⓐ file into Rows 1 and 2, L.

ⓒ move backwards to front row.

With ladies in position, chorus men take their places beside them.

Male principals remain standing.

13. "Now give three cheers." Captain sings from rostrum.

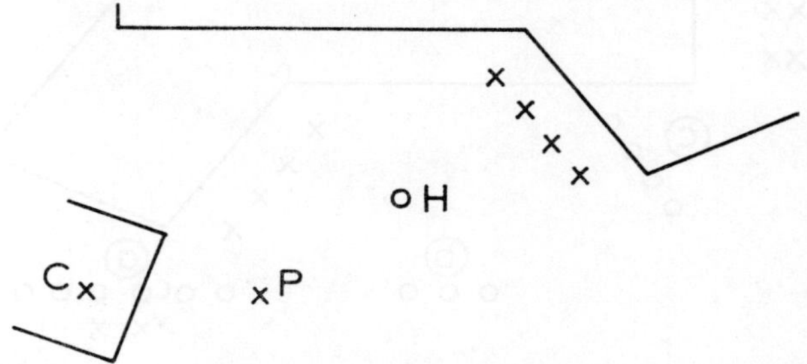

As chorus sings "Hurrah" Sir Joseph enters (II) with Hebe on his left arm. He stops to sing RC front. Hebe continues to centre, but farther back.

14. *Final Postlude* of "When I was a lad." Captain comes down to welcome Sir Joseph, bringing him LC. Sir Joseph fixes monocle in his eye and looks about him. Dick delivers "So we're to have an inspection" to audience, then Sir Joseph approaches him ⓐ with Captain on his left, introducing crew. Dick knuckles his forehead as Sir Joseph speaks to him.

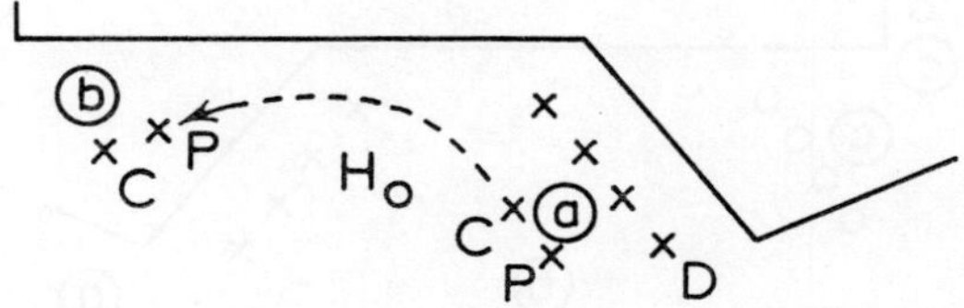

Sir Joseph talks to Ralph, Carpenter, Bo'sun, as Dick continues to address audience. Timing to narrative, Sir Joseph gives Bo'sun a music script, then takes Corcoran by the arm, and leads him behind Hebe, to RC back, obviously reprimanding him. ⓑ

15. "For I hold that on the seas." Sir Joseph sings from ⓑ. As chorus sing "And so do his sisters," Sir Joseph crosses in front of Captain to sit ⑩. Captain follows him to sit ⑨. Hebe takes her seat ⑥.

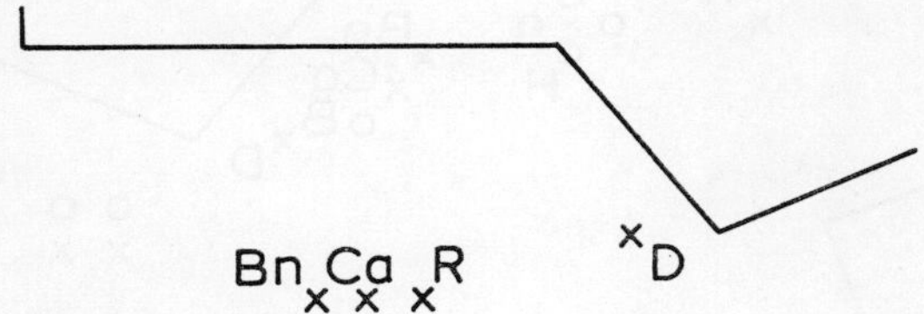

16. *Glee.* At introduction, Bo'sun, Carpenter and Ralph step forward, centre, with music. Dick remains standing in position.

   Postlude of chorus. Carpenter and Bo'sun cross in front of Ralph, shaking hands with him, wishing him well, then take their seats, L.

17. *Narrative.* As Dick, still standing, speaks, Ralph moves restlessly to the right.

   Josephine appears from behind rostrum as Dick says "to try his luck with the lady." Ralph sees her and hurries forward with outstretched hands.

   Dick sits.

18. "Refrain audacious tar" (*Introduction*) Josephine has almost reached RC as Ralph crosses to her. Seeing his hands reaching out to her, she halts and raises a forbidding hand. Stopped, Ralph kneels before her for Verse 1. Ralph stands for Verse 2.

   Last eight bars of singing. Ralph and Josephine very close but almost back to back.

   Postlude. Josephine exits to her seat, Ralph remains.

19. *Finale Act I.*

   Ralph sings from R. As he calls "Messmates, ahoy," all stand, and there is a general movement towards him.

   Right: third row, two tenors step forward.

   second Row, two tenors step out and down one step.

   first Row, one tenor out and down step.

   Middle: Hebe and three sopranos step forward, Hebe in advance.

   Bo'sun and Carpenter come LC, back. Buttercup joins them.

   Left: two basses and two altos step down on to stage.

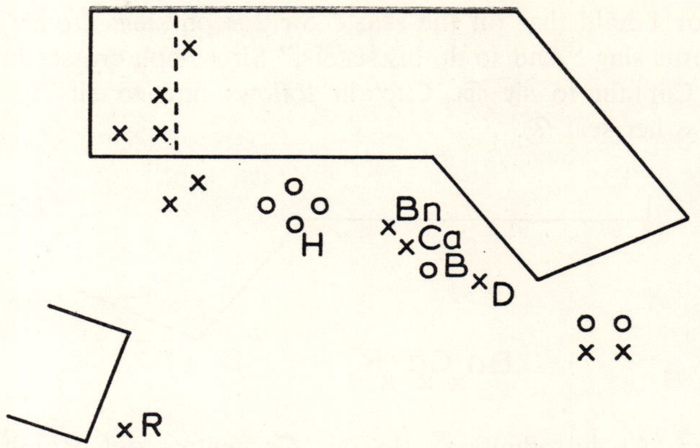

Dick remains seated, gloating.

"Ah, cruel one." Dick comes forward LC, to front.
"My friends, my leave of life I'm taking." Ralph still R, Bo'sun starts to load pistol.

"Of life alas" (*Chorus*). Ralph crosses to centre, Bo'sun comes forward, and after shaking hands, gives him pistol.

"Be warned my messmates." Josephine has crept on and has come front R, to observe more closely.

"Ah, stay your hand." Josephine R.

"Loves me?" (*Ralph*). Ralph still centre.

"Loves you" (*Josephine*). Ralph and Josephine run together, RC middle.

Hebe comes forward on Ralph's left.

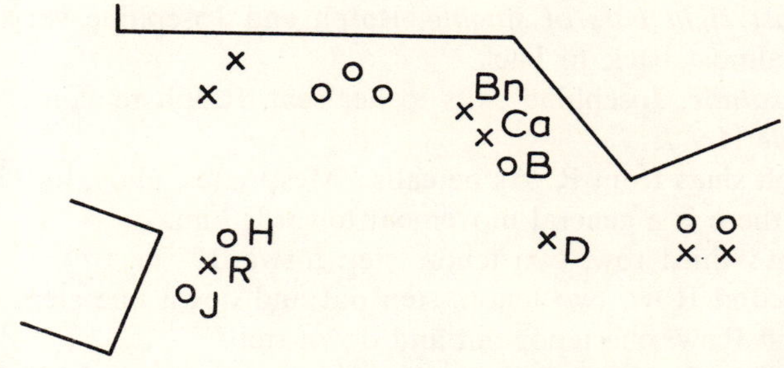

"He thinks he's won his Josephine." Dick still LC front.
"This very night." Ralph, Josephine, Hebe, conspiratorial, heads together.

20. "None can part them then." *Four-bar introduction following.*
Dick lumbers across to Josephine, Ralph, Hebe to sing
"Forbear, nor carry out the scheme."

"Back, vermin, back." Bo'sun and Carpenter cross, seize Dick by the arms to propel him off-stage at (II). Ralph starts to follow, watching from R, so allowing Josephine and Hebe to move centre.

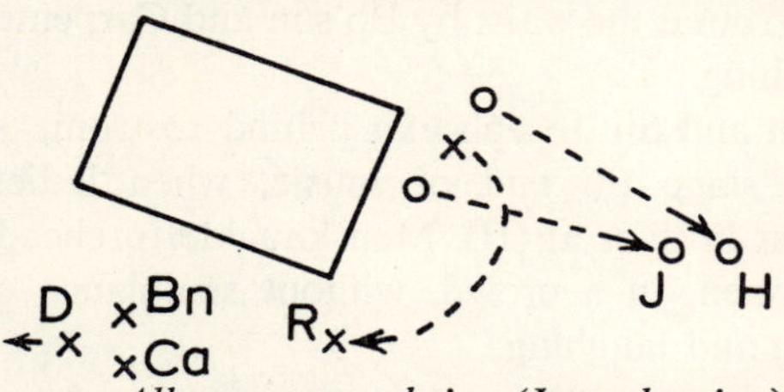

Allegro con brio (*Introduction*). Bo'sun and Carpenter return, laughing, pat Ralph on the back, and all three go to stand RC.

Buttercup comes forward, LC.

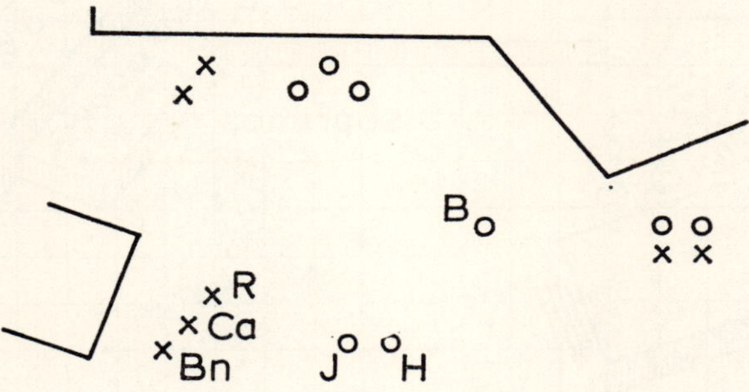

"A British tar" (*eight bars introduction*). All tenors come to form a line across stage back. Dance if desired.

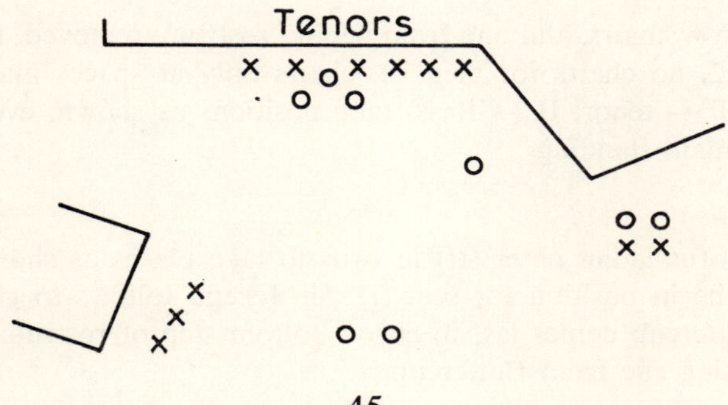

End of chorus singing, during postlude. The following should exit (II) quickly, thus: Bo'sun and Carpenter step back to allow Ralph and Josephine arm in arm to exit first; Hebe follows, the two sailors knuckling their foreheads as she passes; Buttercup, following her is seized round the waist by Bo'sun and Carpenter and all three exit laughing.

During this, Captain and Sir Joseph exit behind rostrum.

Chorus remain on stage till end of music, when ladies, starting from R, file off in twos at (II). Men knuckle foreheads as ladies pass. Then men, in a crowd, without semblance of order, exit (II), talking and laughing.

Basic Seating Plan — Act II

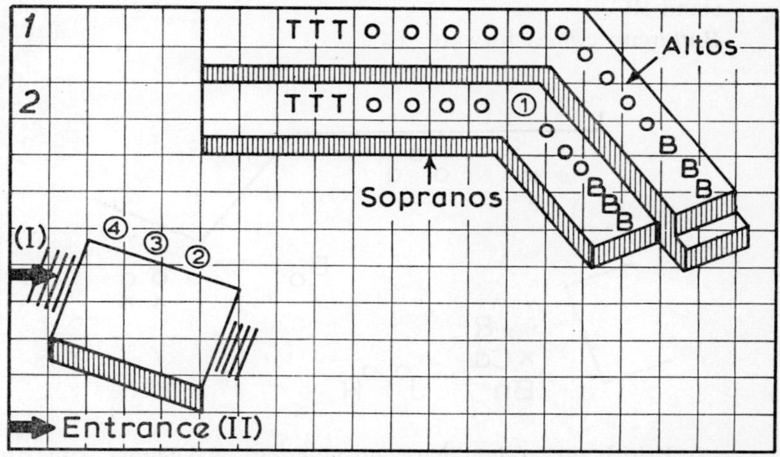

ROW 1 (Raised 2 single steps) ROW 2 (Raised 1 single step)

NOTES

Front row chairs, and one from behind rostrum, removed. In Rows 1 and 2, no chairs for men i.e. chairs only at spaces marked O. Men (T — tenor, B — Bass) take positions as shown, eventually, and remain standing.

ACT II

1. Chorus ladies enter (II) in twos to take places as shown, with Hebe in position for seat ①. Sir Joseph follows to go to ④. Buttercup comes last to sit on bottom step of rostrum. All sit taking cue from Buttercup.

2. *Entracte.*

3. "Fair moon." Captain climbs steps (II) and sings from rostrum. End of song, Buttercup rises.

4. *Duet.* Buttercup sings from stage level, at foot of steps. Corcoran, initially surprised to hear her, listens attentively from rostrum. He descends to her on "Tho' to catch your drift." Half stage R can be used for traditional actions, Verse 2. At the end, Captain, deep in thought, hands behind back, goes to sit ③, followed respectfully by Buttercup, who sits ②.

5. *Josephine's scena.* She enters (II), ascending steps slowly — may even start singing as she ascends. *Recit.* sung from rostrum — on which she may move about in melodramatic fashion. She comes down to RC for Verse 1 of song. She may cross stage at any time to suit her emotions but must finish song in position LC.

6. *Postlude to song.* Sir Joseph and Captain appear from behind 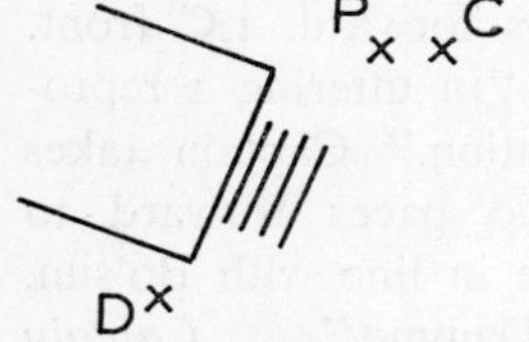 rostrum and stand RC back, 'conversing.' Dick creeps on furtively (II) to crouch at corner of rostrum, to deliver *narrative*. Captain and Sir Joseph mime to suit narrative (e.g. Captain seen to start as Sir Joseph obviously announces his displeasure with Josephine. Captain tries to conciliate him, gesturing to Josephine. Sir Joseph finally agrees.) As narrative ends, Captain leads the way to centre, where they are joined by Josephine for the trio.

7. *Trio.* Traditional 'business.'

Exit (off-stage) dancing, Josephine by (II), Sir Joseph by (I). Captain remains centre.

8. "Kind Captain." Dick limps across to Captain in wheedling fashion.

Verse 3, Dick takes Captain conspiratorially by the arm and leads him across to steps of rostrum.

Postlude. Captain seizes cloak from place behind steps 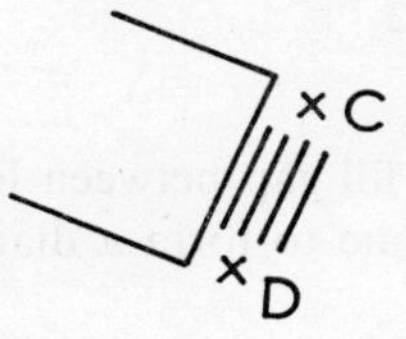 wraps it about him melodramatically and stands behind steps of rostrum, with his back to the audience.

Dick crows with laughter "foiled, foiled" — and crouches just in front of steps, out of line of entry of chorus.

9. "Carefully on tip-toe stealing." Basses, Carpenter and Bo'sun enter (II) furtively, on tip-toe, single file. They move directly across L, and are nearly in position when the crack of the cat-o'-nine-tails is heard. All pause, looking over shoulders. Hold pose, till they sing "It was the cat," when even more furtively they stand in position beside ladies. Bo'sun and Carpenter in front, LC.

"Pull ashore." Tenors enter, going upstage R. 'Business' as before.

"Every step." Ralph and Josephine enter (II), he upstage of her with arm round her waist, crossing to centre, where they huddle fearfully.

"Hold." Captain strides forth to RC.

"Proud officer." Ralph straightens to reply fearlessly.

"He is an Englishman." Bo'sun steps forward, LC front.

"In uttering a reprobation." Captain takes two paces forward to be in line with Bo'sun. "Damme." *Captain* (*first time*). All ladies rise, horrified at "Oh!" Carpenter joins Bo'sun on his left.

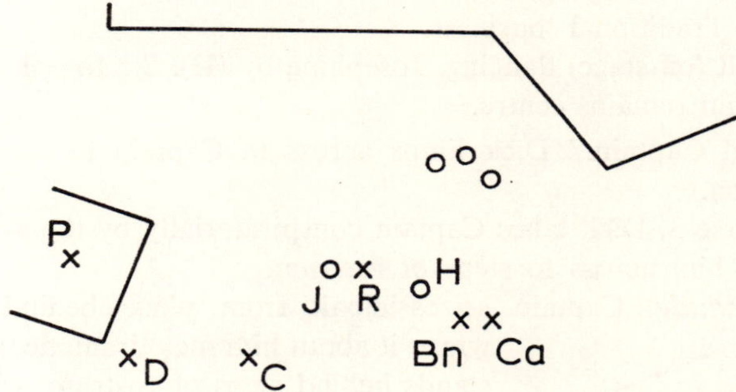

"Did you hear him?" Hebe comes to fill gap between Ralph and Bo'sun. Three altos in front row come to form a diagonal behind.

Sir Joseph enters (I) and stands on rostrum viewing scene through his monocle in amazement.

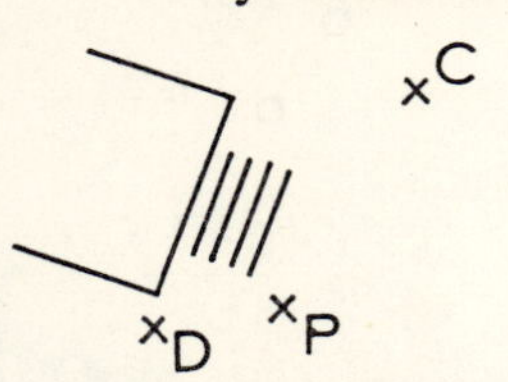

"My amazement." Sir Joseph sings from rostrum. "My Lord." Captain turns to face him, and as Captain sings, Sir Joseph with haughty dignity descends to come on his right. "I will hear of no defence." Sir Joseph on floor level. "Go, ribald." Captain exits behind rostrum, and so off-stage.

10. *Narrative.* Dick steps forward to address audience. Mime to narrative. Sir Joseph queries. Ralph takes a pace forward and faces him. Sir Joseph almost collapses. At "insolent sailor" there is a double mime (which needs careful rehearsal). Dick speaks the words which in a stage performance would be spoken by Sir Joseph, and mimics Sir Joseph's normal actions. Sir Joseph also goes through the actions. These actions should be identical — but neither man observes the other.

11. *Octet.* Ralph, broken, steps back to be clasped by Josephine.

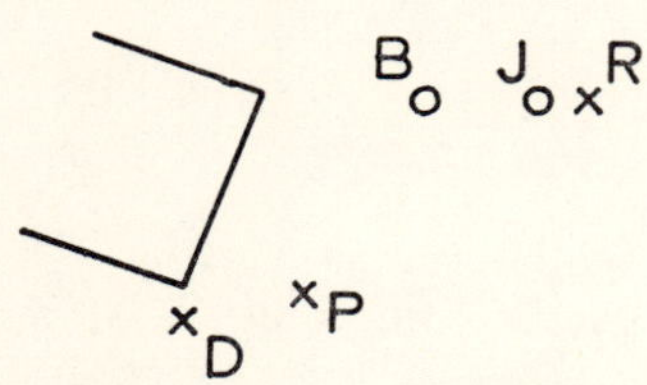

"He'll hear no tone." Buttercup enters from behind rostrum, to take place formerly occupied by Captain.

End of chorus. Bo'-sun and Carpenter lead Ralph off-stage by (II), crossing in front of Sir Joseph. The three altos come forward to fill the gap, LC.

Sir Joseph, watching Ralph exit, starts "My pain and my distress" facing R, then turns to chorus to finish the lines.

12. Buttercup sings from where she stands.

13. After Buttercup's song, Ralph, with Captain on his right, appears on rostrum (both with costumes changed), Bo'sun and Carpenter behind them.

Josephine rushes up steps into Ralph's arms. Captain steps aside and knuckles his forehead to her. Then he goes down steps, and seizing Buttercup round the waist, leads her centre. (These moves should be performed quickly, but without apparent haste — except for Josephine's move.)

14. *Narrative.* As Dick says "What about Sir Joseph?", Hebe moves across coyly, curtseys to Sir Joseph and offers him her hand — which he takes affectedly.

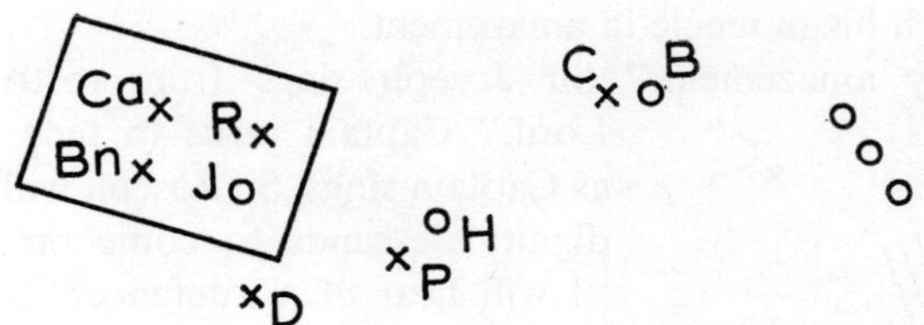

15. *Finale.* Sung in above positions.
   Postlude. Traditional three Hurrahs
16. *End of opera.* Exeunt:
   By (II): Dick.
   By (I): Bo'sun and Carpenter, Josephine and Ralph,
            Sir Joseph and Hebe — he leads her up steps,
            Captain and Buttercup.
   By (II): Three altos; ladies in twos; men in twos, tenors
            pairing with basses.

Suggestions for Costuming

PRINCIPALS	ACT I	ACT II
SIR JOSEPH PORTER	Morning tails with grey topper.	Same.
CAPTAIN CORCORAN	Dinner jacket (white).	Same. Later as for Ralph, Act I.
RALPH	As for Male Chorus, but white shirt, and dark-blue cravat.	Same. Later as for Captain, Act I.
DICK DEADEYE	Light-coloured slacks, cream shirt, red and white spotted cravat, tennis shoes, white socks.	Same.
BO'SUN	As for Male Chorus, but white shirt, and light-blue cravat.	Same.
CARPENTER	As for Bo'sun.	As for Bo'sun.
JOSEPHINE	White garden-party dress, large hat.	Dark outdoor dress, with cape.
HEBE	As for Female Chorus.	Same.
BUTTERCUP	Blouse, skirt (below knee), white thick tights, spotted blue and white bandanna.	Same.

CHORUS	ACTS I, II
MALE	Lightweight white slacks, white or blue open-neck shirts (all the same), tennis shoes, white socks.
FEMALE	Garden-party dresses, large hats.

THE PIRATES OF PENZANCE

Note on Samuel as Narrator

Of all the operas, with the exception of *Trial by Jury*, which has none, *The Pirates of Penzance* has the least amount of spoken dialogue. This serves a concert version well, as there is much less break in continuity, whole scenes being explained within the musical context. In consequence, Samuel is the most suitable character to provide the narrative links. In the Opening Chorus he introduces Frederic, and it is appropriate that he should continue the story.

While it is acceptable that Samuel, as a member of the pirate band, must confess to having been hoodwinked by the Major-General, it would hardly do for the Pirate King to admit to the audience (through narrative) that he had been taken in by the duplicity — he would lose face, his characterisation would be weakened.

The other possible narrator would be the Major-General. But for his imprecise brain to muster the details of the whole plot would seem to be at variance with his character. Moreover, the impact of the appearance of a Major-General confronting the Pirates midway through Act I would largely be lost if he had already made himself known to the audience.

Thus everything points to Samuel as narrator.

Script for Samuel as Narrator

ACT I

Overture.
V.S. No. 1. *Chorus.* "Pour, oh pour the pirate sherry."
SAMUEL As you have heard, Ladies and Gentlemen, we, the famous Pirates of Penzance, held a special carousel to celebrate the coming of age of our apprentice, Frederic. Frederic was a likely lad, but he was inclined to think a lot — too much perhaps — for having just completed his indentures, so becoming a full-blown

member of our band, he declared his intention of leaving us forth-
with. Apparently he should never have joined us in the first place —
it was all a mistake made by his nurserymaid, Ruth, who had
brought him to us many years before, and had enlisted herself as
our Pirate Maid-of-all-Work.

V.S. No. 2. *Song.* "When Fred'ric was a little lad."

SAMUEL Perhaps Ruth, having grown old in our service, had
grumbled a bit about us to Frederic, for he gave us a few home
truths about ourselves. He was very fond of us as individuals, but
detested our calling. Moreover, he said that financially there was
little incentive to remain with us — we didn't seems to make piracy
pay. He told us we were too tender-hearted — we would never
attack a party weaker than ourselves, and so, attacking only stronger
parties, we were always defeated. Again, we would never attack an
orphan. Well, that was true. Being orphans ourselves, we felt very
sorry for them. Thus Frederic tried to persuade us back to civilisation with him, but our leader spoke up for the principles we stood
for.

V.S. No. 3. *Song.* "Oh better far to live and die."

SAMUEL Presenting our best wishes to Frederic, we departed,
leaving Ruth with him. (*Pause, then with a grin*) Oh, yes, Frederic
had suggested she remain with us, but, let us say, that while she
was still a fine figure of a woman, Ruth's charms had faded somewhat; and the King had our full support in giving her to her former
charge. The move suited Ruth, for she had last-chance matrimonial
designs upon the poor lad. I say poor lad because Frederic hadn't
seen a woman for years and was completely ignorant of their
wheedling ways. Ruth played all her feminine tricks coyly, con-
vinced him that their age gap would make no difference to their
marriage, and even made him believe she was still pretty — when
suddenly (*here chorus ladies sing, unaccompanied, a snatch of
"Climbing over rocky mountains"*) Frederic heard girls' voices, and,
investigating, discovered a bevy of beautiful maidens approaching.
He turned on Ruth in some anger!

V.S. No. 4. *Duet.* "Oh false one, you have deceived me."

V.S. No. 5. *Chorus.* "Climbing over rocky mountains."

Continue with musical numbers to the end of the act, without
further narrative.

After V.S. No. 13. *Song,* "I am the very model of a modern a
Major-General" go straight into V.S. No. 14. *Recit.* "Oh men of
dark and dismal fate."

ACT II

SAMUEL Major-General Stanley was very worried at having lied to us about his being an orphan. Much conscience-stricken, he took to wandering in the grounds of his ruined chapel at night, and there he was discovered by his daughters who were much concerned for his welfare in the chill night air. But conscience or not, the Major-General had unknown to us, decided to take action, and had arranged that Frederic would lead an expedition against us.

V.S. No. 1. *Chorus and Solo.* "Oh dry the glistening tear."
V.S. No. 2. *Recit.* "Then, Frederic."
V.S. No. 3. *Chorus and Solos.* "When the foeman bears his steel."
V.S. No. 4. *Recits.*
V.S. No. 5. *Trio.* "When you had left our pirate fold."

SAMUEL   Having met Frederic again, our King and Ruth learned of the force assembling against us. But more important, as Frederic now realised he was still one of us, his sense of duty compelled him to reveal that the Major-General was no orphan. Outraged at this perfidy, the King set forth to collect our band and reap a just revenge.

V.S. No. 6. *Trio.* "Away, away."

Continue with musical numbers to the end, without further narrative.

At the end of V.S. No. 9., *Recit and Chorus*, "No. I'll be brave," Mabel should deliver the standard few lines of libretto to the Police, and the Sergeant likewise.

Basic Seating Plan — Act I

(see figure overleaf)

PROPS

Act I.   Tankards and black jack.
Act II.   Garden Seat (for three).

NOTATION

Mg — Major-General	M — Mabel
Kg — Pirate King	E — Edith
S — Samuel	K — Kate
F — Frederic	R — Ruth
Sg — Sergeant	
T — Tenor (Chorus)	B — Bass (Chorus)

55

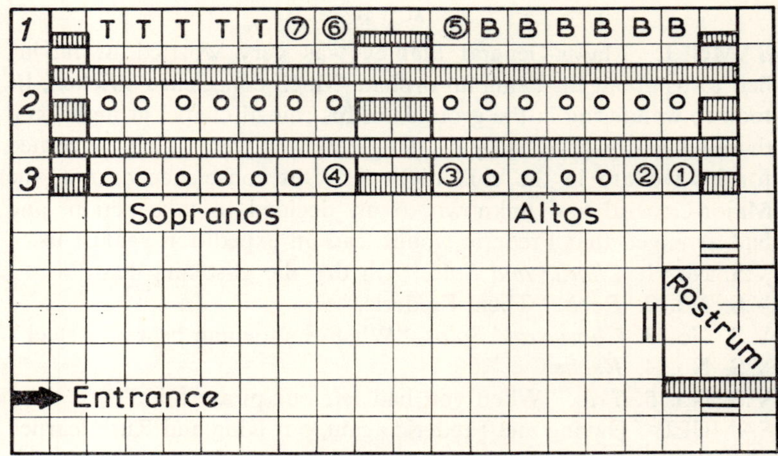

ROW 1 (Raised 2 double steps) ROW 2 (Raised 1 double step)
ROW 3 (Seated floor level)
ROSTRUM (Raised 1 double step)

Production for Script with Samuel as Narrator

ACT I

1. Company enter thus:
   > Row 2 — led by an alto, altos then sopranos, single file, go up centre steps and divide.
   >
   > Row 3 — Mabel to ②, altos, Kate to ③, Edith to ④, sopranos.
   >
   > Rostrum — Frederic, followed by Ruth
   >
   > Remain standing till all on stage, then sit together taking cue from Frederic and Ruth.
   >
   > Frederic sits on rostrum, knees up, chin on knees. Ruth reclines at his feet in humble attitude.

2. *Overture.*

3. *Opening Chorus* (Introduction). Pirates enter, laughing and drinking, as soon as music starts. Order: basses, Samuel, King, tenors.

   Group on front area, standing. Frederic and Ruth remain seated.

   Postlude. All raise tankards to, and shout "Frederic!" on last chord.

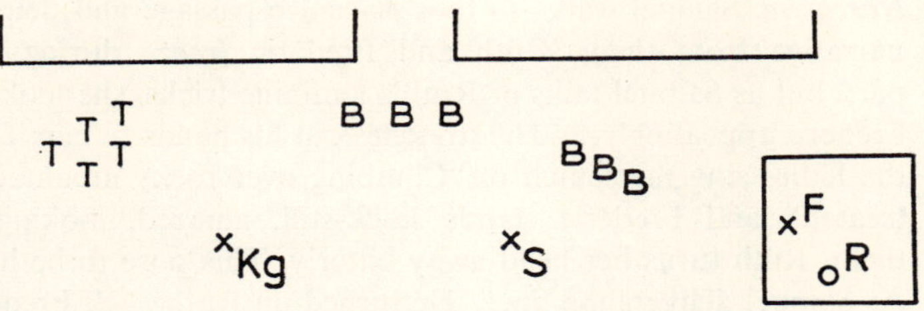

4. *Narrative.* All *freeze* as Samuel steps forward.
5. *Ruth's Solo.* Verse 1 and first half Verse 2 sung on rostrum. Rest of Verse 2 crossing to centre, haranguing pirates. Verse 3, centre.
6. *Narrative.* Samuel again comes forward (all *freeze*) and then steps back for King's solo.

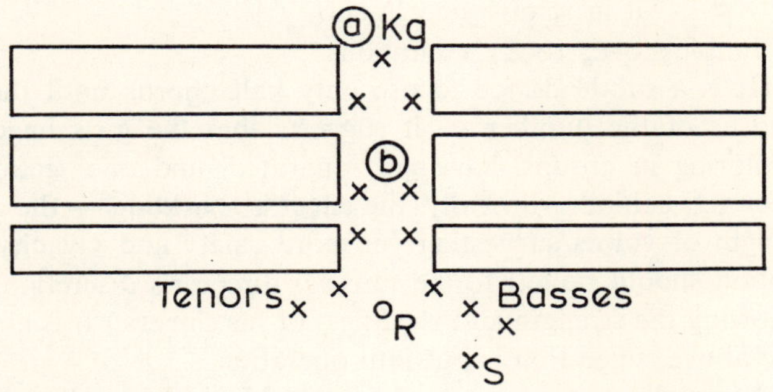

7. *King's Solo.* King steps forward RC; Frederic rises; Ruth, still centre, moves back a little, unobtrusively. King may move about stage as desired, but towards end of Verse 2, having sung the held top C, he mounts steps of centre passage as chorus sings, and poses at top ⓐ to sing "And it is a glorious thing." As chorus sing "It is," in twos they mount steps and hold picture ⓑ at final "Hurrah!," then quickly file into their seats. Pirate King sits ⑦, and Chorus sits with him. As they do so, Ruth crosses in front of Samuel, to kneel about a pace from the rostrum, facing Frederic.

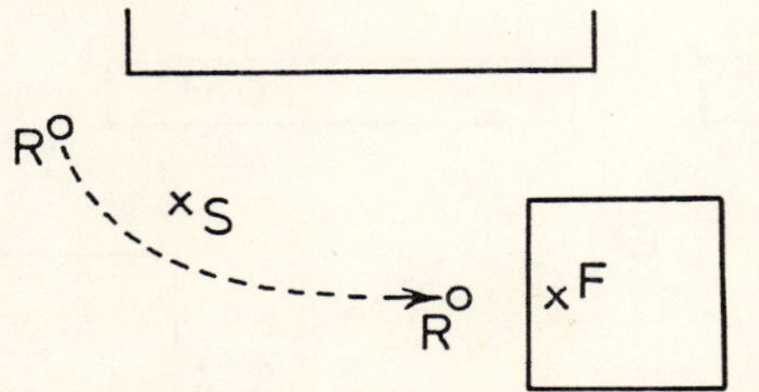

8. *Narrative*. Samuel walks to foot of centre passage and delivers narrative from there. Ruth and Frederic *freeze* during first part, but as Samuel talks of Ruth's feminine tricks, she looks at Frederic appealingly, and he stretches out his hands to her. Then the ladies sing the snatch of "Climbing over rocky mountains" (seated), and Frederic stands stock-still, amazed, looking at them. Ruth turns her head away bitterly. This pose to be held. As Samuel delivers the line, "He turned on Ruth . . ." Frederic tears his gaze from the ladies to scowl at Ruth.

9. "Oh false one." At first chord, Samuel climbs steps to sit ⑥. During duet, Ruth and Frederic may use the stage, but as she is finally spurned, she breaks, weeping, to run up steps to sit ⑤.

10. "What shall I do?" For his Recit, Frederic comes in front of rostrum and kneels behind it in semi-concealment.

11. "Climbing over rocky mountains."

(It is a subtle device to use only half chorus until the final chorus of the number — it suggests that the girls have been exploring in groups, have got separated, and one section has been left behind. Musically, the effect is sparkling — the double weight of voices suggesting yet more gaiety and vivacity. This option should be left to the musical director's discretion — he knowing the strength and weakness of his singers.) It is assumed the above suggestion is put into operation.

As music starts, front row, except Mabel, rises. Kate, Edith and three ladies on each side of them should move and dance.

Led by Kate and Edith, the eight move to rostrum, across stage to form a group RC, ⓐ. Remaining alto and three sopranos on front row follow to fill gap at rostrum. Positions attained for Edith's solo shown ⓑ. (See figure on facing page)

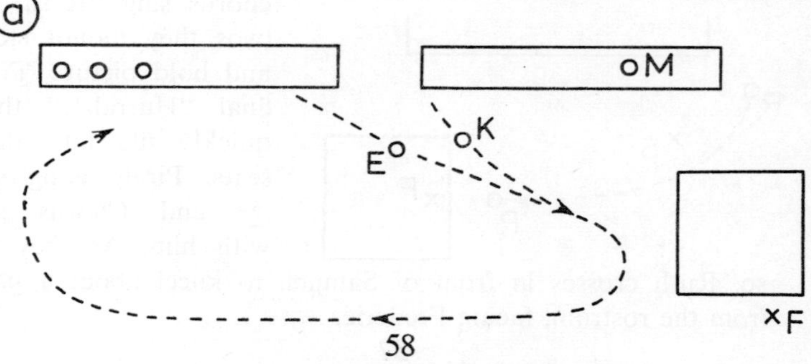

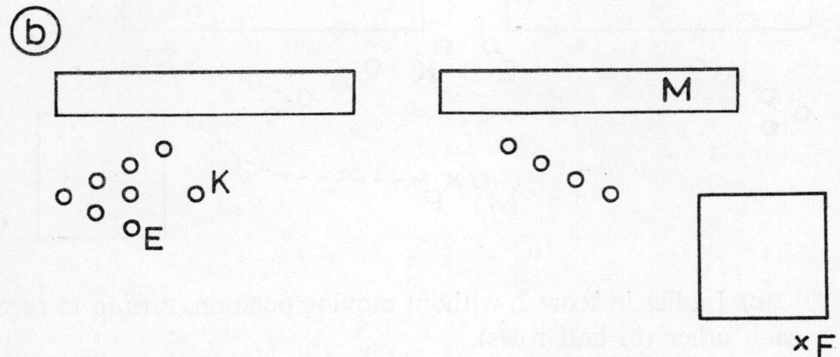

Kate's Solo. Kate runs to sing on back corner of rostrum.
Final chorus. Row two ladies rise. Edith dances with six ladies R, Kate joins and dances with four ladies L.

Postlude. Frederic, who has been watching unobserved, becomes bolder, and rises.

12. "Stop ladies, pray." On two bar introduction, Frederic steps on to rostrum. The ladies shrink from him as he sings.

"Oh, is there not one maiden breast." Verse 1 sung from rostrum. Chorus of Verse 1, Frederic steps down to appeal to Kate and ladies L. Verse 2 sung centre. Chorus Verse 2, Frederic crosses to appeal to Edith and ladies R. His back is turned to rostrum.

Mabel rises on Frederic's last "Not one?" and steps on to rostrum, singing from there.

13. "Poor wand'ring one" (*Postlude*). Frederic joins Mabel on rostrum. Ladies, in groups, huddle round Edith and Kate.

14. "How beautifully blue the sky." Mabel sings her solo on rostrum. Both cross to RC for Frederic's solo, then back to centre to sing duet section.

15. "No, we must not lose our senses."

(a) Ladies on stage again huddle in two groups, but Edith and Kate run together to centre passage.

(b) Frederick and Mabel cross L, in front of ladies, behind rostrum, to sit ①, ②.

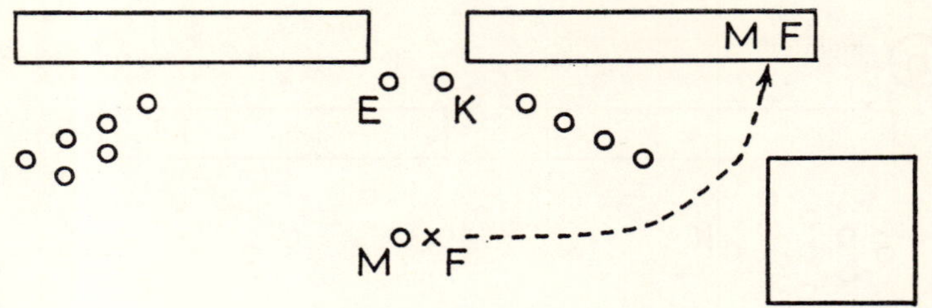

    (c) Ladies in Row 2, without moving position, turn in to face each other (in half rows).

    (d) Pirates rise and start creeping down steps thus:

        Steps centre — Samuel, King, two basses.

        Steps R — four tenors.

        Steps L — three basses.

        Row 1 — one tenor, one bass remain standing there. Ruth keeps seated.

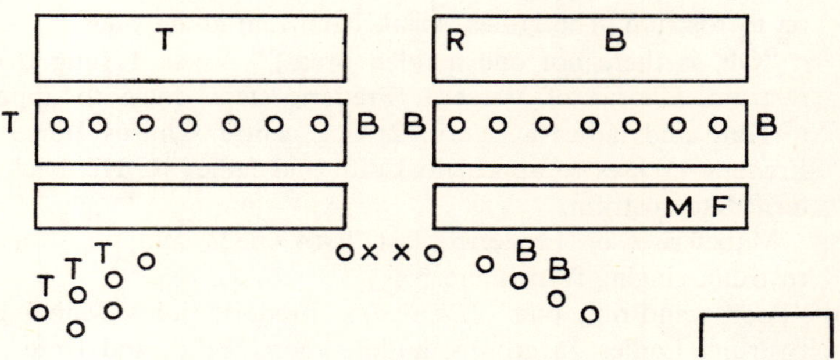

16. "Here's a first rate opportunity." Sung in above positions.

17. "Hold, monsters." Mabel, with Frederic behind, comes on to rostrum. All eyes are turned to her, allowing Major-General to make his entrance R front, unobserved. He sings *Recit* from there, then moves centre for solo.

18. "Oh men of dark and dismal fate."

    Major-General moves RC front.

    Samuel and King move LC middle.

    Edith and Kate close, centre back.

19. These basic positions to be held with dancing or traditional 'business' as required until the end of "Her sisters all will bridesmaids be."

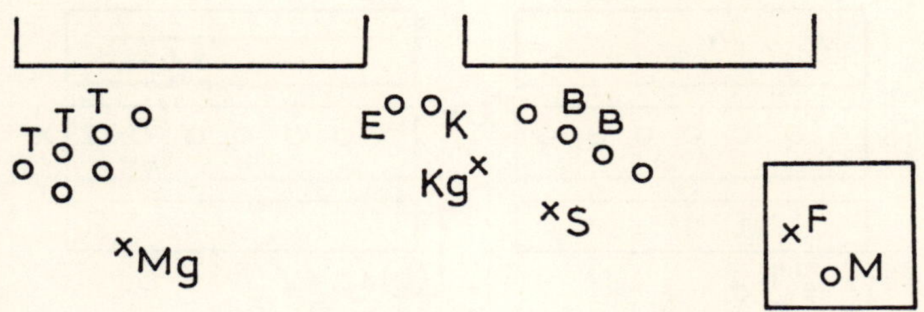

Orchestral Postlude. Ruth creeps down centre steps, bursts between Edith and Kate, crosses in front of King and Samuel, to kneel below rostrum in front of Frederic. Banished, she moves weeping, to sit ①.

20. *Final Chorus.* Same positions.

"Pray observe" (Ladies). Ladies on stage curtsey to pirates beside them. Kate and Edith move to King and Samuel, curtsey to them, then cross R, to stand on either side of the Major-General.

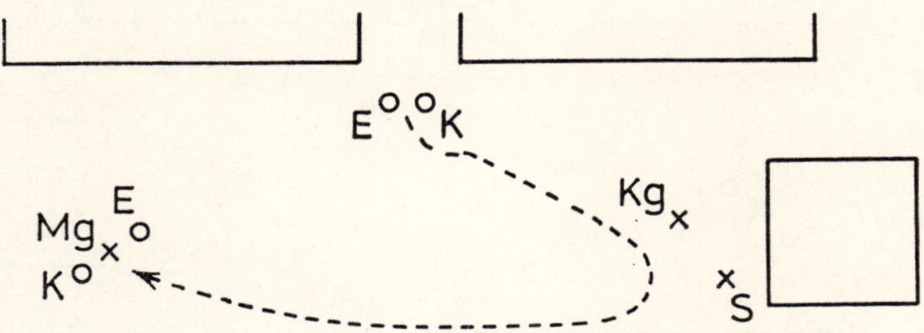

21. "But they give up the felicity" (last time).

Row 2 ladies in twos, come straight down centre, military fashion, march to front, do right turn, crossing in front of Major-General who stands at salute ⓐ, and exit. They are followed immediately by four ladies L, who pass in front of Major-General ⓑ; then by six ladies R, who exit behind him ⓒ.

Pirates are rather amazed at this military precision, and assemble in straight line across stage ⓓ, with King taking salute. They then turn and march off in single file. ⓔ Exit of whole Chorus, male and female, should be accomplished by the time postlude is finished. Principals remain.

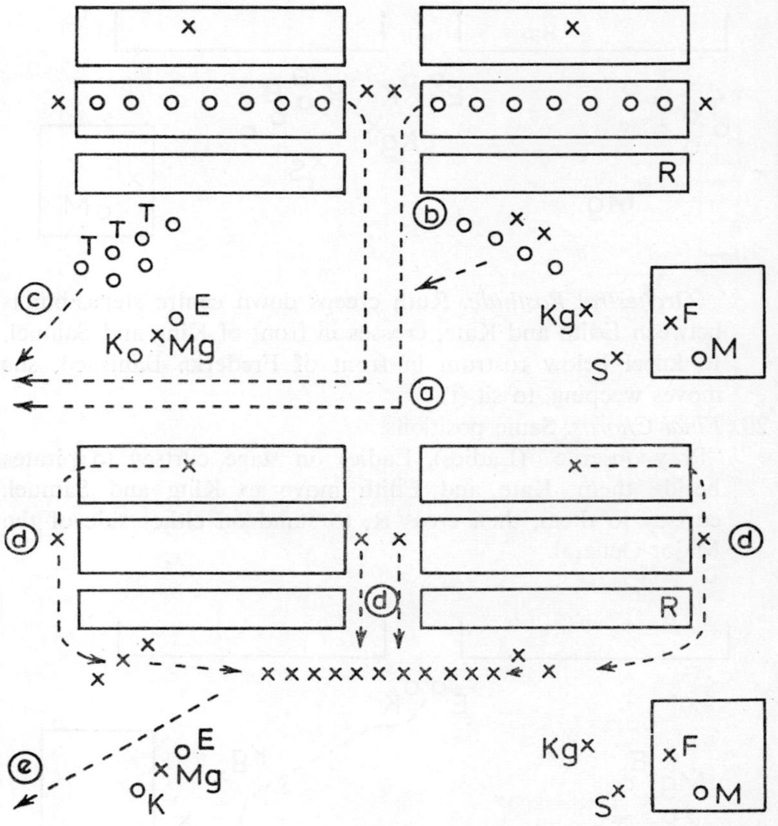

Ruth comes forward between Samuel and King, Frederic and Mabel cross centre.

Hold pose thus: Major-General erect, Kate and Edith on his arms, Frederic and Mabel in embrace; three Pirates, crouched slightly, watch in menacing fashion this family scene.

Then all Principals step forward to front, take one bow together, then exit.

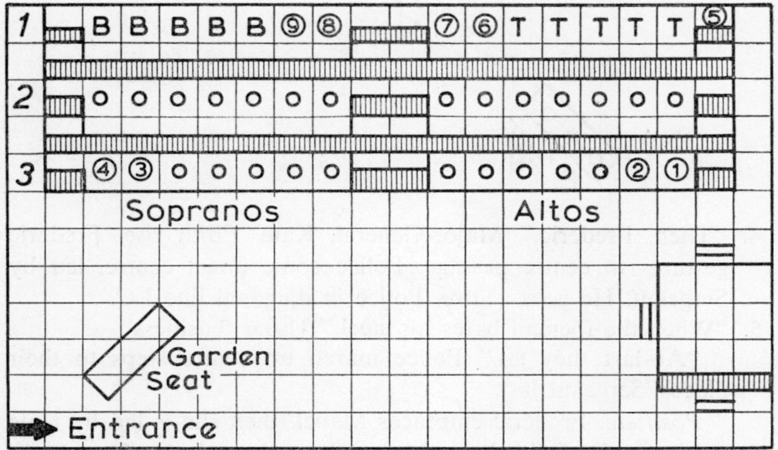

ROW 1 (Raised 2 double steps) ROW 2 (Raised 1 double step)
ROW 3 (Seated floor level)

NOTES

1. Garden Seat to be three-seater.
2. Extra chair ⑤ for Samuel.
3. Note tenors and basses have positions reversed from Act 1.

ACT II

1. Company enters thus:
   > Row 1 — Basses, Sergeant to ⑨, Pirates, King to ⑥, Ruth to ⑦.
   > In twos: go up centre steps and divide.
   > Row 2 — Altos, sopranos — single file.
   > Row 3 — Altos, sopranos — single file.

   Mabel and Frederic, Kate and Edith escorting Major-General — all five to group at seat.

   Major-General, Kate and Edith sit, on which cue company sit together. Mabel and Frederic remain standing. (See next figure)
2. *Narrative.* Sam enters and crosses front to deliver narrative from rostrum; then goes up steps L, to sit ⑤.
3. *Opening Chorus.* Ladies' Chorus rises.

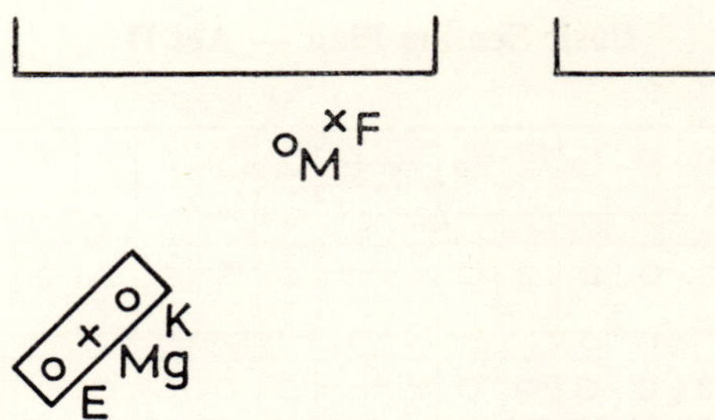

4. "Then, Frederic." Major-General, Kate, Edith rise. Frederic gestures to centre passage. Police come down centre, led by Sergeant. He goes centre, Police in diagonal line LC.
5. "When the foeman bares his steel." Usual 'business'.

"At last they go." Police march up centre steps to their places, Sergeant last.

Postlude. Frederic embraces Mabel, then she is led by Kate to sit ①, ②. Edith leads Major-General to sit ③, ④. All sit.

6. "Now for the Pirates lair." Frederic moves downstage centre.

King and Ruth creep down steps centre to arrive on either side of him.

7. After "Paradox Trio." Principals *freeze* while Samuel comes down to rostrum for *Narrative*. Samuel then returns to his seat.
8. "Away, away" (*Postlude*). King and Ruth stride up centre steps to their seats. Frederic, remaining centre, is joined by Mabel from her seat.

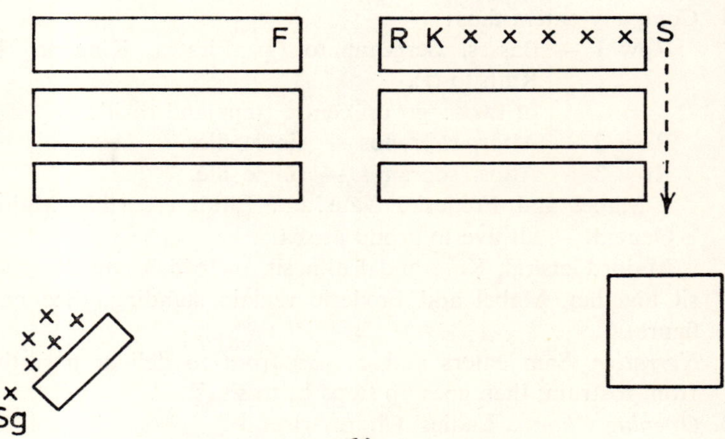

Traditional actions for *duets*, after which Frederic leaves Mabel RC and goes to sit ⑧.

9. "No, I'll be brave." When summoned, Police come down to take former diagonal line LC, with Sergeant centre. Mabel walks behind Sergeant to resume her seat. (See last figure)

10. "A rollicking band of Pirates." Pirates stand and sing all this chorus from Row 1. Police cross R to hide behind seat, as very slowly, Pirates come down steps L, led by Samuel for . . .

11. "With cat-like tread." Slow descent in order: Samuel, Pirates, King, Frederic, Ruth. They should take their time to arrive in positions in time for Samuel's solo. They climb over and beyond rostrum, leaving it for King, Ruth and Frederic.

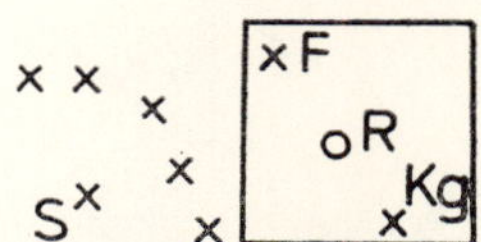

12. "Hush, hush! Not a word." Frederic points R, then he, King and Ruth climb over end of rostrum to crouch in front of it. Pirates climb back over rostrum and hide at far left side.

13. "Sighing softly to the river" (*Introduction*). Major-General comes from his seat centre for song. He should finish it RC.

14. "Now what is this." Ladies' Chorus rises. Edith, Mabel and Kate rush to gather round their father.

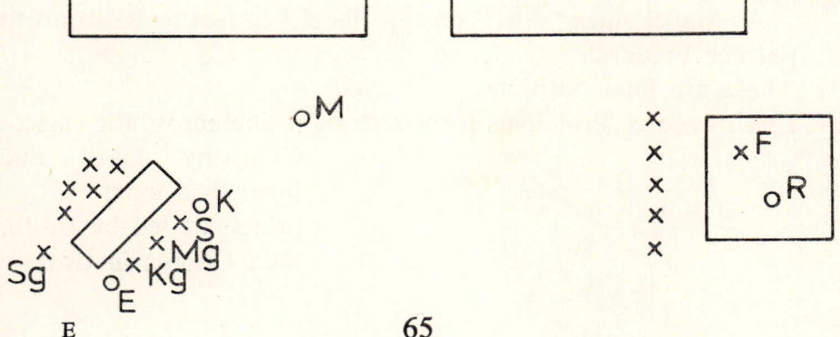

15. "Forward, my men, and seize that general." Samuel and King run right to seize Major-General by the arms. The other Pirates group in front of the rostrum, Ruth and Frederic step on to rostrum.

16. "Yes, we are here." Police come from behind seat, in front and across stage for stylised fight with Pirates, centre.

17. "Take my daughters." Selection of partners takes place during first part of "Poor wand'ring one."

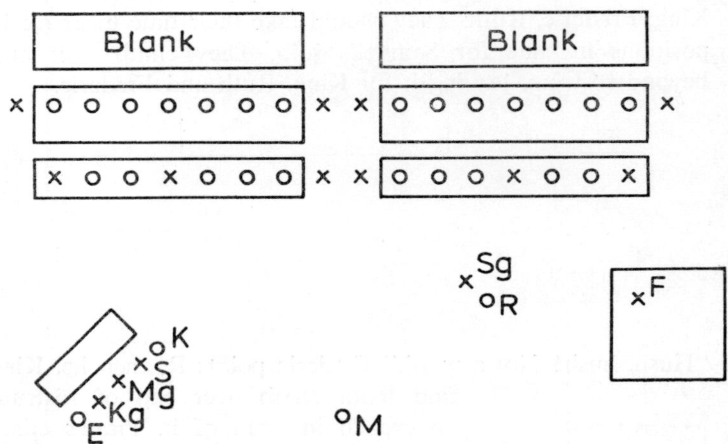

(a) Mabel comes centre front.
(b) King takes Edith, Samuel takes Kate.
(c) Sergeant crosses to rostrum, offers rose to Ruth — she steps down to accept it.
(d) Pirates and Police go to sides and centre of Rows 1, 2, partnering ladies at end of each row. Two men squeeze into middles of front row.

All above should be completed in first verse.

As Mabel sings "Ah!" on top B♭, she moves to Rostrum to partner Frederic.

These are final positions.

18. *End of opera.* Principals form a straight line across the stage.

Company takes one bow, then exit: principals led by Edith, then Chorus in twos.

Suggestions for Costuming

PRINCIPALS	ACT I	ACT II
MAJOR-GENERAL STANLEY	Dinner jacket (white), with medal ribbons	Jacket discarded. Short quilted dressing gown over.
PIRATE KING	Dark slacks, red shirt, flamboyant cravat.	Same.
SAMUEL	Dark slacks, brown shirt, cravat. (Less colourful than King)	Same.
FREDERIC	Light-coloured slacks, white sports shirt, yellow cravat (Much more sober and refined)	Well-cut sports suit. (Very smart and dapper)
SERGEANT OF POLICE	—	As for Police, but with white shirt.
MABEL	White summer dress.	Opening — Same. Later — white nylon nightdress.
EDITH KATE	Pink summer dresses.	Opening — Same. Later — pink nylon nightdresses.
RUTH	White sports blouse, black slacks, white tights, buckled shoes, broad belt, bright bandanna. Alternative: Tight-fitting, high-necked, black sweater; black leather mini-skirt, broad black leather belt, thick black tights, black leather boots, pink bandanna and one pink, dangling ear-ring.	Same.

CHORUS	ACT I	ACT II
PIRATES	Dark slacks, polo or crew-neck sweaters.	Same.
POLICE	—	Dark suits, shirts either all blue (preferable) or all white, black ties, black shoes.
LADIES	Bright summer dresses/floral prints	Opening — Same. Later — Nylon nightdresses. Length optional, but all should be approximately the same. (No 'baby-dolls' or pyjamas).

6

PATIENCE

Script for Patience, Angela and Saphir as Narrators

ACT I

Overture

V.S. No. 1. *Chorus and Solos*. "Twenty love-sick maidens we."

ANGELA There is a strange magic in this love of ours! Rivals as we all are in the affections of our Reginald, the very hopelessness of our love is a bond that binds us to one another. Jealousy is merged in misery. While he, the very cynosure of our eyes and hearts, remains icy insensible.

SAPHIR And yet the man loves — wildly loves.

ANGELA (*Surprised*) Whom? None of us!

SAPHIR No, none of us. His weird fancy has lighted, for the nonce, on Patience, the village milkmaid.

ANGELA On Patience? Oh it cannot be!

SAPHIR But yesterday I caught him in her dairy, eating fresh butter with a tablespoon. Today, he is not well!

ANGELA But Patience claims that she has never loved — that love is, to her, a sealed book. Oh he cannot be serious!

V.S. No. 2. *Recit and Song*. "I cannot tell what this love may be."

ANGELA Ah, Patience, if you have never loved, you have never known true happiness!

PATIENCE But the truly happy always seem to have so much on their minds. The truly happy never seem quite well.

SAPHIR There is a transcendentability of delirium — an acute accentuation of supremest ecstasy — which the earthy might easily mistake for indigestion. But it is not indigestion — it is aesthetic transfiguration! (*To chorus*) Come.

PATIENCE But stay, I have some news for you. The 35th Dragoon Guards have halted in the village, and are even now on their way to this very spot.

ANGELA The 35th Dragoon Guards!

SAPHIR They are fleshly men, of full habit — we care nothing for Dragoon Guards.

69

PATIENCE   But bless you, you were all engaged to them a year ago!

SAPHIR   A year ago! My poor child, you don't understand these things. A year ago they were very well in our eyes, but since then our tastes have been etherealized, our perceptions exalted. (*To chorus*) Come, it is time to lift up our voices in morning carol to our Reginald.

V.S. No. 2a. *Chorus.* "Twenty love-sick maidens we."

V.S. No. 3. *Chorus/Solo.* "The soldiers of our Queen" / "If you want a receipt."

V.S. No. 4. *Chorus and solos.* "In a doleful train."

PATIENCE   (*To audience*) The Dragoons are quite astounded at the ladies' indifference to them, and at the way in which they regard Reginald with admiration as he completes the writing of a poem.

BUNTHORNE   Ah, Patience! Dear Patience!

ANGELA   Will you please read your composition to us, sir?

SAPHIR   This we supplicate. (*Both kneel.*)

BUNTHORNE   Shall I?

ALL THE DRAGOONS   No!

BUNTHORNE   (*To Patience*) I will read it if you bid me.

PATIENCE   (*Indifferent*) You can if you like.

BUNTHORNE   (*Reads*) "Oh Hollow! Hollow! Hollow!" (See libretto.)

ANGELA   How purely fragrant!

SAPHIR   How earnestly precious!

PATIENCE   Well, it seems to me to be nonsense.

SAPHIR   Nonsense, yes, perhaps — but oh, what precious nonsense.

PATIENCE   You seem to have forgotten you are engaged to these other gentlemen.

SAPHIR   It can never be. They are not Empyrean. They are not Della Cruscan. They are not even Early English. Would that they would be Early English before it is too late!

ANGELA   If they could but improve their mode of dress. There is a cobwebby grey velvet, with a tender bloom like cold gravy, which, made Florentine fourteenth century, trimmed with Venetian leather and Spanish altar lace, and surmounted with something Japanese — it matters not what — would at least be Early English! Come, ladies.

V.S. No. 4a. *Chorus.* "Twenty love-sick maidens we."

V.S. No. 5. *Song.* "When I first put this uniform on."

V.S. No. 6. *Recit and Song.* "Am I alone?"

ANGELA Well, I do believe Reginald is declaring his love to Patience!

SAPHIR Oh me miserum.

ANGELA But soft. She repulses him.

SAPHIR Oh rapture — though lack-a-day for poor, desolate Reginald.

PATIENCE (*To the ladies*) What on earth does it all mean? Why does he love me? Why does he expect me to love him? He's not a relation! It frightens me!

ANGELA Why, Patience, what is the matter?

PATIENCE Lady Angela, tell me two things. Firstly, what on earth is this love that upsets everybody. And secondly, how is it distinguished from insanity?

ANGELA Poor blind child! Oh forgive her, Eros! Why, love is of all passions the most essential! It is the embodiment of purity, the abstraction of refinement! It is the one unselfish emotion in this whirlpool of grasping greed!

PATIENCE (*Beginning to cry*) Oh, dear, oh!

ANGELA Why are you crying?

PATIENCE To think that I have lived all these years without having experienced this ennobling and unselfish passion! Why, what a wicked girl I must have been! For it is unselfish, isn't it?

ANGELA Absolutely! Love that is tainted with selfishness is no love. Oh, try, try, try to love! Is it possible you have never loved anybody?

PATIENCE Yes, one.

ANGELA Ah! Whom?

PATIENCE My great aunt.

ANGELA Great aunts don't count.

PATIENCE Then there's nobody. At least — no, nobody. Not since I was a baby. But that doesn't count, I suppose.

ANGELA I don't know. Tell me about it.

V.S. No. 7. *Duet.* "Long years ago."

PATIENCE It's perfectly dreadful to think of the appalling state I must be in! I had no idea love was a duty. No wonder they all look so unhappy. Upon my word, I hardly like to associate with myself. I don't think I'm respectable. I'll go at once and fall in love with (*enter Grosvenor*) a stranger!

V.S. No. 8. *Duet.* "Prithee pretty maiden."

ANGELA Why it's Archibald Grosvenor, the friend and play-fellow of Patience's childhood days.

SAPHIR I have heard of him. Is not he, too, a poet?

ANGELA (*Beginning to become enamoured of him*) Oh, yes. He is the Apostle of Simplicity. He is called 'Archibald the All-Right' — he is infallible.

SAPHIR He has a beauty which surely can have no rival upon earth.

ANGELA He has. He complains that it is his hideous destiny to be madly loved at first sight by every woman he comes across.

SAPHIR (*With a sigh*) Perhaps his claim is not unjustified. Oh, Archibald!

ANGELA (*Watching Patience*) Alas, Patience has fallen to the spell of his beauty. Oh, Archibald!

PATIENCE (*To Grosvenor*) Oh marvellous! I seem now to know what love is! It has been revealed to me — it is Archibald Grosvenor. We will never, never part. But — oh, horror! You are perfection. A source of endless ecstasy to all who know you. So there can be nothing unselfish in loving *you*. To monopolise these features on which all women love to linger — it would be unpardonable! Our duty is clear; we must part, and for ever.

V.S. No. 8a. *Duet.* "Though to marry you."

V.S. No. 9. *Finale Act I.*

ACT II

V.S. No. 1. *Chorus.* "On such eyes."

(This number is usually omitted, but for a concert version it is worth including it to facilitate a smooth entrance for the ladies.)

JANE The fickle crew have deserted Reginald and sworn allegiance to his rival, and all, forsooth, because he has glanced with passing favour on a puling milkmaid! Fools! Of that fancy he will soon weary — and then I, who alone am faithful to him, shall reap my reward. But do not dally too long, Reginald, for my charms are ripe, Reginald, and already they are decaying. Better secure me 'ere I have gone too far!

V.S. No.2. *Recit and Song.* "Sad is that woman's lot."

V.S. No. 3. *Chorus.* "Turn, oh, turn."

ANGELA Sir, will it please you read to us? One of your own poems?

SAPHIR (*As he demurs, prompts him*) Mr. Bunthorne used to read a poem of his own to us every day.

72

GROSVENOR (*Reads*) "Gentle Jane" (see libretto).
SAPHIR There is not one word in that decalet which is calculated to bring the blush of shame to the cheek of modesty.
ANGELA Not one; it is purity itself.
SAPHIR May we hear more, kind sir?
GROSVENOR (*Reads*) "Teasing Tom" (see libretto).
ANGELA Marked you how grandly — how relentlessly — the damning catalogue of crime strode on, till Retribution, like a poisèd hawk, came swooping down upon the Wrong-Doer? Oh, it was terrible!
SAPHIR Oh sir, you are indeed a true poet, for you touch our hearts, and they go out to you!
GROSVENOR Poor, poor, girls! It is best to speak plainly. I know that I am loved by you, but I can never love you in return, for my heart is fixed elsewhere! Remember the fable of the Magnet and the Churn.
V.S. No. 4. *Song.* "A magnet hung in a hardware shop."
V.S. No. 5. *Song.* "Love is a plaintive song."
ANGELA Poor Patience. She is very much in love with our Archibald.
SAPHIR And it is making Mr. Bunthorne very jealous. Do you know, I've heard him call dear Archibald a smug-faced idiot! How ever could we have admired him?
ANGELA Jane still does. She has been advising him to meet Archibald on his own ground and beat him.
V.S. No. 6. *Duet.* "So go to him."
V.S. No. 7. *Trio.* "It's clear that mediaeval art."
ANGELA Oh, Saphir — see, see! The immortal fire has descended upon them, and they are of the Inner Brotherhood — perceptively intense and consummately utter!
SAPHIR How Botticellian! How Fra Angelican! Oh Art, we thank thee for this boon!
ANGELA (*To the men*) We will not deny that we are much moved by this proof of your attachment.
SAPHIR Yes, your conversion to the principles of Aesthetic Art in its highest development has touched us deeply.
ANGELA And if Mr. Grosvenor should remain obdurate. . . .
SAPHIR Which we have every reason to believe he will. . . .
ANGELA We are not prepared to say our yearning hearts will not go out to you.
COLONEL By sections of threes — rapture.

V.S. No. 8. *Quintet.* "If Saphir I choose to marry."
V.S. No. 9. *Duet.* "When I go out of door."
Additional dance. See Production.

PATIENCE   I cannot express the joy that I feel at the change in Reginald. He has promised to model himself on Archibald — from henceforth to be mildly cheerful, to blend amusement with instruction in his conversation. Oh, it will no longer be a duty to love him, but a pleasure — a rapture — an ecstasy! (*Changes mood.*) But, oh horror — if he is absolutely reformed, he will be a perfect being — utterly free from defect of any kind. So I can never be his. Love to be pure, must be absolutely unselfish, and there can be nothing unselfish in loving so perfect a being as he has become.

V.S. No. 10. *Song and Chorus.* "I'm a Waterloo House young man."

BUNTHORNE   Angela — Ella — Saphir — what, what does this mean?

ANGELA   It means that Archibald the All-Right cannot be all-wrong; and if the All-Right chooses to discard aestheticism, it proves that aestheticism ought to be discarded.

PATIENCE   (*To Grosvenor*) Is it quite certain that you will always be a commonplace young man?

GROSVENOR   Always — I've sworn it.

PATIENCE   Why, then, there's nothing to prevent my loving you with all the fervour at my command!

GROSVENOR   Why, that's true.

PATIENCE   My Archibald!

GROSVENOR   My Patience!

BUNTHORNE   Crushed again!

JANE   Cheer up! I am still here. I have never left you and I never will!

BUNTHORNE   Thank you, Jane. After all, there is no denying it, you're a fine figure of a woman!

JANE   My Reginald!

BUNTHORNE   My Jane!

V.S. *Fanfare.*

COLONEL   Ladies, the Duke has at length determined to take a bride!

DUKE   I have a great gift to bestow. Ladies, in personal appearance you have all that is necessary to make a woman happy. In common fairness, I think I ought to choose the only one among you who has the misfortune to be distinctly plain. Jane!

JANE Duke!
BUNTHORNE Crushed again!
V.S. No. 11. *Finale Act II.*

Basic Seating Plan

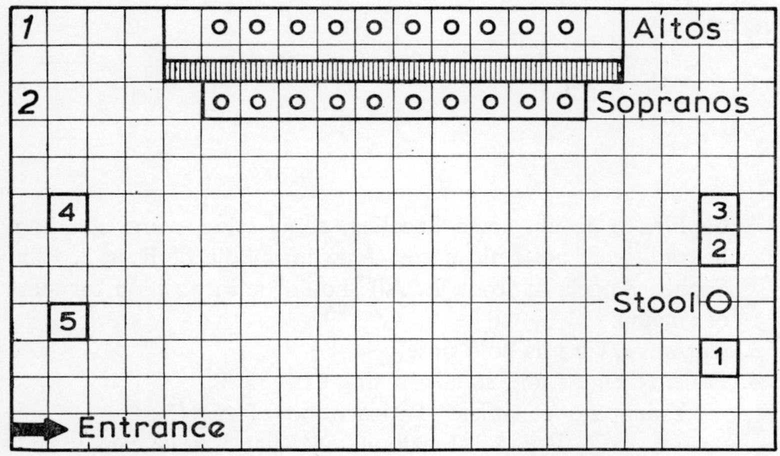

ROW 1 (Raised 1 single step) ROW 2 (Seated floor level)

NOTE

20 seats for ladies.

NOTATION

C — Colonel   A — Angela
M — Major   S — Saphir
D — Duke   E — Ella
B — Bunthorne   J — Jane
G — Grosvenor   P — Patience

(The part of Mr. Bunthorne's Solicitor is omitted.)

Production for Script with Angela, Saphir and Patience as Narrators

ACT I

1. *Overture.*
2. *Opening Chorus.* Ladies glide on in twos, led by Angela and

75

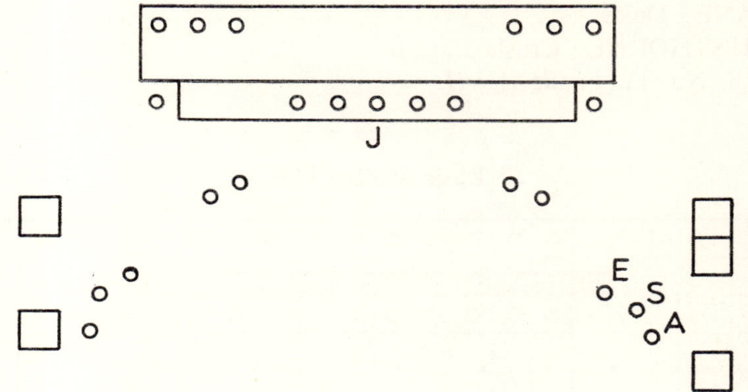

Saphir, to group, some kneeling, some lying, some standing, in traditional aesthetic poses; Jane in middle of Row 2, Ella, Saphir, Angela at front, L. All should be in position for start of singing.

3. *Narrative.* Chorus hold pose.
4. Patience enters and stands to sing extreme R.
   "Your pardon, ladies." Patience moves to RC.

5. "I cannot tell what this love may be." Verse 1 sung RC, Verse 2 sung LC.
6. *Narrative.* Angela and Saphir come on either side of Patience. Ella moves back to join ladies behind.
7. "Twenty love-sick maidens." Ladies, singing, glide to their positions at seats.

Saphir and Angela leave Patience to go to stand at ③, ②.
"Ah, miserie." Patience shakes her head and goes to ①.
Second last bar. All sit.

8. "The soldiers of our queen." Men march on in twos, basses

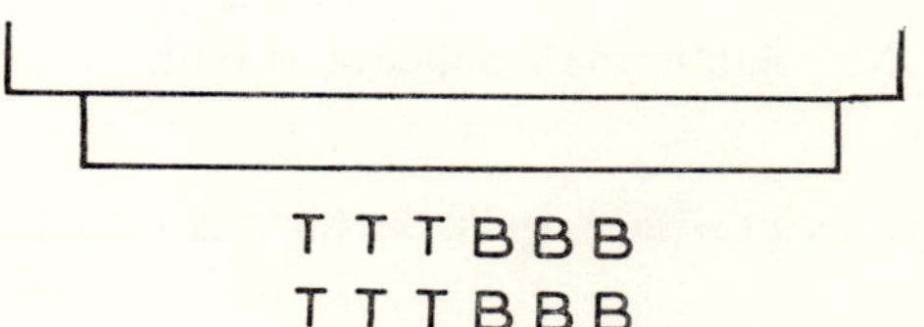

followed by tenors, to stand in two rows centre.
Postlude. Major, Duke, Colonel march on in that order,

76

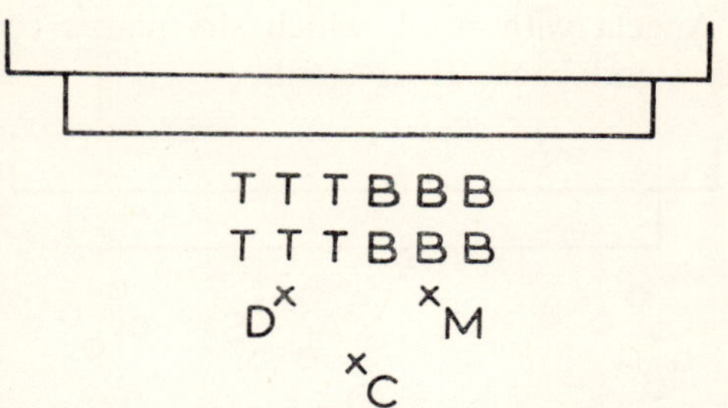

single file, to take positions for Colonel's song.

    Colonel's song (Postlude). Dividing in centre, men do R, L

turn respectively for tenors to march R, followed by Duke, basses L, followed by Major and Colonel.

9. "In a doleful train." All ladies except Patience rise. Six ladies

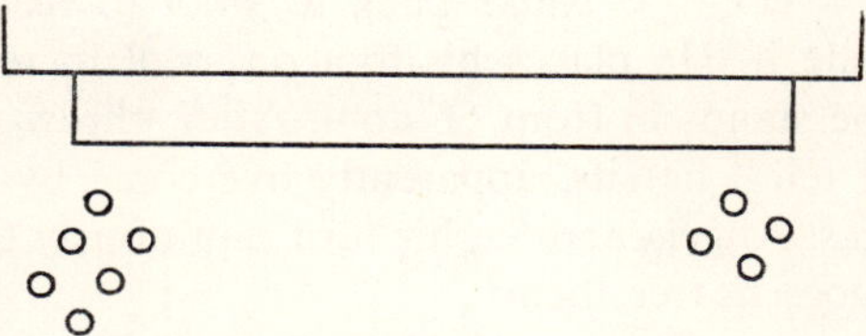

front row R, glide forward in twos to form diagonal lines, RC middle. Four ladies front row L, do the same, LC middle. These ten ladies kneel. As they start to sing, Angela and Saphir

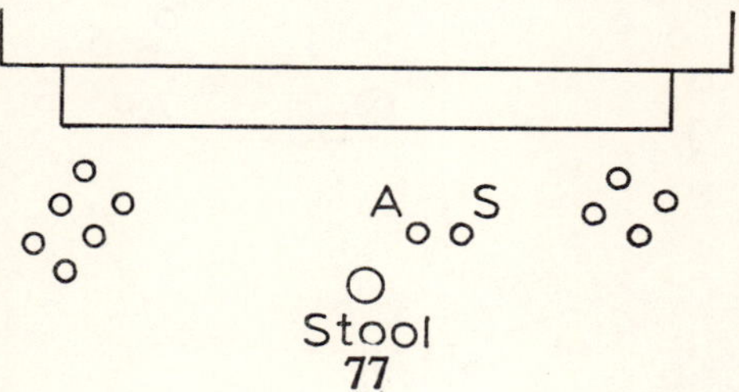

move R, Angela with stool, which she places centre, middle.
Then both stand back, L of stool.

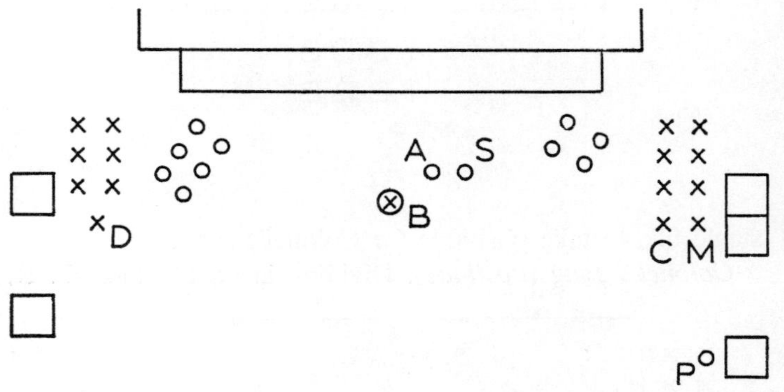

"None so sorrowful." Bunthorne, apparently completely
oblivious of surroundings, enters, to sit on stool, facing slightly
L.

"Now is not this preposterous." Dragoons march forward.
Angela and Saphir sing solos standing.

10. *Narrative*. Patience rises and turns to
face audience. Bunthorne comes down
to her. Angela and Saphir move nearer
Bunthorne, on diagonal. Bunthorne
walks back to stool to read Verse 1 of
poem beside it. He places his foot on stool to recite Verse 2.
Verse 3, he stands in front of stool. After 'throw-away' line of
"I cannot tell", he sits, apparently overcome by the effort —
then *freezes*. Angela and Saphir turn rapturously to each other.
Patience goes nearer them.

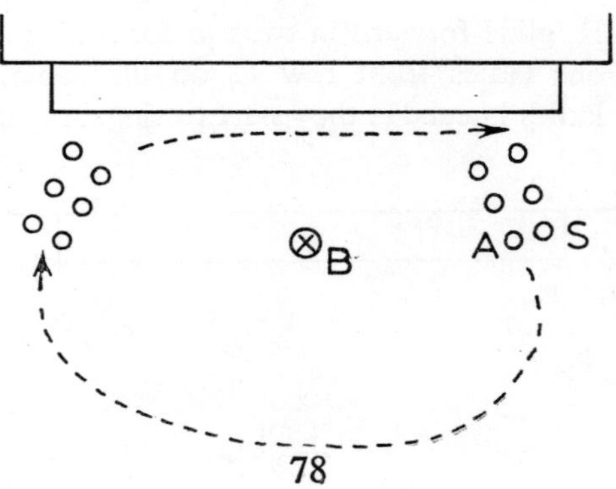

11. "Twenty love-sick maidens we." At narrative, " Come, ladies,"
Angela and Saphir start to lead ladies on L round the front of
the stage, while other six turn back and move L, for all to
glide to positions in front row.
(Note. Positions on front row will now be altered — places to
be taken in order of walking.)
Angela and Saphir proceed beyond all front row, *behind men*
L, to their seats.
   "Ah, miserie." Patience, again shaking her head, resumes
her seat. All ladies sit.
12. "When I first put this uniform on." Colonel marches centre
for solo.
   Second chorus. Colonel marches back to his place at head
of column.

   Postlude. All men do 'about turn' and march back to their
former positions.
13. "Am I alone?" Bunthorne 'comes to life'.
   For recit and song he may use as he pleases, but should
finish LC.
   During applause, Patience rises and Bunthorne and she move
together — he miming that he is paying court to her.
14. *Narrative.* Angela and Saphir run centre back, quickly, to

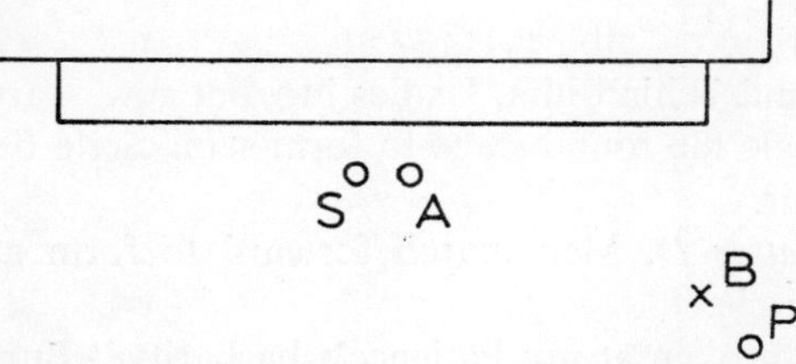

watch, horrified. On Patience rejecting him, Bunthorne with
melodramatic gesture of anguish, leaves her, crossing stage to
sit ④. Angela moves down to Patience.
15. "Long years ago." Patience and Angela move LC middle for
duet. At the end, Angela waves an admonishing finger at
Patience, and rejoins Saphir, centre back.

79

16. *Narrative.* At the end Grosvenor enters to RC.
17. "Prithee pretty maiden." Verses 1, 2, Grosvenor RC, Patience LC. They come together for last two verses, then stand 'conversing.'
18. *Narrative.* Angela and Saphir move LC. They both sigh and turn away to sit as Patience starts to speak to Grosvenor.
19. "Though to marry you." At the end, Patience sits ①, Grosvenor ⑤.
20. *Finale Act I.* All ladies, except Patience, stand.

Introduction. Angela and Saphir take garlands (concealed below their seats) and run to Bunthorne, raise him from his seat, and with care, adjust the flowers about his neck. This action should take up all the introductory music.

"Let the merry symbols sound." Angela and Saphir lead Bunthorne slowly to centre, where he sits on stool. Angela and

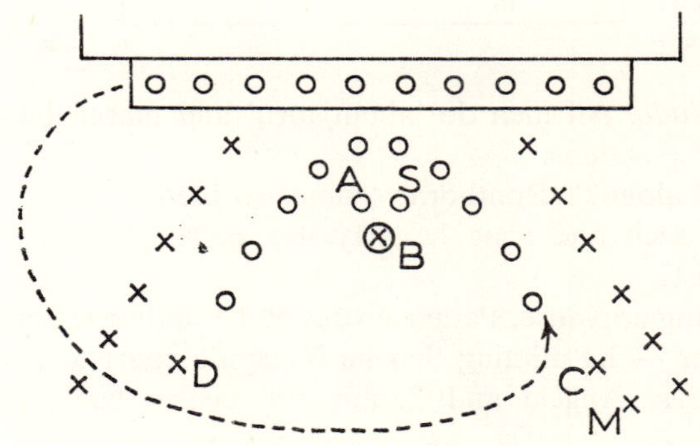

Saphir stand behind him. Ladies in front row, starting from R, dance single file round stage to form semi-circle behind Angela and Saphir.

V.S. *Letter D.* Men march forward to form a V on sides of semi-circle.

"Heart-broken at my Patience's barbarity." Bunthorne rises.
Allegro vivace. Bunthorne stands on stool.

V.S. *Letter M.* Jane steps forward on right of Angela, downstage of her. Ella steps to left of Saphir, level with her.

V.S. *Letter Q.* Patience rises and sings extreme L.

"She wants a ticket." Bunthorne runs to Patience.

V.S. *Letter Y*. Saphir steps forward in line with Duke. Then Angela steps forward in line.

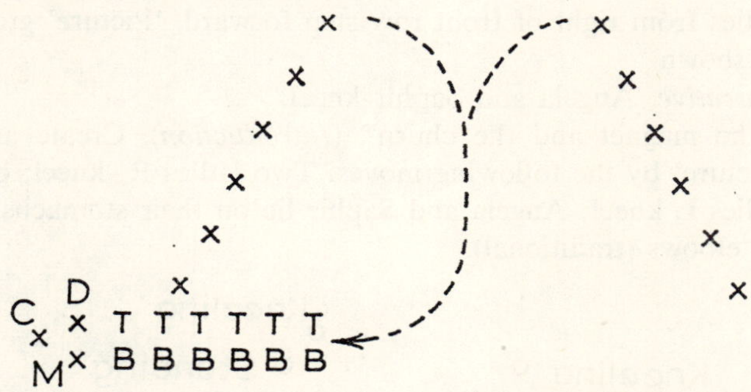

"I hear the soft note" (*Introduction*). Line completed by the six soloists.

Postlude. Grosvenor rises to stand extreme R.

(Note. V.S. *Letter E*. Angela is marked to sing "But who is this." In narrative she has already shown she knows of Grosvenor. If possible, therefore, this solo should be given to Ella. If it proves to be set too low for Ella's soprano voice, Angela may sing it — the small point may well pass unnoticed.)

"I am a broken-hearted troubadour." Grosvenor advances R.C. front.

"Then, we love you." All ladies on stage (except Patience and Jane) kneel with hands outstretched to Grosvenor.

After Grosvenor's "Horror," ladies rise again.

Immediately last bar is sung, Angela and Saphir run to take Grosvenor's arms and rush off with him, followed by ladies on stage, then ladies from the back row — a sense of flurry here. Bunthorne follows with affected indifference, Jane in stately fashion, Patience demurely.

Men, who stood to attention the moment they ceased to sing, now *march* out in twos, led by Colonel, Duke and Major after him.

ACT II

Basic seating plan as for Act I except centre stool removed, seat ⑤ moved up beside seat ④.

1. V.S. No. 1. Ladies' chorus, led by by Angela and Saphir (Ella with sopranos) glide on in twos — altos paired with sopranos, altos upstage line. Angela and Saphir go to stand at ③ and ②, ladies to positions at seats. This movement should be accomplished before singing starts, and all should be seated, taking cue from Angela and Saphir. Sing seated, without action.
2. Jane enters, carrying cello, stands and speaks RC.
3. *Jane's solo.* Sung RC.
   Postlude. Jane exits with cello.
4. V.S. No. 3. All ladies rise.
   Grosvenor enters to stand RC front.
   "On such eyes." Angela and Saphir forward to centre middle.

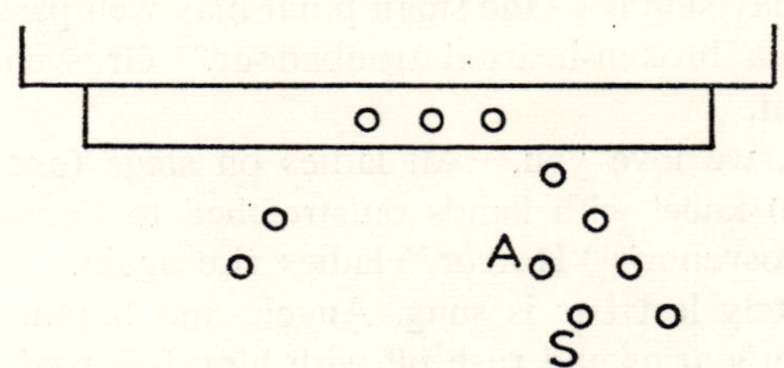

Four ladies from left of front row come behind them. Two ladies from right of front row step forward. 'Picture' grouping as shown.
5. *Narrative.* Angela and Saphir kneel.
6. "The magnet and the churn" (*Introduction*). Create another 'picture' by the following moves. Two ladies R, kneel; outside ladies L kneel; Angela and Saphir lie on their stomachs, lean on elbows (traditional).

Kneeling

Kneeling   Standing

Lying   Kneeling

Postlude. Grosvenor turns and exits R, followed by all ladies, in twos — except Angela and Saphir. They rise to stand and watch, then, sighing, turn and sit ③, ②.
7. "Love is a plaintive song." Patience enters to sing Verse 1 RC, Verse 2 LC, then sits ①.

8. *Narrative*. Angela and Saphir rise and move a little from their seats. As Angela mentions Jane, Bunthorne and Jane enter, he affectedly, she obviously haranguing him. Angela and Saphir sit.

9. "So go to him." Jane and Bunthorne may use stage for traditional 'business'.

    Postlude. Jane carries Bunthorne R, to sit Jane ⑤, Bunthorne ④.

10. *Trio*. As men enter, Angela and Saphir stand at their seats. Men traditional 'business', centre.

    Postlude. Angela and Saphir move LC middle, unobserved by men.

11. *Narrative*. Angela speaks to Saphir, without men noticing (men still holding pose).

    "How Botticellian." Saphir, followed by Angela comes forward to congratulate men.

12. *Quintet*. Traditional 'business' and dance.

    Postlude. All five exit, dancing.

13. "When I go out of door." Bunthorne dances centre, to be joined by Grosvenor. Traditional 'business'. Grosvenor exits.

(Note. Even in stage production, Grosvenor has to make a very quick costume change during only one page of libretto. Here the libretto has been cut to a speech for Patience. In order, therefore, to give time for the change, it is suggested that an appropriate

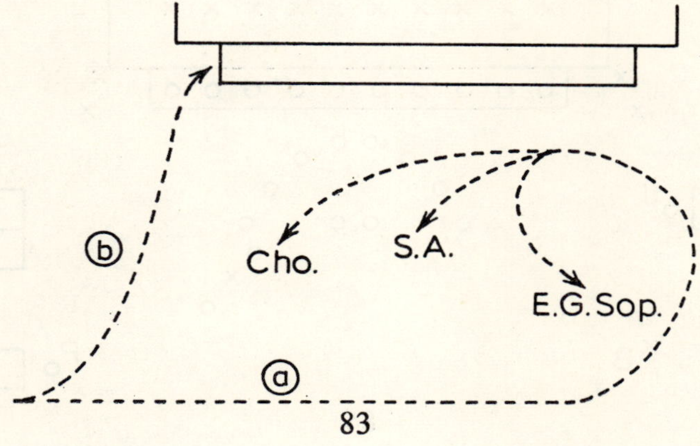

length of the duet be played during which time Bunthorne dances, happily, centre. He ends by sitting on front row, extreme R.)

14. *Narrative.* Patience stands at her seat to address audience.

15. "I'm a Waterloo House young man." Enter full company, dancing gaily in this order: Grosvenor arm-in-arm with Ella and a soprano; Saphir and Angela; then front row ladies in twos. They dance across front of stage to make a loop — Grosvenor and his partners curve back to LC. Angela and Saphir break to centre; ladies arrive in arc ⓐ. During this,

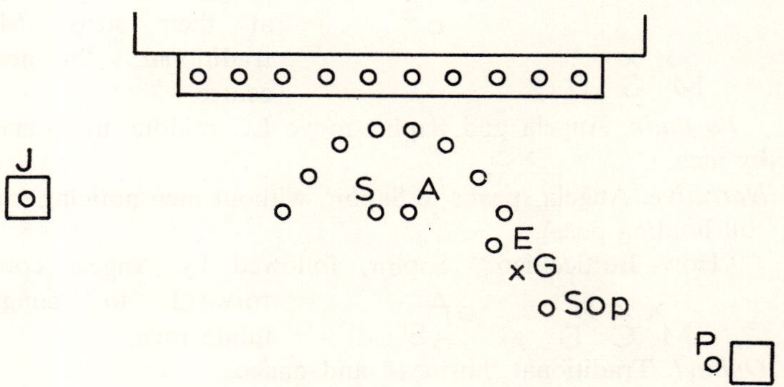

altos have danced in twos to take position this time at front row seats, ⓑ. Men follow, marching in twos to take position on back row — two go beyond to LC back, two remain RC back. Bunthorne, astonished comes to stand extreme R. Jane rises but stays at her seat.

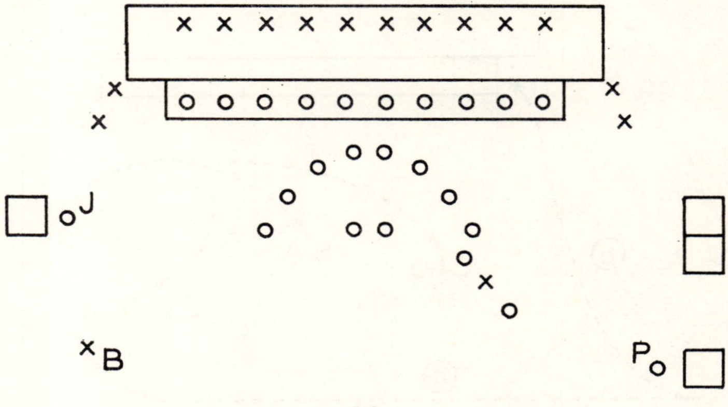

16. *Narrative.* When Patience accepts Grosvenor, he crosses to her. Bunthorne, saying "Crushed again," turns R in disgust, to be faced by Jane who has come forward and now slaps him on the shoulder.

    Fanfare. Major, Colonel, Duke in that order (in Act I costume) march to RC, passing in front of Jane and Bunthorne. When Duke selects her, Jane rushes in front of Bunthorne to embrace Duke.

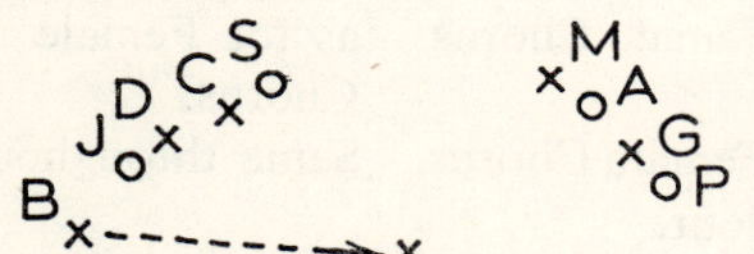

17. *Finale Act II.*

    Introduction. Angela and Saphir take Major and Colonel respectively as partners. For his verse Bunthorne minces affectedly to centre, lying as traditional at the end, gazing at lily.

18. *End of opera.* All take one bow.

Exeunt Jane and Duke; Colonel and Saphir, Major and Angela, Grosvenor and Patience.

Ladies in twos, men in twos.

Bunthorne who has held his pose during bow and exits, now rises and walks off affectedly.

PRINCIPALS	ACT I	ACT II
COLONEL MAJOR DUKE	White dinner jackets with medal ribbons.	As for Bunthorne or Grosvenor (Act I).
BUNTHORNE	Velvet suit, lace frilled shirt, floppy bow tie.	Same.
GROSVENOR	Corduroy suit, modern shirt, kipper tie.	Opening — same. Finale — well-cut sports jacket, cravat.
ANGELA SAPHIR ELLA	As for Female Chorus.	Opening and Finale as for Female Chorus.
JANE	As for Female Chorus, dark colour.	Same throughout.
PATIENCE	Skirt above knee, white draw-string blouse, white tights.	Same.

CHORUS	ACT I	ACT II
MALE	Dinner jackets, preferably white (all or none).	Same.
FEMALE	Midi/maxi dresses — any style, but sombre or pastel colours	Opening — same. Finale — mini dresses, bright colours.

7

IOLANTHE

Note on Narrative for Celia and Leila

Initially the two fairy narrators address the audience directly, but within a very short time they communicate the plot by allowing the audience to eavesdrop on their very feminine conversations.

Celia and Leila must be seen as friends who meet frequently to exchange the latest gossip. In this, Leila is always that bit better informed than Celia, who acts as a feed, by posing questions — and here, these are the questions for which the audience require the answers to further the understanding of the plot. Leila is presented as the more extrovert of the two — if she does not know what will happen, she is prepared to make a guess; and she is the type of person who adds weight and humour to her conversation by characterising and mimicking the persons about whom she is talking.

Script for Celia and Leila as Narrators

ACT I

Overture.
V.S. No. 1. *Chorus.* "Tripping hither."
V.S. No. 2. *Invocation.*
LEILA (*To audience*) It will be lovely to have Iolanthe back with us. She was the life and soul of Fairyland, and these last twenty-five years without her have been very dull.
CELIA (*To audience*) You see, our Queen banished her because (*pause — then in melodramatic whisper to audience*) she married a mortal.
LEILA (*To audience*) The crime was punishable by death, but Iolanthe was so loved by all of us that the Queen agreed to banish her, on condition that she left her husband and never communicated with him again.
CELIA (*To Leila*) The only thing I can't understand is why Iolanthe chose to live at the bottom of a stream.

LEILA   (*To Celia*) Oh, didn't you know? (*She draws Celia aside to give her the gossip.*) Shortly after she left her husband by the Queen's command, Iolanthe had a son — who incidentally doesn't know of his father's existence. Iolanthe wanted to be near him as he grew up.

CELIA   (*To Leila*) A son! How exciting! What's he like?

LEILA   (*To Celia*) Well — he's twenty-four. You'd never think to look at Iolanthe that she had a son of twenty-four, but that's one of the advantages of being a fairy — we never grow old. He's an Arcadian shepherd; and he's handsome. But see for yourself. Here he comes.

V.S. No. 3. *Song.* "Good morrow, good mother."

CELIA   Who's he going to marry?

LEILA   Phyllis, an Arcadian shepherdess, a ward of the Lord Chancellor. I'm afraid things aren't going too well for Strephon, though. The Lord Chancellor won't give his consent to the marriage. And Strephon hasn't told Phyllis that his mother is a fairy. I don't know how she will take that. I have a feeling that we might have to help him in some way.

V.S. No. 4. *Solo and Chorus.* "Fare thee well."

V.S. No. 5. *Duet.* "Good morrow, good lover."

V.S. No. 6. *Chorus.* "Loudly let the trumpet bray."

V.S. No. 6a. *Entrance of Lord Chancellor.*

V.S. No. 7. *Song.* "The law is the true embodiment."

V.S. No. 8. *Trio and Chorus.* "My well-loved Lord."

V.S. No. 9 *Recit.* "Nay tempt me not."

V.S. No. 10. *Song and Chorus.* "Spurn not the nobly born."

V.S. No. 11. *Chorus and Solos.* "My lords, it may not be."

CELIA   (*To Leila*) It's obvious that all the House of Peers are in love with Phyllis.

LEILA   Yes. And I believe the Lord Chancellor has taken a fancy to her as well!

CELIA   Poor Strephon!

LEILA   He doesn't give up trying. He's approaching the Lord Chancellor again, but I'm sure all he will get is the answer that he considers the marriage unsuitable, and therefore duty compels him to refuse permission. Oh, yes, and he's bound to give Strephon one of his little homilies. (*She mimes the pedantic manner and assumes the dry voice of the Chancellor.*) I have always kept my duty strictly before my eyes, and it is to that fact that I owe my advancement to my present distinguished position.

V.S. No. 12. *Song.* "When I went to the Bar."

CELIA   I should think Strephon will turn to his mother for advice now.

LEILA   Of course. Oh my! Iolanthe does seem terribly shaken when he mentioned the Lord Chancellor. I think she'll advise him to appeal to our Queen.

V.S. No. 13. *Finale Act I.*

ACT II

V.S. No. 1. *Song.* "When all night long."

V.S. No. 2. *Chorus.* "Strephon's a member of parliament."

CELIA   (*To audience*) I'm afraid the House of Peers is annoyed with us.

LEILA   (*Haughty, mimicking the affected speech of the Lords*) Annoyed! I should think so! Why this ridiculous protegé of yours is playing the deuce with everything.

CELIA   (*Giggling*) I know. Our system shortens the debates. We influence the members and compel them to vote just as Strephon wishes them to.

LEILA   (*Still mimicking*) This comes of women interfering in politics. It so happens that if there is an institution in Great Britain which is not susceptible of any improvement at all, it is the House of Peers.

V.S. No. 3. *Song.* "When Britain really ruled the waves."

LEILA   Charming persons, aren't they?

CELIA   Distinctly. For self-contained dignity, combined with airy condescension, give me a British Representative Peer.

LEILA   But they won't speak to us if Strephon keeps on with his reforms.

CELIA   But we can't stop him now. (*To Leila.*) Aren't they lovely? (*To Mountararat and Tolloller*) Oh, why did you go and defy us, you great geese?

V.S. No. 4. *Duet.* "In vain to us you plead."

QUEEN   Oh shame, shame upon you! Is this your fidelity to the laws you are bound to obey? Know ye not that it is death to marry a mortal?

LEILA   Yes, but it's not death to *wish* to marry a mortal.

CELIA   If it were you'd have to execute us all!

QUEEN   Oh, this is weakness! Subdue it!

LEILA   We are not all as tough as you are!

QUEEN   Tough! Do you suppose that I am insensible to the

effect of manly beauty? Look, there (*pointing to sentry*) is a man whose physical attributes are simply godlike. That man has a most extra-ordinary effect upon me. If I yielded to a natural impulse, I should fall down and worship that man. But I mortify this inclination; I wrestle with it, and it lies beneath my feet! That is how I treat my regard for that man!

V.S. No. 5. *Song*. "Oh foolish fay."

CELIA   (*To Leila*) Oh, dear. It's an awful thing to be in love with someone who doesn't love you. I suppose Phyllis has her problems too.

PHYLLIS   (*To audience. She is half crying*) I can't think why I'm not in better spirits. I'm engaged to two noblemen at once. That ought to be enough to make any girl happy. But I'm miserable! Don't suppose it's because I care for Strephon, for I hate him! No girl *could* care for a man who goes about with a mother considerably younger than himself!

LEILA   (*To Celia*) Very similar problems. The noble Lords both want her — but neither will yield to the other.

CELIA   (*To Leila, clapping her hands excitedly*) Oh, perhaps they'll fight a duel!

LEILA   (*To Celia, knowingly*) Not they. The challenge will be made. (*Affectedly*) It's the family tradition. (*With some disdain*) But the English Lord won't offer himself as a pin-cushion like the demmed Froggies for the sake of a woman. They'll wriggle out of it.

CELIA   How?

LEILA   (*Very affectedly*) I have a very strong regard for you, George. You are very dear to me Thomas. We were boys together. If I were to survive you my existence would be hopelessly embittered.

CELIA   Ah! The sacred ties of friendship are paramount?

LEILA   Exactly!

V.S. No. 6. *Quartet*. "Tho' p'raps I may encur your blame."

V.S. No. 7. *Recit and Song*. "Love, unrequited."

CELIA   Well, well. Even the Lord Chancellor has been affected by Cupid's darts!

LEILA   Oh yes. And he's very sorry for himself. It's one thing to be in love with Phyllis, but another for him to marry her. (*Mimicking the Chancellor*) Your Lordships, the feelings of a Lord Chancellor who is in love with a Ward of Court are not to be envied. What is his position? Can he give his own consent to his own marriage with his own Ward? Can he marry his own Ward without his own consent? And if he marries his own Ward without his own consent, can he commit himself for contempt of his own Court? And if he commit himself for contempt of his own Court, can he appear by counsel before himself, to move for the arrest of his own judgement? Ah, my Lords, it is indeed painful to have to sit upon a woolsack which is stuffed with thorns such as these!

CELIA (*Applauding and laughing*) Oh, Leila! What will he do?

LEILA He'll turn for support to Lord Mountararat and Lord Tolloller — and receive it! If neither of them can agree to yielding Phyllis to the other, they will both yield to him. As he is a man more powerful than they, no odium will fall upon them. Their faces will be saved. (*Knowingly*) The politician is capable of resolving any dilemma in his own favour, my dear.

V.S. No. 8. *Trio.* "If you go in."

V.S. No. 9. *Duet.* "If we're weak enough to tarry."

LEILA I am so happy that Phyllis and Strephon are reconciled to each other.

CELIA So am I. It was a sensible thing for him to tell her that his mother was a fairy. . . .

LEILA (*Breaking in*) . . . and that if she sees him kissing any of us pretty fairies, he is embracing an elderly aunt!

CELIA But what can they do now that the Lord Chancellor has resolved to marry Phyllis?

LEILA (*Taking her aside and speaking confidentially*) I'm afraid it's up to Iolanthe. Only a few of us know — and certainly Strephon doesn't — that the Lord Chancellor was the mortal Iolanthe married.

CELIA Strephon's father! Well that solves the problem. Obviously the Chancellor cannot marry again.

LEILA But he thinks Iolanthe died, and childless. And she is bound, under penalty of death, not to undeceive him.

V.S. No. 10. *Recit and Ballad.* "My Lord, a suppliant at your feet."

V.S. No. 11. *Recit and Chorus.* "It may not be."

LEILA Hold! If Iolanthe must die, so must we all; for, as she has sinned so have we!

QUEEN What?

CELIA We are all fairy duchesses, marchionesses, countesses, viscountesses and baronesses.

MOUNTARARAT It's our fault. They couldn't help themselves.

QUEEN It seems they *have* helped themselves, and pretty freely, too! (*Pause.*) You have all incurred death; but I can't slaughter the whole company! And yet the law is clear — every fairy must die who marries a mortal!

CHANCELLOR Allow me, as an old Equity draughtsman, to make a suggestion. The subtleties of the legal mind are equal to the emergency. The thing is really quite simple — the insertion of a single word will do it. Let it stand that every fairy shall die who *doesn't* marry a mortal, and there you are, out of your difficulty at once!

QUEEN We like your humour. Very well! Private Willis!

SENTRY Ma'am!

QUEEN To save my life, it is necessary that I marry at once. How should you like to be a fairy guardsman?

SENTRY Well, ma'am, I don't think much of the British soldier who wouldn't ill-convenience himself to save a female in distress.

QUEEN You are a brave fellow. You're a fairy from this moment. And you, my Lords, how say you, will you join our ranks?

MOUNTARARAT (*To Tolloller*) Well, now that the Peers are to be recruited entirely from persons of intelligence, I really don't see what use *we* are, down here, do you, Tolloller?

TOLLOLLER None whatever.

QUEEN Good! Then away we go to Fairyland.

V.S. No. 12. *Finale Act II.*

Basic Seating Plan

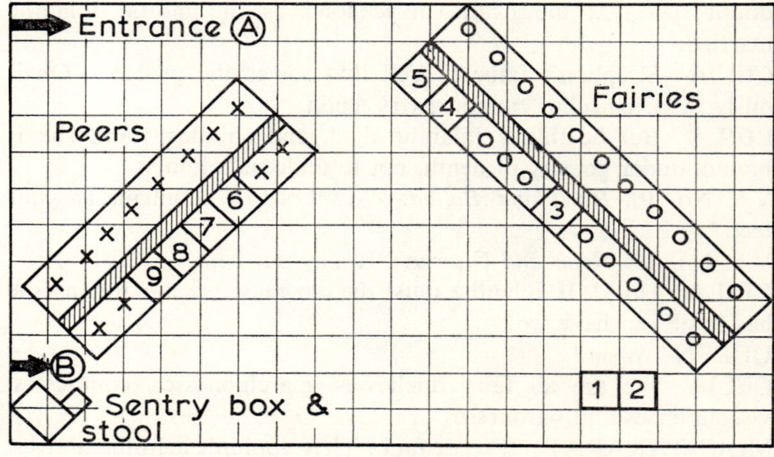

BACK ROWS   Raised 1 single step

1. Sentry box, with stool at side, for Act II only.
2. Distribution of parts for singing — soprano/alto, tenor/bass — at discretion of musical director.
3. Front row of fairies (except Queen and Iolanthe) are also dancers, with Celia and Leila as leaders, *i.e.* eight or ten dancers.
4. Seats ①, ② for Celia and Leila on floor level.

PROPS

Pipes of Pan. Wand for Queen.

NOTATION

Ld — Lord Chancellor	Q — Fairy Queen
M — Lord Mountararat	I — Iolanthe
T — Lord Tolloller	C — Celia
W — Private Willis	L — Leila
S — Strephon	P — Phyllis

Production for Script with Celia and Leila as Narrators

ACT I

1. *Overture.*
2. *Opening Chorus* (Introduction). Fairies enter at Ⓐ in twos, led by Celia and Leila. They and front row come downstage to dance. Fairy Queen takes her place, standing at ③. Back-row fairies follow single file, to take positions, standing, in back row.

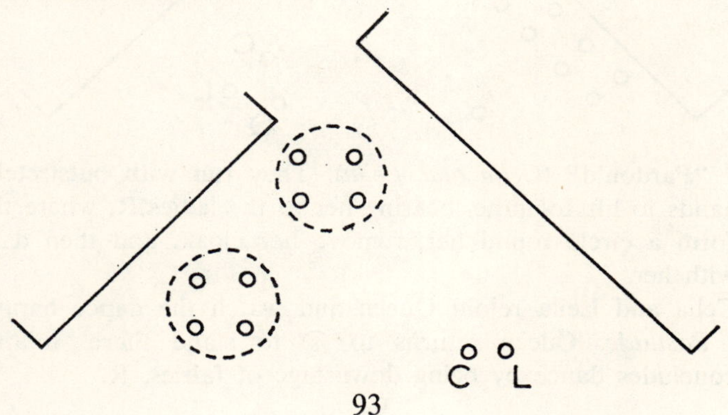

Dance can be as elaborate as stage permits. The eight dancers form one (or two) groups;
Celia and Leila dance together LC, and sing their solos from there.
Positions at end of chorus.

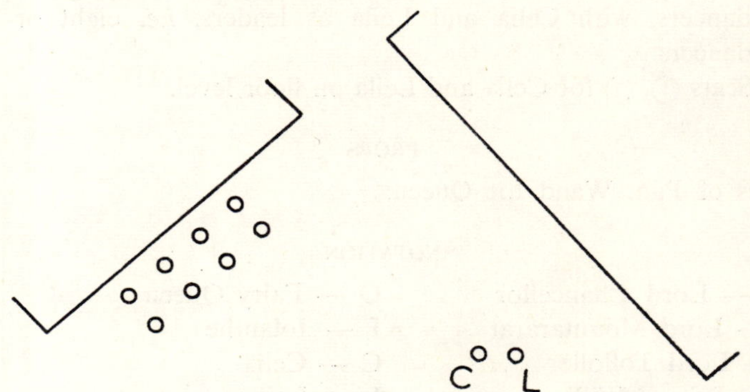

3. *Invocation* (Introduction). Fairies on stage in diagonal lines face centre entrance. Queen comes LC, Celia and Leila behind her.

Iolanthe enters Ⓐ slowly and comes down centre, singing, to end kneeling RC, to face Queen.

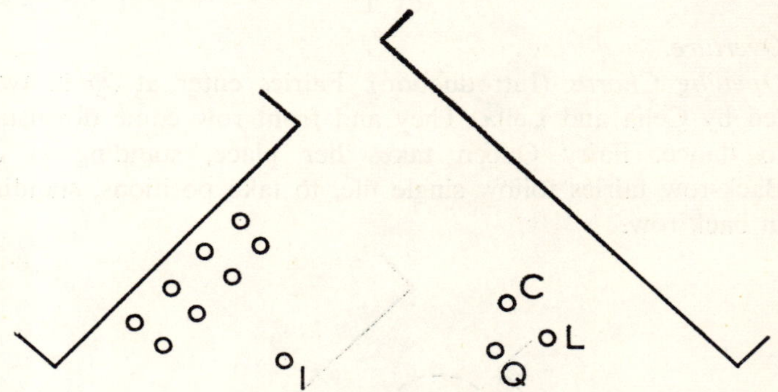

"Pardon'd" (*Celia and Leila*). They run with outstretched hands to lift Iolanthe, bearing her to the ladies R, where they form a circle round her, remove her cloak, and then dance with her.
Celia and Leila rejoin Queen and watch the dance happily.
Postlude. Queen returns to ③ to stand there. Iolanthe concludes dance by being downstage of fairies, R.

Celia and Leila side-by-side, LC.
All *freeze* for narrative.

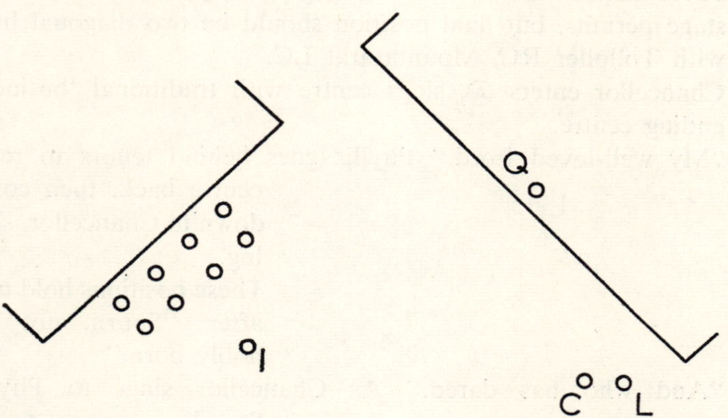

4. *Narrative* delivered standing at seats.
5. Strephon enters Ⓑ, going straight to his mother.
    "Yes, he's to be married" (*Chorus*). Iolanthe and Strephon dance RC.
6. *Narrative*. All *freeze*.
7. "Fare thee well." Same positions.
    "Aye, call us" (*Chorus*). Iolanthe kisses Strephon, then joins the eight fairies, who dance. Fairies eventually reach their places in front row. Iolanthe at ④.
    All sit together, on bar following "ring."
8. Phyllis enters Ⓑ. She and Strephon dance RC.
9. "None shall part us." Sung RC.
    At the end. Embrace, Strephon goes to sit ⑤, Phyllis to ⑧.

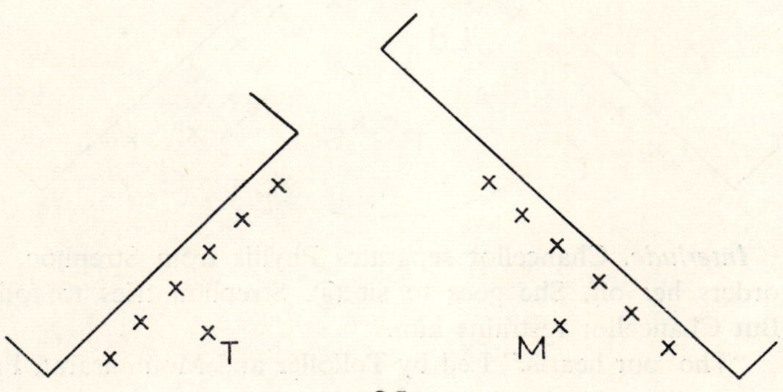

10. *Entrance of Peers.* Very stately march to enter Ⓐ—in pairs with basses L, tenors R, led by Mountararat and Tolloller. Procession before and during singing may be as elaborate as stage permits, but final position should be two diagonal lines, with Tolloller RC, Mountararat LC.

11. Chancellor enters Ⓐ, sings centre with traditional 'business' ending centre.

12. "My well-loved Lord." Phyllis goes behind tenors to reach centre back, then comes down to Chancellor, singing.

These positions hold until after "Spurn not the nobly born."

13. "And who has dared." As Chancellor sings to Phyllis, Strephon comes to fill gap between Chancellor and Mountararat.

"I claim my darling's hand." Phyllis crosses to Strephon.

" Let's depart" (*Chorus*). Tenors follow Tolloller, single file, in stately march across stage to line up in front of basses. (Mountararat has gone back, to end of line of basses.) This should be achieved just before the ten-bar Interlude.

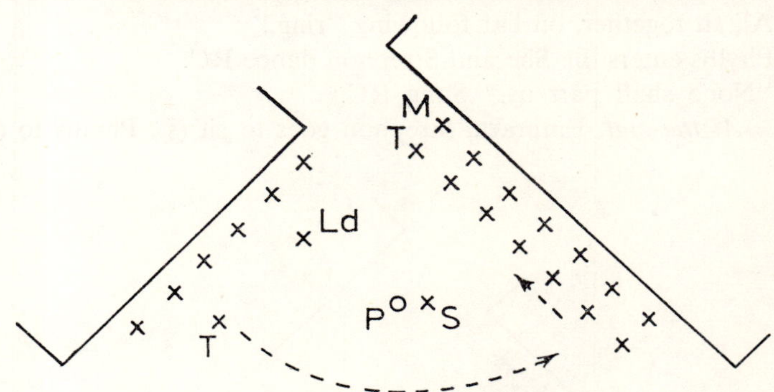

Interlude. Chancellor separates Phyllis from Strephon, and orders her off. She goes to sit Ⓑ. Strephon tries to follow, But Chancellor restrains him.

"Tho' our hearts." Led by Tolloller and Mountararat, Peers

process to their positions at seats R. All sit on final bar, Tolloller ⑨, Mountararat ⑥.

14. *Narrative*. Chancellor and Strephon *freeze*.
Celia and Leila stand, talking conversationally and taking glances at Phyllis, Chancellor and Strephon.
Then they sit.

15. "When I went to the Bar." Sung centre.
Postlude. Chancellor retires to sit ⑦. Strephon half follows, reaching RC, middle stage.

16. "When darkly looms the day" (*Introduction*). At this point, *narrative*, spoken through music, commences. Strephon turns L to move towards Iolanthe. Iolanthe rises and comes to meet him. They walk slowly, arm-in-arm to LC front with Strephon on Iolanthe's right.
"When darkly looms the day" (*Singing*). Men (not Chancellor), Phyllis, Mountararat and Tolloller rise.

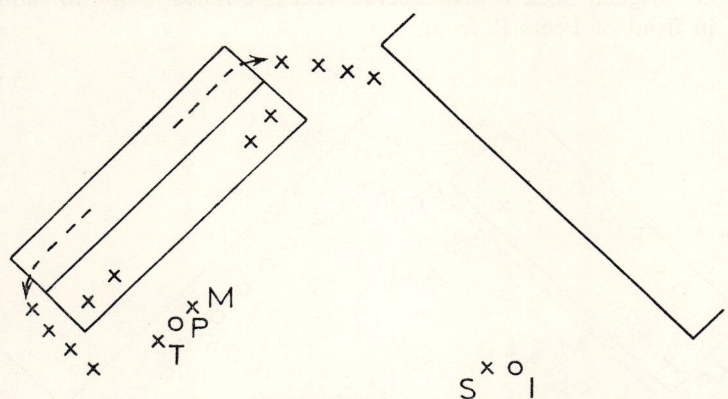

"When tempests." Phyllis, Mountararat and Tolloller tip-toe to RC. Peers: front row remain; back row, four tip-toe to extreme R, four tip-toe to centre, extreme back. After laughter, at *piu vivo*, Chancellor comes down centre.

"That's very true" (*Chorus*). Iolanthe slips unnoticed back L, well away from Chancellor, to exit Ⓐ.

V.S. *Letter O*. All fairies stand. Front Row, led by Celia and Leila, trip across front of stage, round in front of Peers R, behind principals, to position.

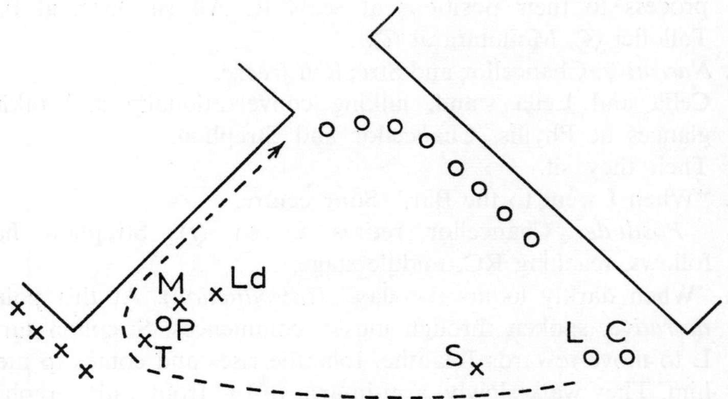

"Why you want us." Back-row fairies dance R, in front of Peers centre back. The first six go to stand on rostrum R, *i.e.* original back row of Peers. Next five fairies come to stand in front of Peers R front.

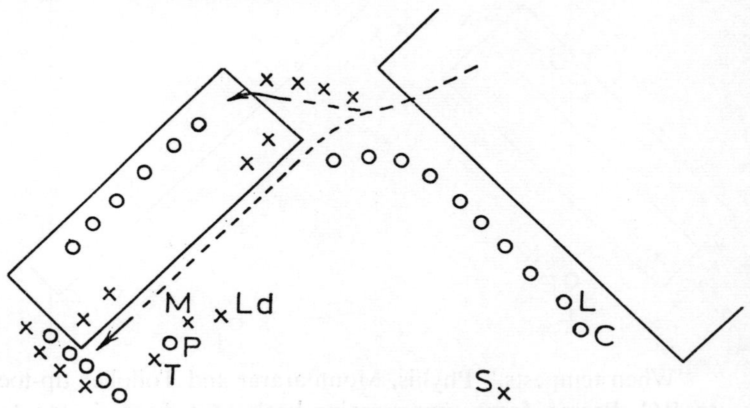

"Enter all the little fairies." Queen makes a regal move to between Chancellor and Strephon.

Thereafter traditional 'business' until V.S. *Letter L.*
"'Twill plunge them." Four fairies nearest centre move R to join five fairies R.

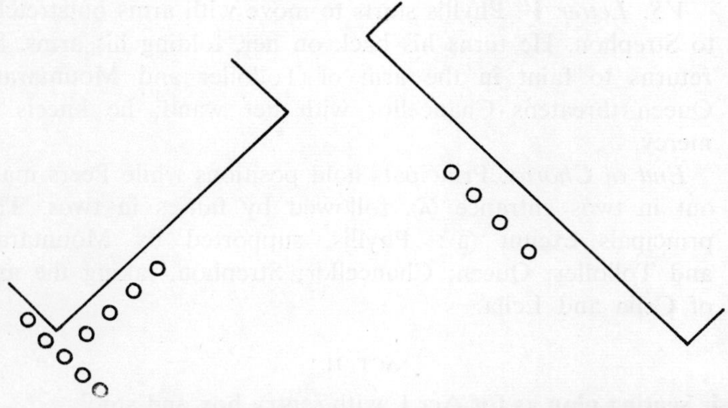

"Your powers we dauntlessly pooh-pooh." These four move
back to rejoin fairies L, who move down to front. Five fairies
R follow at end of line. Thus thirteen fairies in line.

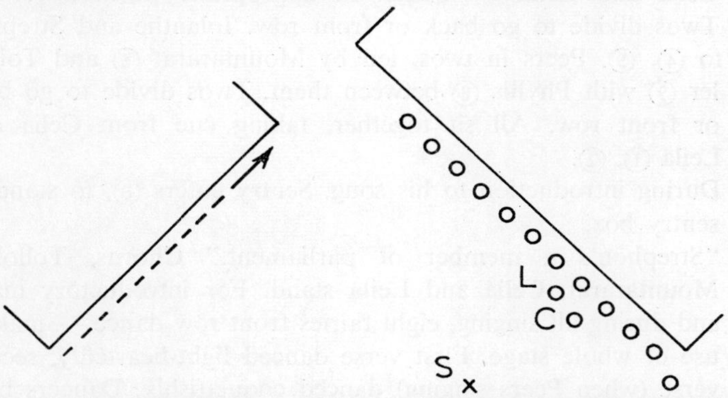

"Our lordly style." Four Peers R, march to stand in front
of four at back. Two Peers in front row march up to join
other two.

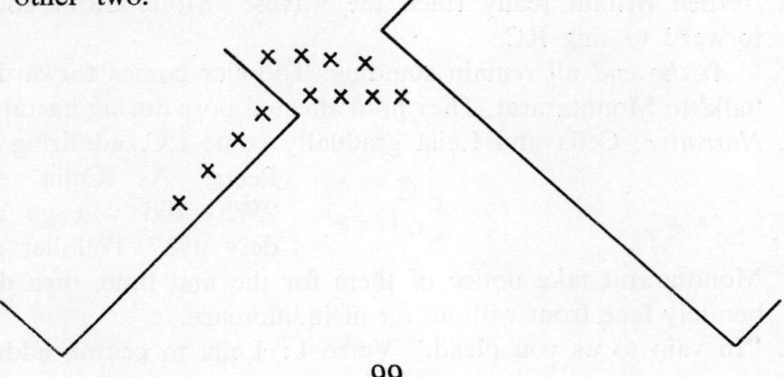

99

VS. Letter V. Phyllis starts to move with arms outstretched to Strephon. He turns his back on her, folding his arms. She returns to faint in the arm of Tolloller and Mountararat. Queen threatens Chancellor with her wand; he kneels for mercy.

End of Chorus. Principals hold positions while Peers march out in twos entrance Ⓐ, followed by fairies in twos. Then principals exeunt Ⓑ: Phyllis, supported by Mountararat and Tolloller; Queen; Chancellor; Strephon, taking the arms of Celia and Leila.

ACT II

Basic seating plan as for Act I, with sentry box and stool.

1. Company enters Ⓐ, in this order: Fairies in twos, led by Celia and Leila — Queen in appropriate position for ③. Twos divide to go back or front row. Iolanthe and Strephon to ④, ⑤. Peers in twos, led by Mountararat ⑥ and Tolloller ⑨ with Phyllis ⑧ between them. Twos divide to go back or front row. All sit together, taking cue from Celia and Leila ①, ②.
2. During introduction to his song, Sentry enters Ⓑ, to stand in sentry box.
3. "Strephon's a member of parliament." Chorus, Tolloller, Mountararat, Celia and Leila stand. For introductory music and during all singing, eight fairies front row dance — making use of whole stage. First verse danced light-heartedly, second verse (when Peers singing) danced coquettishly. Dancers back to front row at the end.
4. *Narrative*. All *freeze*.
5. "When Britain really ruled the waves." Mountararat comes forward to sing RC.

   At the end all remain standing. Tolloller comes forward to 'talk' to Mountararat. They hold affected pose during narrative.
6. *Narrative*. Celia and Leila gradually come LC, admiring the Peers. As Celia says "Why did you go and defy us?" Tolloller and Mountararat take notice of them for the first time, then deliberately face front with an air of indifference.

ᵒC
M ˣ ˣT   ᵒL

7. "In vain to us you plead." Verse 1: Leila to centre, addres-

100

sing Mountararat and Tolloller. Celia joins her for chorus. Verse 2: Celia goes nearer the two men. At second chorus, Queen rises.

At the end Mountararat and Tolloller wheel right (*i.e.* turning their backs on Celia and Leila) and walk with dignity to their seats. Peers all sit as two men do. All fairies remain standing. Celia and Leila distressed, comfort each other and move back LC.

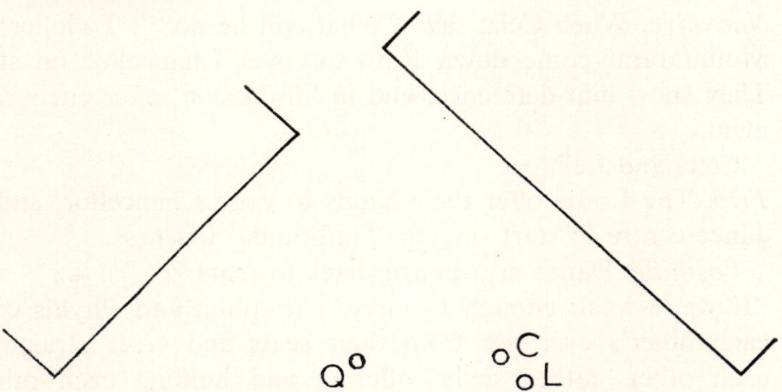

8. *Narrative.* Queen comes down centre. She sings her song from there.

Postlude. with a crushing look at Celia and Leila, Queen sweeps back to her seat. Fairy chorus sits with her.

9. *Narrative.* As Celia begins, Phyllis walks slowly down to RC, with head bowed. As Leila says "Very similar problems," Tolloller and Mountararat come on either side of Phyllis. The men assume affected poses to suit narrative. Phyllis keeps looking from one to the other as they change their attitudes. Celia and Leila then sit.

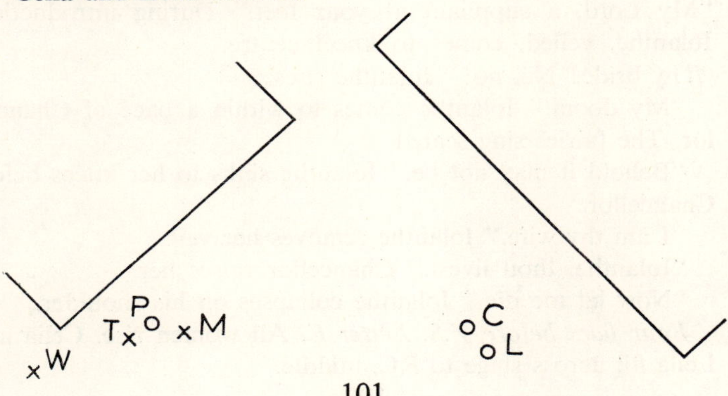

10. "Tho' p'raps I may incur your blame." Sung from above positions.

Postlude. Tolloller and Mountararat turn in to Phyllis, each offers her an arm courteously and they lead her back to her seat, where all three sit.

11. *Nightmare Song.* Chancellor enters Ⓑ, to sing centre.

Postlude. He collapses on stool at sentry box, leaning his back against the box.

12. *Narrative.* When Celia says "What will he do?", Tolloller and Mountararat come down R to discover Chancellor on stool. They show him deference, and in 'discussion' offer encouragement.

Celia and Leila sit.

13. *Trio.* The Lords offer their hands to raise Chancellor, and all dance centre to start singing. Traditional 'business.'

Postlude. Dance arm-in-arm back to seats Ⓙ, Ⓖ, Ⓕ.

14. "If we're weak enough to tarry." Strephon and Phyllis catch each other's eye, rise from their seats and cross straight to each other, rather shyly, offering and holding each other's upstage hand. After a shy kiss, they dance down centre hand-in-hand, to sing.

Postlude. They dance upstage to Iolanthe, who stands to greet them. She kisses Phyllis. They stand 'talking' seriously during narrative.

15. *Narrative.* As Leila mentions the Chancellor, Phyllis and Strephon sit Ⓔ, Ⓓ, Iolanthe remaining standing. At the same time, Chancellor rises, pensively; and as Celia says "Strephon's father," he walks down to R front, deep in thought.

16. "My Lord, a suppliant at your feet." During introduction, Iolanthe, veiled, comes to kneel centre.

17. "Thy bride! No, no!" Iolanthe rises.

"My doom." Iolanthe comes to within a pace of Chancellor. The fairies sing seated.

"Behold it may not be." Iolanthe sinks to her knees before Chancellor.

"I am thy wife." Iolanthe removes her veil.

"Iolanthe, thou livest." Chancellor raises her.

"Now let me die." Iolanthe collapses on his shoulder.

Four bars before V.S. Letter E. All women rise. Celia and Leila flit across stage to RC, middle.

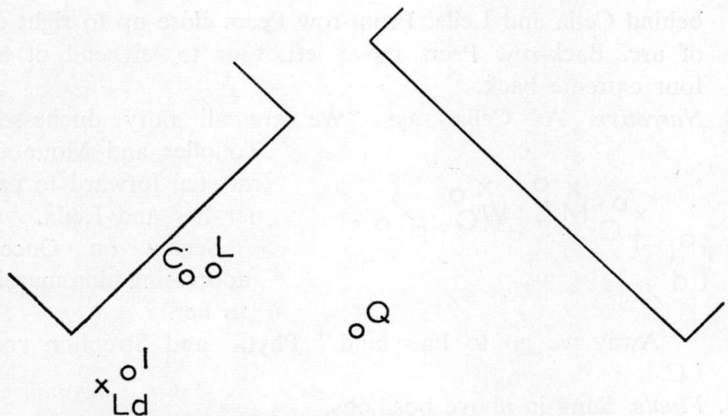

V.S. Letter E. Queen advances centre.
V.S. Letter F. Men rise. Front-row fairies flit to arc,
Back-row fairies wave their arms in attitude of desolation.

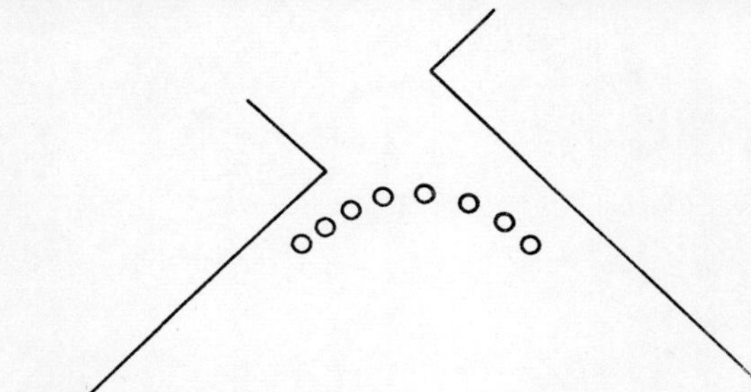

V.S. Letter H. Tolloller and Mountararat come directly

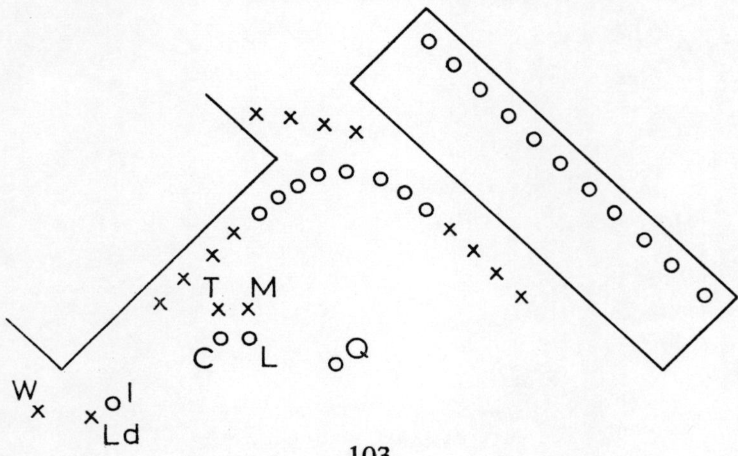

behind Celia and Leila. Front-row Peers close up to right end of arc. Back-row Peers move left, four to left end of arc, four extreme back.

18. *Narrative.* As Celia says "We are all fairy duchesses," Tolloller and Mountararat step forward to partner her and Leila.

Sentry on Queen's addressing him, marches to her.

"Away we go to Fairyland." Phyllis and Strephon come LC.

19. *Finale.* Sung in above positions.
20. *End of Opera.* All take one bow.
Exeunt principals, at Ⓑ, in couples, starting from right.
Exeunt chorus at Ⓐ, in twos, fairies partnering Peers.

Suggestions for Costuming

PRINCIPALS	ACT I	ACT II
CHANCELLOR	Black jacket and pin-stripe trousers.	Same.
MOUNTARARAT	Evening tails.	Same.
TOLLOLLER	As for Mountararat.	Same.
SENTRY		Modern soldier's uniform.
STREPHON	Sports jacket, light-coloured slacks, cravat.	Same.
FAIRY QUEEN	Voluminous white ball gown.	Same.
CELIA } LEILA	As for Female Chorus, but preferably identical.	Same.
IOLANTHE	As for Celia and Leila. Drab cloak for opening.	Same (no cloak), transparent veil.
PHYLLIS	Mini dress with broad, low neckline, white tights, white shoes.	Same.

CHORUS	ACTS I, II
MALE	Dinner jackets (black).
FEMALE	Diaphanous, knee-length dresses, pastel colours, white tights; ballet shoes. (Mini-skirts to be avoided. If femininity is to be emphasized, it should be by accenting low necklines, not the legs.)

8

PRINCESS IDA

Script for Hilarion, Cyril, Florian et al as Narrators

ACT I

Overture
V.S. No. 1. *Chorus and Solo.* "Search throughout the panorama."
V.S. No. 2. *Song.* "Now hearken to my strict command."
V.S. No. 3. *Recit and Song.* "To-day we meet."
V.S. No. 4. *Chorus.* "From the distant panorama."
V.S. No. 5. *Trio.* "We are warriors three."
V.S. No. 6. *Song.* "If you give me your attention."
FLORIAN Here's a to-do! King Gama arrives en suite, but with no daughter to wed Prince Hilarion.
CYRIL Where is she?
FLORIAN In her Castle Adamant. There she is Principal of a university, with over a hundred students — all female!
CYRIL A hundred girls! A hundred ecstasies!
FLORIAN No, Cyril, you would have no luck there. The ladies are interested only in study. No males of any kind are allowed within the walls of the castle. Why, the ladies rise every morning to the crowing of an accomplished hen!
CYRIL Poor Hilarion. Considering Ida has beauty and grace, with virtue and courage coupled to this apparent hatred of man, he will have some task to storm her defences.
V.S No. 7. *Finale Act 1.*

ACT II

V.S. No. 8. *Chorus and Solos.* "Towards the empyrean heights."
V.S. No. 9. *Chorus.* "Mighty maiden with a mission."
V.S. No. 10. *Recit and Aria.* "Minerva! O hear me."
IDA Women of Adamant, fair Neophytes —
Who thirst for such instruction as we give,
Attend, while I unfold a parable.
The elephant is mightier than Man,
Yet man subdues him. Why? The elephant

Is elephantine everywhere but here (*tapping her forehead*),
And Man, whose brain is to the elephant's
As Woman's brain to Man's — (that's rule of three) —
Conquers the foolish giant of the woods,
As Woman in her turn, will conquer Man.
In Mathematics, Woman leads the way:
The narrow-minded pedant still believes
That two and two make four! Why, we can prove,
We women — household drudges as we are —
That two and two make five — or three— or seven;
Or five-and-twenty, if the case demands!
Diplomacy? The wiliest diplomat
Is absolutely helpless in our hands,
He wheedles monarchs — woman wheedles him!
Logic? Why, tyrant Man himself admits
It's waste of time to argue with a woman!
Then we excel in social qualities:
Though Man professes that he holds our sex
In utter scorn, I venture to believe
He'd rather pass the day with one of you,
Than with five hundred of his fellow-men!
In all things we excel. Believing this,
A hundred maidens here have sworn to place
Their feet upon his neck. If we succeed,
We'll treat him better than he treated us:
But if we fail, why, then let hope fail too!
Let no one care a penny how she looks —
Let red be worn with yellow — blue with green —
Crimson with scarlet — violet with blue!
Let all your things misfit, and you yourselves
At inconvenient moments come undone!
Let hair-pins lose their virtue: let the hook
Disdain the fascination of the eye —
The bashful button modestly evade
The soft embraces of the button-hole!
Let old associations all dissolve.
In other words — let Chaos come again!
(As customary since 1954, Lady Blanche's Song is omitted.)
V.S. No. 12. *Trio.* "Gently, gently, evidently."
HILARION So this is princess Ida's Castle. The girls here must
be lovely if such high walls are needed to keep intruders out.

CYRIL   Probably the walls are necessary to keep the girls in!
FLORIAN   What are these? (*He examines some robes.*)
HILARION   Well done, Florian. These must be the academic robes worn by the undergraduates. Let's try them on!
V.S. No. 13. *Trio.* "I am a maiden cold and stately."
FLORIAN   Look out! Here comes the Princess! What shall we do?
HILARION   We must brave it out. Madam. (*All bow.*) We are three students, girls of good family background, who wish to join this university.
IDA   If you wish to join our ranks, it will be quite acceptable — provided you obey the rules to the letter. There are a hundred girls here, all good, all learned, all beautiful. They are prepared to devote their love to you. Do you promise to return their affection?
HILARION   Upon our honour, madam.
IDA   But there is more. Will you promise never to marry any man?
FLORIAN   Indeed! We never will.
IDA   Consider it carefully. You must prefer our girls to all mankind!
CYRIL—We should be fools if we didn't, when you think how beautiful . . . .
HILARION   (*treads on his foot*) Steady on. You're going too far.
IDA   If you are prepared to submit to these regulations, I'm sure a happy time awaits you here.
CYRIL   If, as you say, a hundred girls wait to welcome us with smiles and open arms, I've no doubt we shall be very happy.
V.S. No. 14. *Quartet.* "The world is but a broken toy."
HILARION   Well, we've taken the plunge now. We are now buds of blushing beauty and must so remain (*Cyril and he laugh.*)
FLORIAN   (*Whispering anxiously.*) Hilarion! We've been seen. Damn, it's my sister. It's years since I saw her, but she's bound to recognise me.
HILARION   You'll have to let her into our secret.
FLORIAN   Psyche! Don't you know me? It's Florian.
PSYCHE   Florian!
FLORIAN   This is Prince Hilarion, to whom Ida is engaged. And Cyril too. You'll remember how we used to play together as children.
PSYCHE   (*Warmly*) Of course I do! (*Fearfully*) But don't you

realize it's death for you to enter here? We have all promised to renounce mankind! We are all taught, and being taught, believe, that Man, sprung from an Ape, is an Ape at Heart.

V.S. No. 15. *Song.* "A lady fair, of lineage high."

FLORIAN Psyche, who is that?

PSYCHE Oh, Melissa! The Vice-Principal's daughter. We are lost.

MELISSA No, no. I shan't breath a word. How strange! Are you indeed young men? I had been told that men were hideous, idiotic and deformed. Why, you are quite as beautiful as women — no, more so. Your cheeks haven't that pulpy softness of a woman's. (*She feels Florian's chin.*) And your chins — how curious.

FLORIAN—I'm afraid it's rather rough.

MELISSA Don't apologise — I like it.

V.S. No. 16. *Quintet.* "The woman of the wisest wit."

PSYCHE Melissa, what will you say to your mother? She's bound to find out.

MELISSA Don't worry. She has always set her heart on being Principal here. If Hilarion can marry Ida, then mother will achieve her ambition. Oh, I'm sure she can be persuaded to assist us.

V.S. No. 17. *Duet.* "Now wouldn't you like to rule the roast."

V.S. No. 18. *Chorus and Solos.* "Merrily ring the luncheon bell."

V.S. No. 19. *Song.* "Would you know the kind of maid?"

IDA Infamous creature!

HILARION (*Shaking Cyril*) I'll give you something to sing about.

CYRIL Hilarion, are you mad?

IDA (*Horrified*) Hilarion? Why, these are men! We are betrayed. Girls, run. Monsters, if you dare approach one step, I . . . . (*See Production.*)

PSYCHE Oh, the river! Save her!

BLANCHE He can't, he can't. It's too deep.

PSYCHE No! He's caught her. Yes! She's saved, she's saved!

V.S. No. 20. *Finale Act II.*

ACT III

V.S. No. 21. *Chorus and Solo.* "Death to the invader."

IDA Women of Adamant, we have to show
    That Woman, educated to the task,
    Can meet Man, face to face, on his own ground,
    And beat him there. Now let us set to work.
    Where is our lady surgeon?

110

MELISSA Madam, I must tell you she is not prepared to assist. She says she's happy to cut off arms and legs in theory, but not in practice. And the fusiliers, madam, are unarmed. They have left their rifles in the armoury in case in the heat of battle they should go off!

IDA Away, away. I'll meet these men alone
    Since all my women have deserted me.
    So fail my cherished plans — so fails my faith —
    And with it hope, and all that comes of hope.

V.S. No. 22. *Song.* "I built upon a rock."

MELISSA Madam — your father claims an audience. King Hildebrand is loathe to war with women, and has freed your father to present his proposal to you — that King Gama's sons alone may fight your three prisoners.

FLORIAN That's a cunning move!

HILARION Yes. And I should think my father has applied psychological warfare in his dealings with Gama, too. We shall see — for here he comes.

V.S. No. 22. *Song.* "Whene'er I spoke sarcastic joke."

IDA My poor old father. How you must have suffered. Well, I yield. Open the gates — and admit the warriors.

V.S. No. 24. *Chorus.* "When anger spreads its wing."

V.S. No. 25. *Song.* "This helmet, I suppose."

V.S. No. 26. *Chorus.* "This is our duty plain."

IDA Hold! We yield to you.
    So ends my cherished scheme! Oh, I had hoped
    To bend all women with my maiden throng,
    And make them all abjure tyrannic Man!
    If I had carried out this glorious scheme,
    At my exalted name Posterity
    Would bow in gratitude!

CYRIL But madam, the question then arises "How is that Posterity to be provided?"

IDA (*Shaken*) I never thought of that.
    I have been wrong — I see my error now.
    Take me, Hilarion — "We will walk the world
    Yoked in all exercise of noble end!
    And so through those dark gates across the wild
    That no man knows! Indeed, I love thee —
    Come!"

V.S. No. 27. *Finale Act III.*

Basic Seating Plan

Ten 1		× × × × × × × × × × × ×		Bass
Sop 2		o o o o o o o o o o o o		Alto
3		1 2 3 4 5 6 7 8 9 10 11 12		

→ Entrance

ROW 1 (Raised 2 double steps) ROW 2 (raised 1 double step)
ROW 3 (Seated floor level)

PROPS

Act. II. Three Academic robes, picnic hamper, hip flask.
Act. III. Six swords.

NOTATION

K — Hildebrand   G — Gama   I — Ida
H — Hilarion   A — Arac   B — Blanche
C — Cyril   S — Scynthius P — Psyche
F — Florian   Gu — Guron   M — Melissa

Note. Sacharissa's Solo, Act II (*Opening Chorus*) to be sung by Melissa.

Production for Script with Hilarion, Cyril, Florian et al as Narrators

ACT I

1. Company enters thus:
   Row 1. Men single file — basses then tenors. Basses go up steps L, tenors up steps R.
   Row 2. Ladies single file — altos then sopranos. Altos go up steps L, sopranos up steps R.

112

Row 3. Florian, Cyril, Hilarion, Hildebrand respectively to
⑫, ⑪, ⑩, ⑨. Four chorus ladies — two altos, two sopranos
— to ⑧, ⑦, ⑥, ⑤. All sit together, taking cue from
principals.

2. *Overture.*
3. "Search throughout the panorama." Chorus and Florian rise.
4. "Now hearken to my strict command." Hildebrand, Cyril,
Hilarion rise. Hildebrand sings centre; and on "funeral bell,"
resumes his seat with authoritative air.

   End of chorus. All sit except Hilarion.
5. "Today we meet." Hilarion comes forward LC.
6. "From the distant panorama." All rise. Hilarion goes L. front,
Cyril and Florian come LC middle, Hildebrand centre.

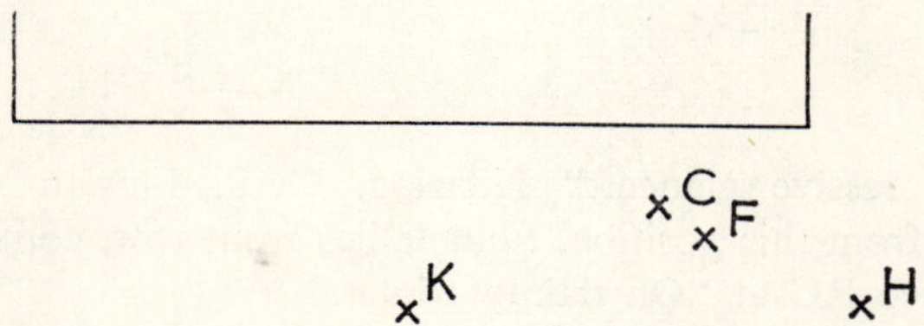

7. "We are warriors three." Arac, Guron and Scynthius enter,
marching ponderously to stand and sing on diagonal R.

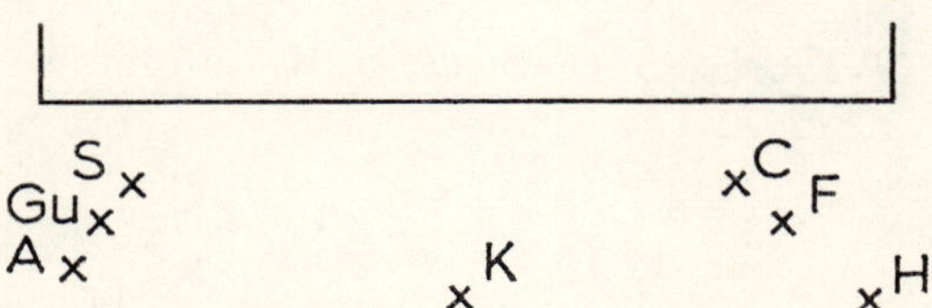

8. "If you give me your attention" (*Introduction*). Gama enters
petulantly, to stand and sing in front of his sons.

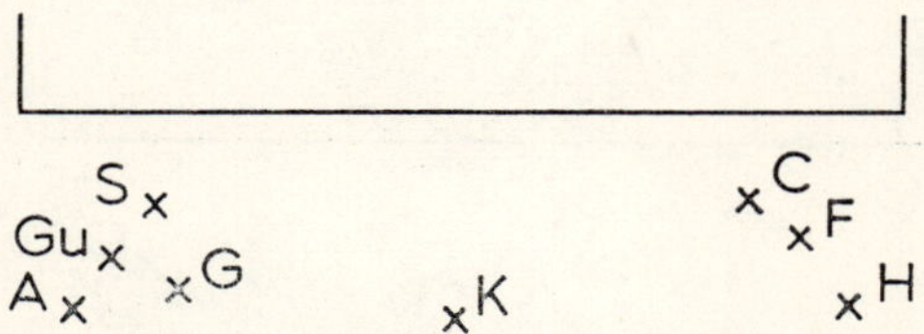

9. *Narrative.* All *freeze* while Cyril and Florian come downstage
front, talking to each other.

10. "Perhaps if you address the lady." Gama totters over to Hildebrand.

"You'll remain as hostage here." Arac, Guron, Scynthius march to sit together ①, ②, ③. Gama follows, muttering to himself and looking over his shoulder at Hildebrand, who assumes a pose of authority. Gama sits ④. As soon as Gama sits, Hildebrand returns to sit ⑨.

11. "Come, Cyril." Hilarion joins Cyril and Florian, LC front.

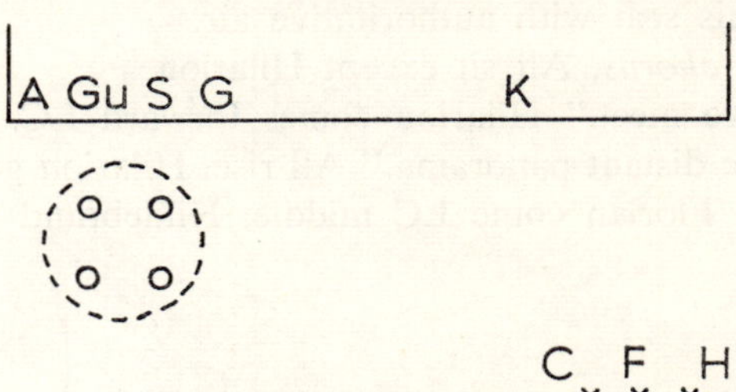

"Expressive glances." Hilarion, Cyril, Florian sing their verses from this position. Four ladies front row, come forward to dance RC at "Oh dainty triolet."

Postlude. Dancers bow to Cyril, Florian and Hilarion who step back on a diagonal and return bow. Then dancers return to their places on front row.

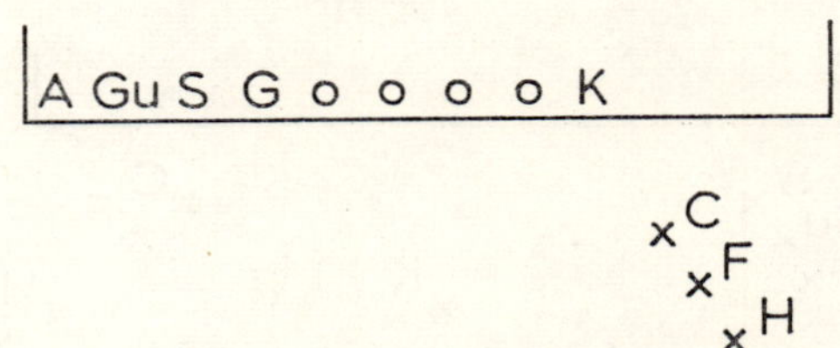

12. "Must we, till then." Gama rises and totters centre middle addressing Hildebrand who comes forward to him.
"Hear, hear!" Three men rise as one.

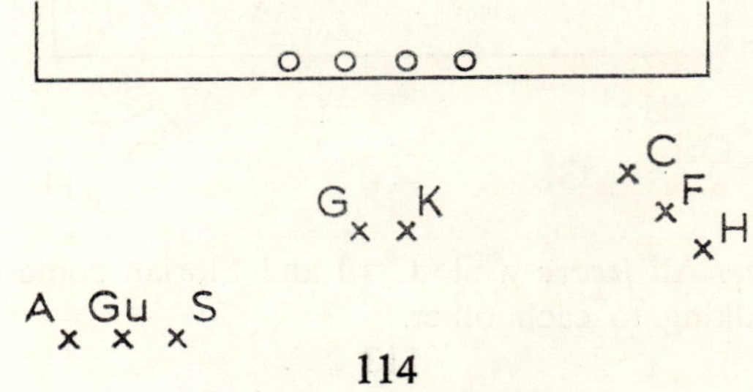

114

13. "For a month to dwell." Three men march forward to R front.

End of singing. Three men do right turn and march off single file ponderously, followed by Gama. Hildebrand follows regally; then Cyril, Florian, Hilarion, in line of three. Then ladies, single file; men, single file.

ACT II

Basic seating plan as for Act I.

Three robes placed on seat ①. Picnic hamper placed right of steps R.

1. Row 1, Row 2 enter as before.
   Row 3. Single file in this order: Blanche, Melissa, two altos, two sopranos, Psyche, to sit ⑪ to ⑤.
2. "Towards the empyrean heights." All ladies chorus rise.
   "Pray what authors should she read?" Melissa and Psyche step forward two paces from their seats and sing to each other, in manner of tutor (Melissa) questioning a student (Psyche).
   Postlude. Melissa and Psyche return to their places, remaining standing.
3. "Mighty maiden." Blanche rises. Ida enters to stand and sing RC.
4. *Ida's Speech.* She may use the stage as she pleases, striding about in mannish fashion, lecturing, gesticulating to make points. Towards the end she approaches seat ④, and having delivered "Let Chaos come again" with a dramatic gesture, she holds pose for a moment, then sits. All ladies sit together after Ida.
5. "Gently, gently, evidently" (*Introduction*). Cyril, Hilarion, Florian creep on in that order, melodramatically, to sing RC.
6. *Narrative.* They separate a little, looking about them. Florian discovers robes on seat ①, and as he holds one up, the others come quickly to him.
7. "I am a maiden cold and stately." Sung LC, with traditional 'business.'

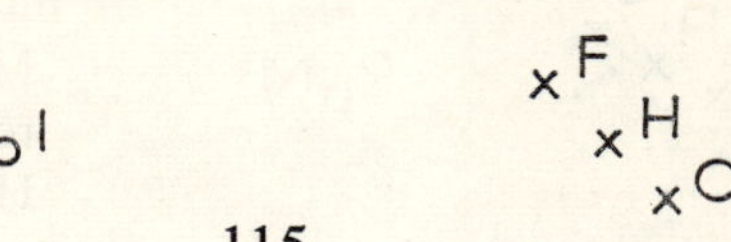

115

8. *Narrative.* Ida rises and comes towards them. Florian, clutching Hilarion's arm, drags him back a little.

9. "The world is but a broken toy." Sung from above positions.

   Postlude. Ida inclines her head graciously to the men, and returns to her seat.

10. *Narrative.* Hilarion and Cyril now relax. Psyche rises and Florian notices her. As she comes forward he takes the bull by the horns and approaches her.

    "This is Prince Hilarion." Florian brings over Hilarion and Cyril.

11. "A lady fair of lineage high." Verse 1, Psyche sings to Florian.

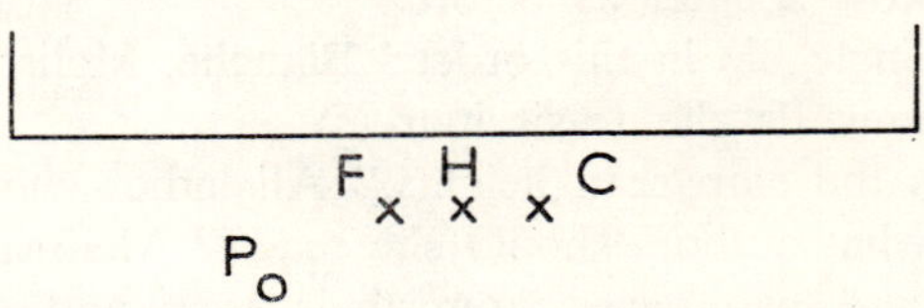

Verse 2, she steps L and sings to Hilarion. Verse 3, she steps L and sings to Cyril. Final chorus she sings on Cyril's left.

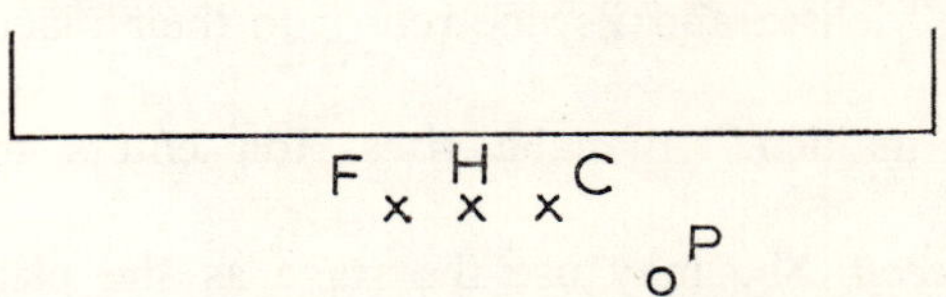

12. *Narrative.* Melissa comes forward to Psyche's left, unnoticed by her. Florian points her out, and Psyche is terrified. Melissa puts her mind at ease, then steps across her to look at the men (like an inspection parade). "I had been told . . .," said to Cyril. "Why you are . . .," to Hilarion. "Your cheeks . . .," to Florian, crossing to his right as she speaks.

13. "The woman of the wisest wit." Initial positions.

Dance after Verse 1, to finish:

Dance after Verse 2, to finish:

Men bow to ladies then retire to sit Florian ①, Hilarion ②, Cyril ③.

14. *Narrative.* On conclusion, Psyche goes to sit ⑤.
15. "Now wouldn't you like to rule the roast" (*Introduction*). Melissa approaches her mother with a deep curtsey. Blanche rises and both come down LC.

    Postlude. Both dance, curtsey deeply to each other, then part — Blanche to return to her seat, Melissa to exit.
16. "Merrily ring the luncheon bell" (*Introduction*). Ladies' chorus rise. Four ladies front row go to collect hamper. As they return with it, Blanche rises and directs the ladies to place it centre back. The four ladies group round it. During this, Cyril has taken out a hip flask and drinks from it. As chorus start to sing, Florian, Hilarion and Cyril rise, and Cyril, turning his back on the seated Ida, takes another swig from the flask, to be rebuked by Hilarion. The men now come forward RC, Cyril still with flask in his right hand.

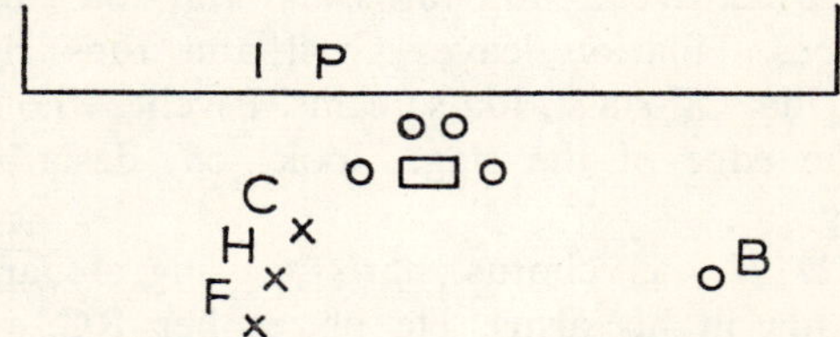

Cyril approaches the hamper and is about to investigate its contents when Blanche starts to sing "Hunger, I beg to state." Cyril remains politely at the hamper.

    "Yes, yes, we'll learn our appetites to subdue" (*Chorus*). Cyril thrusts a hand into the hamper and pulls out a sandwich, then sings "Madam, your words so wise."

    "Merrily ring the luncheon bell" (*Repeat*). Ida and Psyche now come forward extreme R. Cyril eats his sandwich and has another drink from his flask.

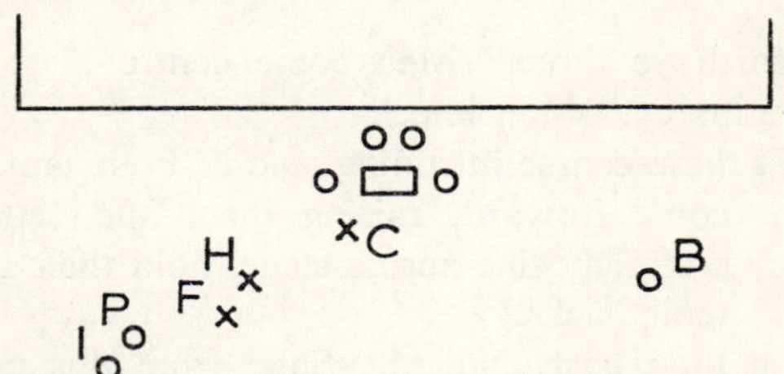

17. *Kissing Song.* Verse 1, Cyril sings where he is standing at the hamper. Between verses he takes another swig, and lurches

front to left of Blanche to sing Verse 2. Florian restrains Hilarion with some difficulty.

Postlude. Cyril grasps Blanche round the waist and gives her a resounding kiss on the cheek. Blanche screams.

18. *Narrative*. As Ida speaks, Hilarion breaks from Florian and strides over to Cyril and shakes him.

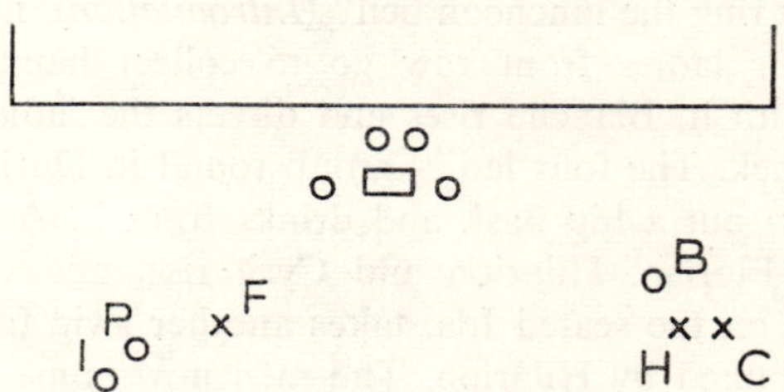

"We are betrayed." Ida turns and runs off stage, speaking as she goes. Hilarion leaves Cyril and runs right to exit, following Ida. Off-stage, Ida screams. Psyche, who has followed Ida to the edge of the stage, looks off, describing what is happening.

19. *Finale Act II*. As chorus starts to sing, Hilarion returns, carrying Ida in his arms. He places her RC, where she is tended by Psyche. Hilarion, followed by Florian, goes LC to be joined by Cyril.

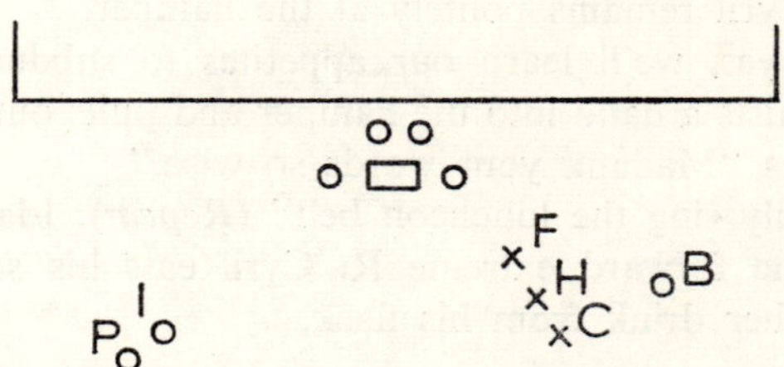

"Stand forth ye three." Men come centre in same diagonal
"Have mercy." Men kneel.

"Arrest these coarse intruding spies." Four ladies at hamper come forward, raising men, and setting them in a straight line across stage, hold their hands behind their backs.

"Whom thou hast chained." Sung from this position.

Postlude. Men led off the stage by the four ladies. As they exit, Melissa enters to sing on Psyche's right.

"Rend the air with wailing." Men's chorus rise. Hildebrand
enters, followed by Arac, Guron and Scynthius in single file,
the three sons with hands tied behind their backs. Arrogantly,
Hildebrand crosses in front of Ida to take centre stage, the
three men forming a line LC. These positions to be retained

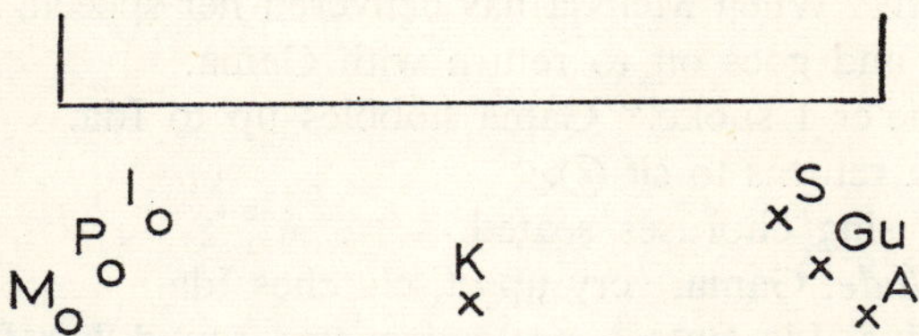

till the end of the Act, though, if desired, Hildebrand can
approach Ida to chastise her — to which she would reply by
assuming a haughty posture.

End of Act. Exeunt in this order: Hildebrand, swaggering
arrogantly; three men plodding single file; Ida, resolute,
followed by Melissa and Psyche; Lady Blanche, haughty.
Then ladies, single file; men, single file.

ACT III

Basic seating plan as for Act I.

1. Row 1, Row 2 enter as before.
   Row 3. Single file in this order: two altos, Florian, Cyril,
   Hilarion, two sopranos, Melissa, Psyche, Blanche to places
   ⑪ to ②. (Florian, Cyril, Hilarion still in robes, have their
   arms tied behind their backs.)
   Taking cue from principals, all sit together, except Florian,
   Cyril, Hilarion, who remain standing.
2. "Death to the invader." All ladies rise.
   "Thus our courage." Melissa steps forward two paces —
   sings very demurely.
   "But 'twould be an error." Melissa now puts on a show of
   bravery, and marches across L as she sings. During following
   chorus she strides back manfully to centre, and holds pose
   there.
3. *Narrative.* Ida enters to RC middle. Her first speech is declamatory. Melissa goes up to her to reply.
   "Away, away." All ladies sit. Melissa, bobbing a curtsey to
   Ida slips behind her and exits.

119

"So fail my cherished plans." Ida, still RC, moves slowly front.

4. "I built upon a rock." Ida sings RC front.

   Postlude. Ida, disconsolate, moves back, when to her enters Melissa.

5. *Narrative*. When Melissa has delivered her speech, she curtsies to Ida and goes off to return with Gama.

6. "Whene'er I spoke." Gama hobbles up to Ida.

   Melissa returns to sit ④.

   Ladies sing choruses seated.

   Postlude. Gama, very upset, clutches Ida.

7. *Narrative*. Ida puts a protective arm round her father.

   Then she assumes a dramatic pose for "Open the gates."

8. "When anger spreads his wings." Chorus rises. Four ladies front row, lead Florian, Cyril, Hilarion, still bound, to stand L, at right angles to stage. Once in position, girls free their bonds.

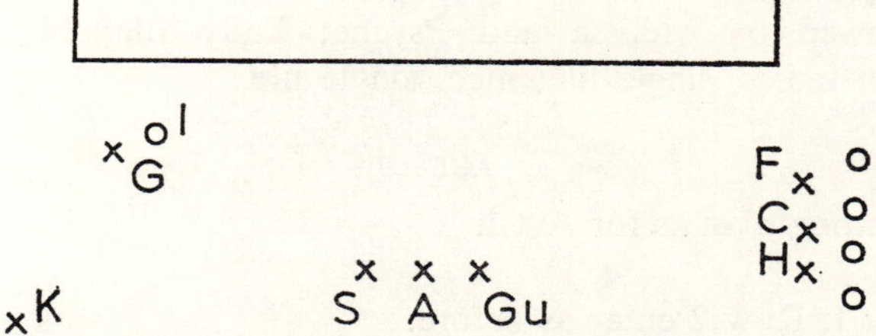

Hildebrand enters to stand R, front. Guron, Arac, Scynthius march heavily past (behind him and in front of Gama and Ida) to stand in a line centre.

9. "This helmet, I suppose" (*Introduction*). Psyche, Melissa and soprano (at back of four ladies) come behind Scynthius, Arac and Guron to assist in taking off armour.

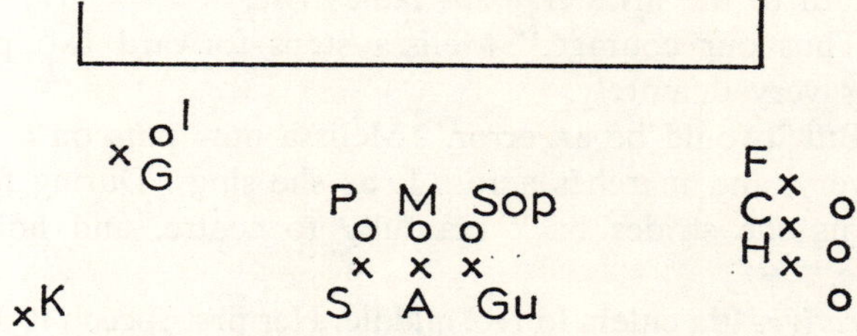

Final chorus. Psyche, Melissa and soprano go back to stand at seats directly behind the three men, taking armour with them and depositing it on the seats.

Postlude. Three men do left turn and march to face Florian, Cyril and Hilarion.

10. "This is our duty plain." As chorus sing, men fight; three ladies creep in arc around them joined by soprano.

"Hilarion! Hilarion!" Scynthius, Arac, Guron, fall on ground with other three men flourishing swords over them.

11. *Narrative.* "Hold! We yield to you." Ida steps forward dramatically. She holds pose, and on the pause Blanche comes forward to join Gama. Scythius, Arac and Guron pick themselves up to stand back at seats ⑧ to ⑩. Four ladies go to original column.

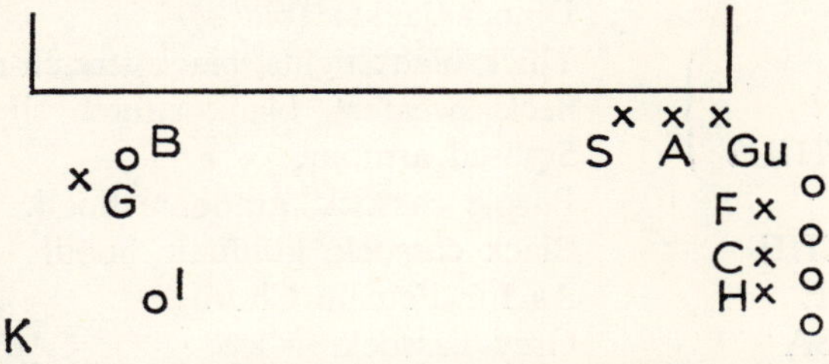

As this action is taking place Ida drops pose and assumes a dejected attitude for "So ends my cherished scheme." At "If I had carried out this glorious scheme," Ida becomes more positive, more declamatory, more like her old self.

"I see my error now." Ida changes attitude to appreciation of Hilarion's worth.

"Take me, Hilarion." She stretches out both arms to Hilarion. He crosses immediately to her.

12. "With joy abiding." Psyche and Cyril, Melissa and Florian join line. Four ladies group in a circle to dance.

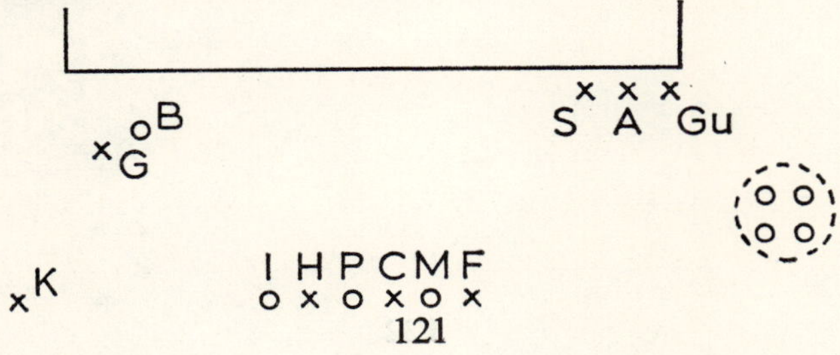

13. *End of opera.* All take one bow, then exeunt: Ida and
Hilarion, Psyche and Cyril, Melissa and Florian, Hildebrand
and Gama (all in twos).

Blanche; dancers in twos; Scynthius, Arac, Guron — single
file.

Ladies, single file; men, single file.

Suggestions for Costuming

PRINCIPALS	ACTS I, II, III
HILDEBRAND	Evening dress tails.
HILARION	Act I. Dinner jackets (white).
CYRIL	
FLORIAN	Acts II, III. Red cassocks.
GAMA	Dinner jacket (black).
ARAC	Thick black tights, black stretch-nylon crew-neck sweaters, black stretch slippers.
GURON	
SCYNTHIUS	Stylised armour.
IDA	Purple cassock, graduate hood.
BLANCHE	Black cassock, graduate hood.
PSYCHE	As for Female Chorus.
MELISSA	Grey cassock.

CHORUS	ACTS I, II, III
MALE	Dinner jackets (black).
FEMALE	Act I. Cocktail dresses knee length.
	Acts II, III. Red cassocks.

9

THE MIKADO

Script for Pooh-Bah as Narrator

ACT I

Overture
V.S. No. 1. *Chorus*. "If you want to know who we are."
V.S. No. 2. *Song*. "A wand'ring minstrel I."
V.S. No. 3. *Song*. "Our great Mikado."
POOH-BAH I am a particularly haughty and exclusive person, of pre-Adamite ancestral descent. You will understand this when I tell you that I can trace my ancestry back to a protoplasmal primordial atomic globule. Consequently my family pride is something inconceivable. I can't help it. I was born sneering. But I struggle hard to overcome this defect. I mortify my pride continually. When all the great officers of State resigned in a body, because they were too proud to serve under an ex-tailor, did I not unhesitatingly accept all their posts at once? It is consequently my degrading duty to serve this upstart as First Lord of the Treasury, Lord Chief Justice, Commander-in Chief, Lord High Admiral, Master of the Buckhounds, Groom of the Back Stairs, Archbishop of Titipu, and Lord Mayor, both acting and elect, all rolled into one. And at a salary! A Pooh-Bah paid for his services! I a salaried minion! But I do it! It revolts me, but I do it! (*He has been working himself into a state of some frenzy. Now he recollects himself.*) This young fellow, Nanki-Poo, appears to have fallen in love with Yum-Yum, the ward of Ko-Ko, that cheap tailor, now Lord High Executioner of Titipu. Hearing that Ko-Ko had been condemned to death for flirting, he has returned with renewed hope, seeking further information. I should consider such detail to come under the head of a State Secret — but as I retail State Secrets at a low figure, I might allow myself to be persuaded to give some guidance.
V.S. No. 4. *Song*. "Young man despair."
V.S. No. 4a. *Recit*. "And I have journeyed for a month."

V.S. No. 5. *Chorus*. "Behold the Lord High Executioner."
V.S. No. 5a. *Song*. "As some day it may happen."
V.S. No. 6. *Chorus*. "Comes a train of little ladies."
V.S. No. 7. *Trio*. "Three little maids."
POOH-BAH How de do, little girls, how de do? (*see Production*.) Go away little girls. Can't talk to little girls like you. Go away, there's dears.
V.S. No. 8. *Quartet and Chorus*. "So please you, sir."
POOH-BAH Oh my protoplasmal ancestor! I am not in the habit of saying 'How de do, little girls, how de do?' to anybody under the rank of a Stockbroker. I am much relieved that these young persons have departed. Ah, but one has contrived to remain. Yum-Yum has discovered Nanki-Poo. The laws against flirting being excessively severe, she will doubtless repel him initially — I believe that is the custom of young persons. So he will counter it by revealing his true identity — as none other than the Son of the Mikado.

You may be surprised that I am acquainted of this fact, but it is my customary practice to ascertain the credentials of all who arrive in Titipu. Thus I am aware also that Nanki-Poo has fled his father's Court to escape the attentions of the elderly Katisha who had claimed his hand in marriage. With these facts before her, I have no doubt that Yum-Yum will succumb to the charms of Nanki-Poo's wooing — or his rank!
V.S. No. 9. *Duet*. "Were you not to Ko-Ko plighted."
POOH-BAH. Pish-Tush is now deep in consultation with Ko-Ko, who has just received a letter from the Mikado — with the contents of which, of course, I am cognisant. The Mikado is struck by the fact that no executions have taken place in Titipu for a year, and decrees that, unless somebody is beheaded within one month, the post of Lord High Executioner shall be abolished, and the city reduced to the rank of a village — a most distasteful eventuality which would involve us all in irretrievable ruin. Ko-Ko, already condemned to death for flirting, would seem the obvious choice as a victim, but he will doubtless decline, as self-decapitation is an extremely difficult, not to say dangerous thing to attempt. I should be delighted to offer myself as Lord High Substitute. Such an appointment would realise my fondest dreams. But no, at any sacrifice I must set bounds to my insatiable ambition.
V.S. No. 10. *Trio*. "I am so proud."
POOH-BAH. The problem is for Ko-Ko's solving — he must

fulfil the function of his office. He must find a substitute. But where? — Nanki-Poo!

Ko-Ko finds him disconsolate at being unable to marry Yum-Yum, and is contemplating suicide. Ko-Ko offers to behead him handsomely with a grand public ceremonial. (As Chancellor of the Exchequer, I shall have to review the financial aspect critically.) But Nanki-Poo demurs — perhaps Yum-Yum would be too distressed. Then he strikes a bargain with Ko-Ko. If he can marry her tomorrow, Ko-Ko may behead him at the end of the month. Unpleasant as is the thought of losing his bride-to-be, Ko-Ko has no alternative but to comply.

V.S. No. 11. *Finale Act I.*

ACT II

V.S. No. 1. *Chorus.* "Braid the raven hair."

YUM-YUM Yes, I am indeed beautiful! Sometimes I sit and wonder, in my artless Japanese way, why it is that I am so much more attractive than anybody else in the whole world. Can this be vanity? No! Nature is lovely, and rejoices in her loveliness. I am a child of Nature, and take after my mother.

V.S. No. 2. *Song*, "The sun whose rays."

V.S. No. 3. *Madrigal.* "Brightly dawns our wedding day."

POOH-POOH—The traditional joyous contemplation of marriage is rather tempered by the fact that, acting as Ko-Ko's Solicitor, I had discovered that by the Mikado's Law, when a married man is beheaded, his wife is buried alive.

V.S. No. 4. *Trio.* "Here's a how-de-do."

POOH-BAH Yum-Yum now seems less attracted to the idea of marriage to Nanki-Poo. Ko-Ko, however, is much more gleeful, until Nanki-Poo refuses to live without Yum-Yum and threatens to commit suicide this afternoon. This puts Ko-Ko in a quandary as the Mikado is due to arrive at any moment and will demand details of the execution arrangements — a suicide case will not prove acceptable to him. So Ko-Ko decides to call upon me to perjure myself — to make an affidavit that Nanki-Poo has been duly executed. Naturally, I shall require a ready-money transaction for this — *and* for undertaking as Archbishop of Titipu to marry Nanki-Poo and Yum-Yum at short notice — on which part of the bargain Nanki-Poo insists.

V.S. No. 5. *Entrance of Mikado and Katisha.*

V.S. No. 6. *Song.* "A more humane Mikado."

125

POOH-BAH Inevitably, my part in the subterfuge went according to plan, but Ko-Ko is now somewhat disconcerted when the Mikado, disappointed at missing the execution, asks for a detailed account of the performance.

V.S. No. 7. *Trio*. "The criminal cried."

POOH-BAH (*Self-satisfied*) This account of the titanic struggle — particularly my embellishment of the fiction — appears to have pleased His Majesty. But wait! Katisha has obtained the Death Certificate. She will see Nanki-Poo's name. Oh! The penalty for encompassing the death of the heir apparent is something lingering — with either boiling oil or melted lead! The Mikado is sure to insist on our execution this very afternoon. *And I wasn't there!*

V.S. No. 8. *Glee*. "See how the fates."

POOH-BAH I must confess that even I can see no solution — unless Nanki-Poo comes to life again. (*Contemplative*) And he would refuse to do so as he should then have to marry Katisha. No! I have it! Ko-ko, poor fellow (*he laughs*) must first marry Katisha, then Nanki-Poo can be resurrected with impunity.

V.S. No. 9. *Duet*. "The flowers that bloom in the spring."

V.S. No. 10. *Recit. and Song*. "Alone and yet alive."

V.S. No. 11. *Song*. "On a tree by a river."

V.S. No. 12. *Duet*. "There is beauty in the bellow of the blast."

POOH-BAH Having as Registrar, married Ko-Ko and Katisha, and presented them to the Mikado, it now falls upon me to use my powers of eloquence to provide the Mikado with a full explanation. (*He brings on Nanki-Poo and Yum-Yum.*) Your Majesty, the Heir Apparent is *not* slain! The sequence of events leading up to his presumed death occurred thus. . . . When your Majesty says, 'Let a thing be done,' it's as good as done — practically, it *is* done — because your Majesty's will is law. Your Majesty says, 'Kill a gentleman,' and a gentleman is told off to be killed. Consequently, that gentleman is as good as dead — practically, he *is* dead — and if he is dead, why not say so?

MIKADO I see. Nothing could possibly be more satisfactory!

V.S. No. 13. *Finale Act II*.

Basic Seating Plan

PROPS

Act I. Guitar and ballads, ceremonial axe or sword, small bags of money. Mikado's letter (scroll), fans for all.

Act II. Mirror on stand, death certificate.

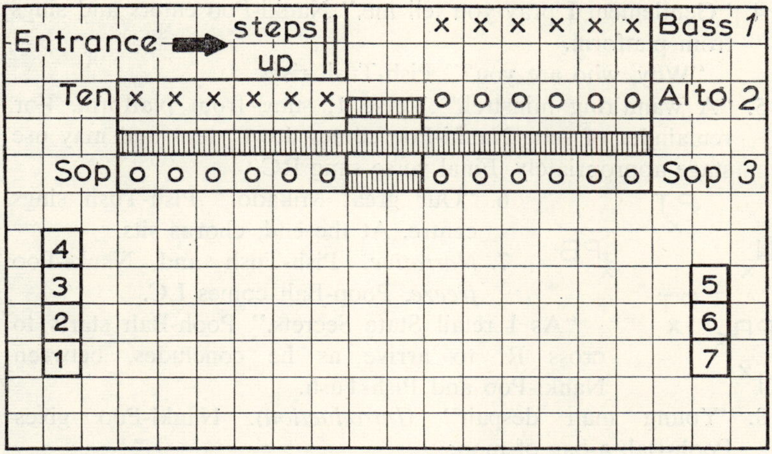

Entrance ➡ steps up ‖						x x x x x x	Bass	1
Ten x x x x x x	▭	o o o o o o	Alto	2
▭▭▭▭▭▭▭▭▭▭▭				
Sop o o o o o o	▭	o o o o o o	Sop	3

4
3
2
1
5
6
7

ROW 1 (Raised 1 double step) ROW 2 (Same level)
ROW 3 (Seated floor level)

NOTATION

M — Mikado	PT — Pish-Tush	K — Katisha
N — Nanki-Poo	Y — Yum-Yum	S — Ko-Ko's sword
KK — Ko-Ko	PS — Pitti-Sing	bearer (child)
PB — Pooh-Bah	Pe — Peep-Bo	

(Note The old music version of having Go-To's part sung by
Pish-Tush is used.)

Production for Script with Pooh-Bah as Narrator

ACT I

1. Men enter in twos, tenors on right, splitting to stand at seat
positions — tenors R, basses L. Pooh-Bah and Pish-Tush
follow, going to ⑦, ⑤. Men keep standing out of respect
for them, and sit after they sit.

2. *Overture.*

3. *Opening chorus.* Chorus rises, and men kneel and stand alter-
nately to allow for traditional marionette actions. Pooh-Bah
and Pish-Tush remain seated, and do not sing.

127

4. "Gentlemen, I pray you tell me." Nanki-Poo enters and sings from platform.

"Why, who are you?" Pish-Tush rises.

5. "A wand'ring minstrel." Verse 1, sung from platform. For remainder of song Nanki-Poo comes down steps and may use stage appropriately. Final verse sung RC.

6. "Our great Mikado." Pish-Tush sings centre. At the end, chorus sits.

7. *Narrative.* Pish-Tush and Nanki-Poo *freeze*, Poop-Bah comes LC.

"As I retail State Secrets." Pooh-Bah starts to cross R, to arrive as he concludes, between Nanki-Poo and Pish-Tush.

8. "Young man despair" (*Introduction*). Nanki-Poo gives Pooh-Bah a bag of money.

Postlude. Pooh-Bah and Pish-Tush cross L, to stand at their seats. Nanki-Poo remains RC.

9. "And I have journeyed for a month." Nanki-Poo, addressing Pooh-Bah, sings RC. Pooh-Bah replies from his standing position.

At the end, Nanki-Poo goes to sit ①, Pish-Tush and Pooh-Bah sit.

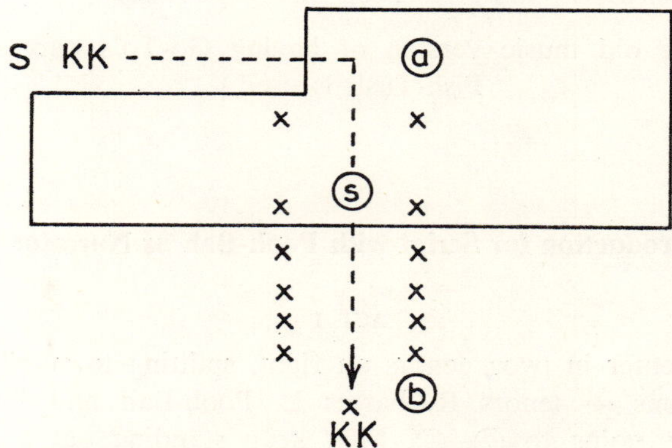

10. "Behold the Lord High Executioner," Chorus rises. Starting from centres, men march to form an aisle of two straight lines from platform, turning to face each other — to be in position at end of introduction.

and poses on platform (a), then comes down between lines, bowing on each "defer," to arrive just beyond men by end of chorus verse (b). Sword Bearer stops at (s).

Ko-Ko, carrying sword, followed by Sword Bearer, enters

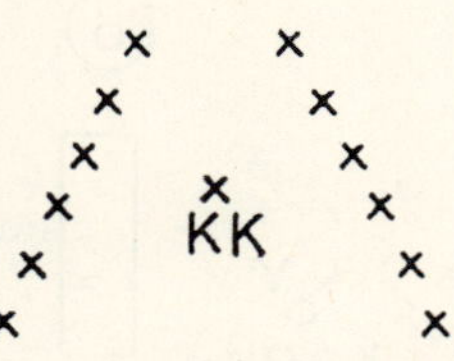

"Taken from a county jail" (*Ko-Ko*). Sung from position (b).

"Taken from a county jail" (*Chorus*). Men march out from centre to form a V.

Postlude of chorus. Ko-Ko hands sword to Sword Bearer, who goes up steps and exits.

11. "As some day it may happen." Traditional 'business'.
Last chorus. Ko-Ko dances sideways L, to sit (6).
Postlude. Chorus march back to seats and sit.

12. "Comes a train of little ladies." Girls enter and come down stage in twos, splitting beyond seats to form two double arcs — sopranos R, altos and sopranos L.

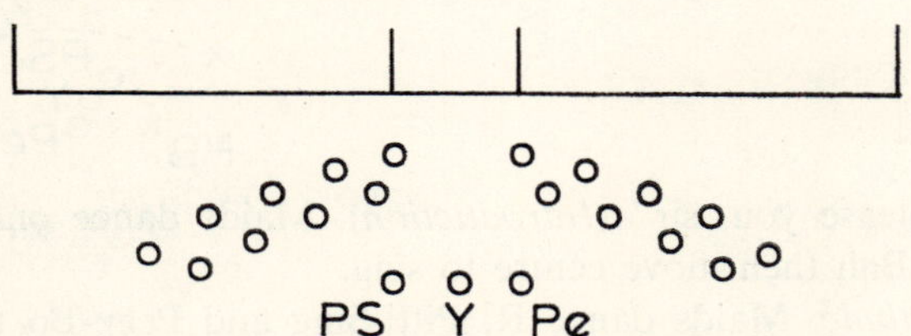

13. "Three little maids." Nanki-Poo, Ko-Ko, Pooh-Bah rise. Yum-Yum, Pitti-Sing, Peep-Bo come down centre to sing — traditional 'business'.

Postlude. Ko-Ko takes Pooh-Bah by the elbow and propels him unwillingly to RC.

14. *Narrative*. Ko-Ko brings maids over to meet Pooh-Bah. They do so giggling and hissing behind their fans. First Peep-Bo makes her curtsey (a), then passes behind him in a circle,

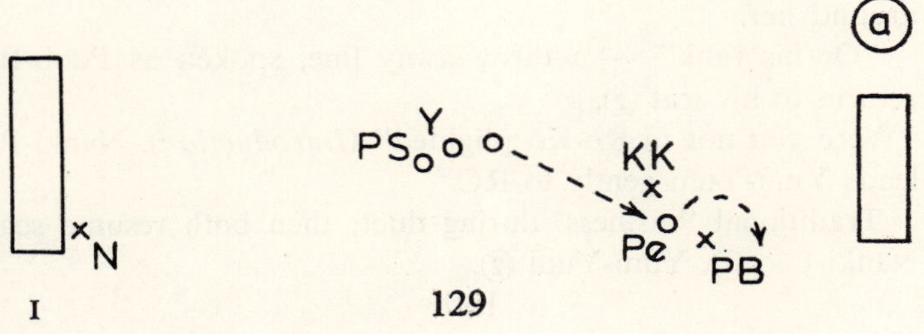

studying him closely. As Yum-Yum follows, Pooh-Bah delivers "How de do, little girls, how de do?" Yum-Yum follows Peep-Bo, and already they are whispering about Pooh-Bah behind

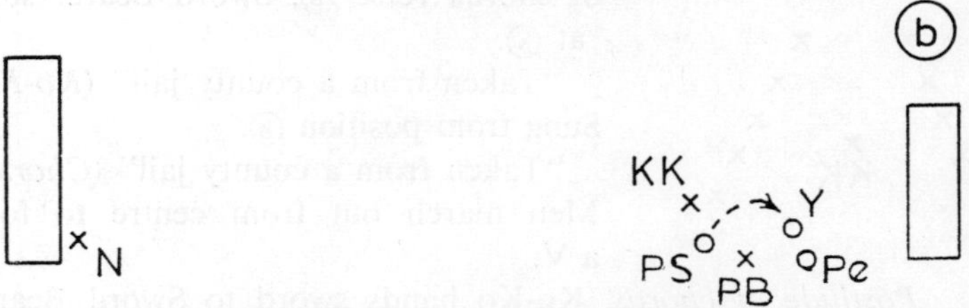

his back when Pitti-Sing curtseys, ⓑ. As she runs behind him, Pooh-Bah realizes he is being laughed at and says "Go away." Ko-Ko follows Pitti-Sing to sit ⑥, position ⓒ.

15. "So please you, sir" (*Introduction*). Maids dance once round Pooh-Bah then move centre to sing.

 Postlude. Maids dance R, Pitti-Sing and Peep-Bo to sit ③, ④; Yum-Yum to stand beside Nanki-Poo. Chorus move up centre in twos, to seats — sopranos front row, altos to middle row.

Chorus sit on final chord.

16. *Narrative*. Pooh-Bah initially not very composed. As he mentions Yum-Yum, Nanki-Poo and she react to narrative.

 "Son of the Mikado." Yum-Yum kneels to Nanki-Poo. He bends over her, holding her hand, during Katisha explanation. After "hand in marriage" he raises her and puts his arm around her.

 "Or his rank" — a throw-away line, spoken as Pooh-Bah returns to his seat ⑦.

17. "Were you not to Ko-Ko plighted" (*Introduction*). Nanki-Poo leads Yum-Yum gently to RC.

 Traditional 'business' during duet; then both resume seats, Nanki-Poo ①, Yum-Yum ②.

18. *Narrative.* Pish-Tush with Ko-Ko on his left, comes centre —
Ko-Ko wearing spectacles, reading a letter. As they reach
centre, Pooh-Bah stands to deliver narrative.

"I should be delighted." Pooh-Bah speaks this to Ko-Ko and
Pish-Tush who look up delightedly, then crestfallen as
Pooh-Bah refuses office. As he speaks, Pooh-Bah walks to
join them.

19. *Trio.* All sit cross-legged, centre.
Postlude. All rise, Pooh-Bah ponder-
ously. He makes his way LC for narrative, leaving the other
two 'in discussion', centre.

PT KK PB

20. *Narrative.* At "substitute," Nanki-Poo rises. At "Nanki-Poo,"
Pish-Tush and Ko-Ko cross to RC to greet Nanki-Poo, who
comes to meet them.

21. *Finale Act I.*

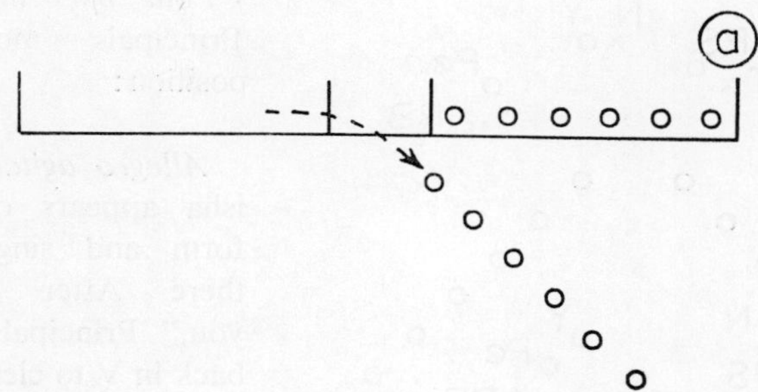

Introduction. Sopranos R, move at solemn pace to stand in
diagonal line L. ⓐ

"With aspect stern." Sopranos L, same to stand R. ⓑ

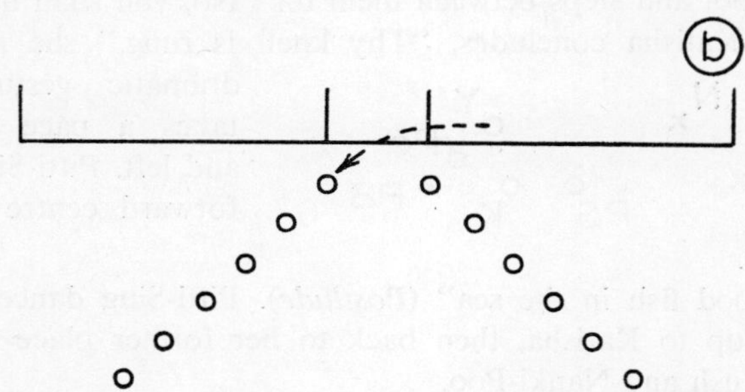

"Don't hesitate." Maids same to stand centre. ⓒ

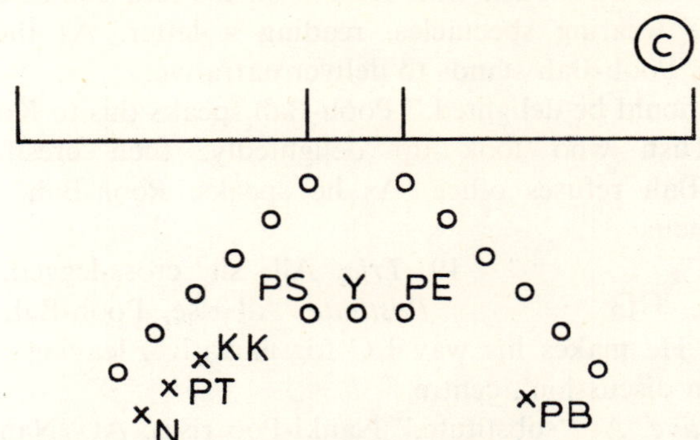

"Congratulate me." Ko-Ko steps forward.
" 'Tis Nanki-Poo." Ko-Ko brings Nanki-Poo forward.
"Take her." Ko-Ko hands Yum-Yum to Nanki-Poo.

Four bars interlude. Principals move to position:

Allegro agitato. Katisha appears on platform and sings from there. After "all of you," Principals sweep back in V to clear space for her to come downstage.

"Ah, 'tis Katisha." Nanki-Poo sings across gap to Yum-Yum; then starts to cross to her. But by then Katisha has reached that spot and steps between them for "No, you shall not go."

As Katisha concludes, "Thy knell is rung," she makes a dramatic gesture and takes a pace forward and left. Pitti-Sing steps forward centre to sing to her.

"Good fish in the sea" (*Postlude*). Pitti-Sing dances tauntingly up to Katisha, then back to her former place between Pish-Tush and Nanki-Poo.

"Ha! Ha! I know." Yum-Yum flits round chorus, both on stage and standing back, whispering to them.

After "Ye torrents roar," Katisha storms upstage to platform, and from there sings "Prepare for woe."

"Away you go" (*Chorus*). Nanki-Poo and Yum-Yum come together centre.

Final Postlude. Katisha sweeps off, followed by tenors and basses in twos, then altos in twos, then sopranos on stage in twos.

Then Nanki-Poo and Yum-Yum; Pitti-Sing and Peep-Bo; Pish-Tush and Pooh-Bah; with Ko-Ko trotting in the rear.

ACT II

Basic seating plan as for Act I, with addition of two seats on platform for Mikado and Katisha.

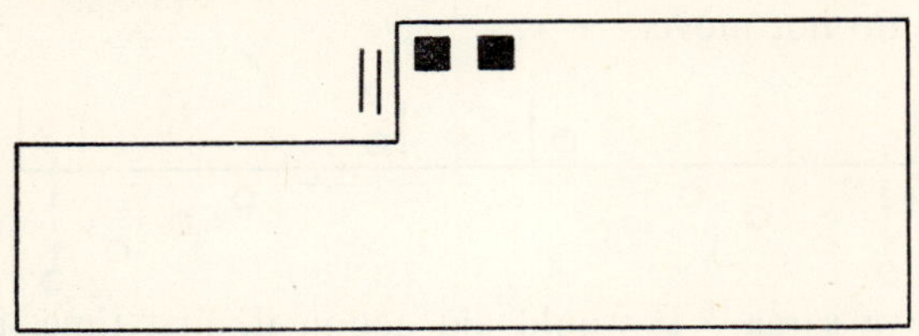

1. *Opening chorus.* During Introduction company enters thus:
Pooh-Bah and Ko-Ko, to stand at ⑦, ⑤.
Nanki-Poo and Pish-Tush, to stand at ①, ③.
Girls in twos led by Peep-Bo. Girls take positions at seats as before Peep-Bo goes to stand at ④.

Y° °PS Yum-Yum and Pitti-Sing (carrying mirror on stand), to stand centre. They kneel, and on this cue, all sit.

"Braid the raven hair." Chorus sing seated.
As traditionally, Pitti-Sing attends to Yum-Yum's toilet.

Postlude. Pitti-Sing goes to sit ⑥, taking mirror, which she conceals behind her chair.

2. Yum-Yum stands to deliver her speech, and sings centre.

3. *Madrigal (Introduction).* Pitti-Sing, Nanki-Poo and Pish-Tush join Yum-Yum.

× × o o
PT N Y PS

At the end. Pitti-Sing and Pish-Tush resume their seats.

4. *Narrative.* Pooh-Bah rises. Nanki-Poo and Yum-Yum, in each others arms *freeze*.

5. "Here's a how-de-do." Commence with only Yum-Yum and Nanki-Poo 'on'.

133

"Here's a state of things." Ko-Ko rises to dance, singing, round stage. Traditional 'business' thereafter.

6. *Narrative.* Nanki-Poo, Yum-Yum and Ko-Ko *freeze* final pose of "Here's a how-de-do."

"I shall require a ready money transaction." Ko-Ko crosses to Pooh-Bah and hands him a bag of money, then passes behind him to sit ⑤.

"To marry Nanki-Poo and Yum-Yum." Nanki-Poo and Yum-Yum walk R, arm-in-arm to sit ①, ②.
Pooh-Bah then sits ⑦.

7. *Entrance of Mikado and Katisha.*

Introduction. Principals remain seated. Girls rise. Front row, from ends, step forward solemnly to form a V. Girls nearest centre do not move.

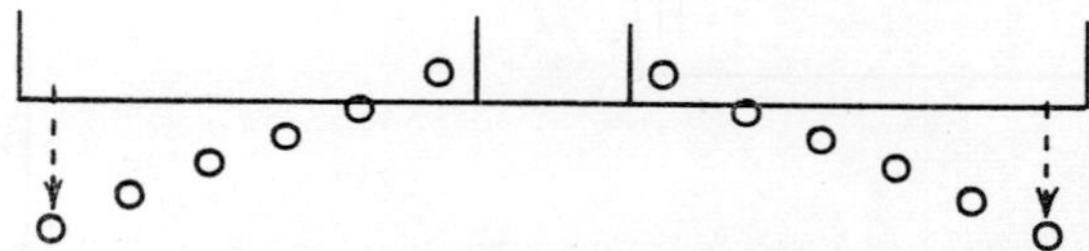

"Miya sama." It would aid action if, first time, girls only sang "Miya sama." Then at *six-bar interlude,* men enter in twos, to take positions, standing, at their seats. Second time all sing "Miya sama". At *ten-bar interlude,* Mikado and Katisha appear on platform, stand, and sing from there — at this point all principals rise.

8. *Mikado's Song.* Mikado comes down during introduction, to sing centre.
Traditional 'business' of Mikado sweeping round on girls on stage can be followed.

Final chorus. Mikado goes back to platform, to pose with fan raised at conclusion.

Postlude. Girls move backwards to front row. All sit.

9. *Narrative.* Pooh-Pooh delivers narrative standing, then sits.

10. "The criminal cried." Verse 1, Ko-Ko rises, steps R two paces for solo.

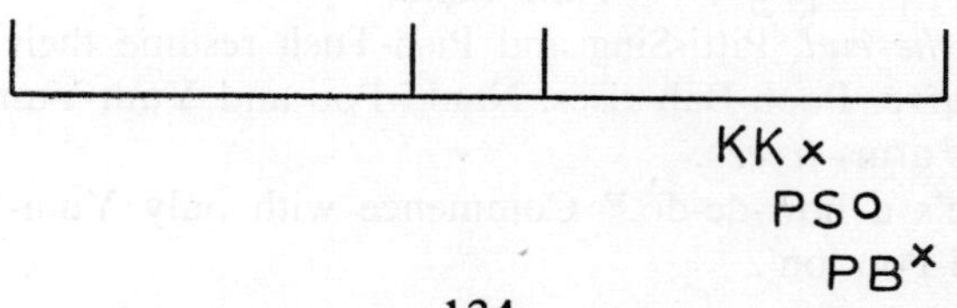

Verse 2, Pitti-Sing joins him, starting a diagonal line.

Verse 3, Pooh-Bah joins her, completing the diagonal. Chorus sing seated.

11. *Narrative.* Pooh-Bah addresses audience from his position on this diagonal.

12. "See how the fates." Mikado and Katisha rise and sing from platform.

Postlude. Mikado and Katisha sit. Others remain standing in diagonal.

13. *Narrative.* Pooh-Bah again addresses audience from same position. As he says, "Nanki-Poo can be resurrected with impunity," Nanki-Poo and Yum-Yum rise to stroll RC.

14. "The flowers that bloom in the spring."

Verse 1 position:

<pre>
                                          x KK
                                          o PS
               Y   x PB
              o
           N
            x
</pre>

Verse 2 position:

<pre>
                              KK   PS
               Y   x   o
              o   x PB
           N
            x
</pre>

Traditional actions.

Postlude. All resume their seats, Ko-Ko dragging his feet unhappily.

15. "Alone and yet alive." Katisha comes downstage slowly, singing *Recit*, to stand centre for song.

16. "Tit-willow." Ko-Ko shyly comes LC middle, to sing. Katisha turns to look back at him.

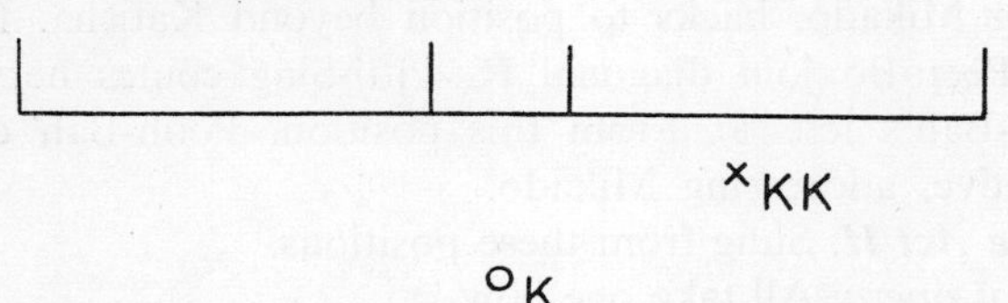

17. *Duet.* Traditional 'business', with Ko-Ko and Katisha ending in position LC middle. Pooh-Bah goes up to them.

18. *Narrative*. Immediately whole company rises. Pooh-Bah leads

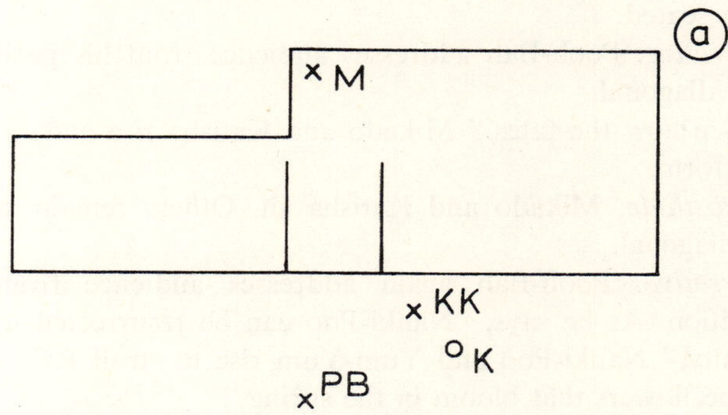

Ko-Ko and Katisha back a little to present them to Mikado (on platform). Mikado looks surprised. Pooh-Bah then comes centre middle to address audience ⓐ. He goes RC to lead Nanki-Poo and Yum-Yum to position opposite Ko-Ko and Katisha.

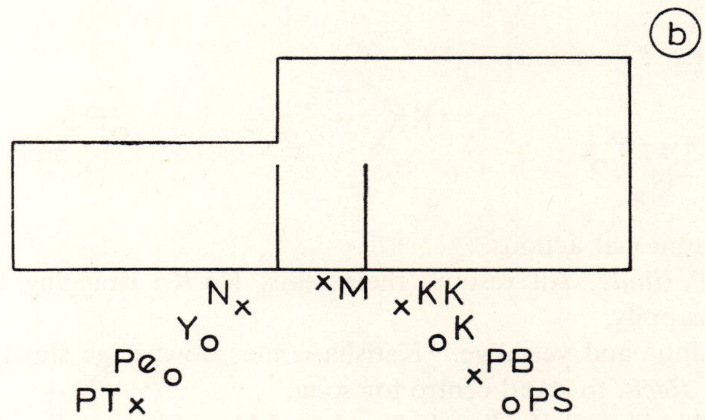

Mikado, astounded, starts to come down steps. Pooh-Bah, facing Mikado, backs to position beyond Katisha. Pish-Tush and Peep-Bo join diagonal R. Pitti-Sing comes nervously to Pooh-Bah's left ⓑ. From this position, Pooh-Bah completes narrative, addressing Mikado.

19. *Finale Act II*. Sung from these positions.

20. *End of opera*. All take one bow.
    Exeunt: Mikado, Nanki-Poo and Yum-Yum, Ko-Ko and Katisha, Peep-Bo and Pish-tush, Pooh-Bah and Pitti-Sing. Girls in twos, men in twos.

Suggestions for Costuming

The use of silk or tricel dressing-gowns for *all* is suggested as most appropriate.

MEN. Gowns should be below the knee, worn with white silk scarf, bare legs, sandals.
WOMEN. Kimono style silk/tricel gown (mandarin collar), white tights, ballet shoes, flowers in hair.
THREE LITTLE MAIDS (Act I). Identical kimonos preferable.
YUM-YUM (Act II). Bridal gown to be white kimono.
KATISHA. Gown to be full-length.
Paper (not plastic) fans to be provided for whole company. Katisha and Mikado to have large cloth fans.

10

RUDDIGORE

Note on Production

Four days after the first performance in 1887, bowing to the criticism of a prudish Victorian public, Gilbert altered the spelling of the title from *Ruddygore* to the present *Ruddigore*. From that time onwards the opera has been subjected to numerous amendments and cuts.

The overture has been rewritten at least once, the Finale Act II, twice. Solo and Chorus parts in Dame Hannah's song have been changed. A song for Robin, "Away, remorse", no longer appears in the vocal score — no great loss perhaps. But the duet, "The battle's roar is over", is too often omitted today with no justification whatever. It is a very fine piece of lyrical writing — textually and musically — and forms an integral part of the work.

Of particular importance for a concert version is the confusion both in vocal scores and libretti, depending on date of printing, as to when full female chorus is used, and when bridesmaids only. There are distinct inconsistencies. Musical director and producer must make up their minds on this point. The writer feels that there are places where bridesmaids only should be used — and has detailed these in the production. At the same time it is admitted that so to divide the ladies, gives the female chorus a very minimal amount of work in the concert version.

Which point stresses a useful function of *Ruddigore* as a concert version — a quick production for, say, fund-raising. Herein, a dedicated section of a society could produce the work under a 'crash-course' of rehearsals very quickly indeed — and with only fourteen chorus (seven male, seven female, i.e. bridesmaids only) plus eight principals.

Note on Dame Hannah as Narrator

This script is one in which the Narrator does not relate as a commentator, what *has* happened. Hannah unfolds the action as it proceeds. She speaks in the present tense. She should be seen as the grandmotherly type from children's story books, telling about the everyday doings of the village — not gossiping maliciously, but in the chatty, conversational tone of the elderly. She is the old woman who sits in her window and observes the passing scene, and is happy to talk about it to anyone who drops in for a cup of tea. (She may even knit on stage, if desired.)

Such an approach makes a very dramatic impact, when, turning to the modified libretto, she finds herself not an onlooker, but an active participant in the happenings of the village.

Script for Dame Hannah as Narrator

ACT I

Overture.

V.S. No. 2. *Song and Full Chorus.* "Sir Rupert Murgatroyd."

HANNAH   Ay, our little village of Rederring has been under the influence of that curse for generations. It has affected me, for Sir Roderic Murgatroyd, one of the baronets, was to have married me long years ago, but when I learnt of the curse, madly as I loved him, I fled him. I never saw him again, and he is dead now, poor soul; but his nephew, Despard, rules in his place.

Still, life goes on apace, and youth is always forming its own fashions and modes of behaviour. There's a group of professional bridesmaids formed, anxious to get my niece, Rose Maybud, married. She's a real beauty, and having been very strictly brought up, is always a stickler for etiquette. But she has a mind of her own; and she won't be hurried into choosing any young man just to suit the bridesmaids.

V.S. No. 1. *Chorus of Bridesmaids.* "Fair is Rose."

V.S. No. 3. *Song.* "If somebody there chanced to be."

V.S. No. 4. *Duet.* "I know a youth."

HANNAH   Now there would be a match for Rose — Robin Oakapple, a young gentleman-farmer. But he's so shy. So unlike his foster-brother, Dick Dauntless, who's just returned from sea. He's a real sailor — no false modesty about him. If he likes a woman, he tells her so. Oh! here he comes — just watch how the bridesmaids ogle him!

V.S. No. 5, 6. *Chorus of Bridesmaids.* "From the briny sea."
       Song. "I shipped d'ye see."

V.S. No. 7. *Song.* "My boy, you may take it from me."

HANNAH   Dick is in no way 'diffident, modest and shy', for having met Rose, he promptly proposes to her. And she, her sense of etiquette on approach to strangers overruled by his forcefulness, yields to him.

V.S. No. 8. *Duet*. "The battle's roar is over."

V.S. No. 9. *Chorus of Bridesmaids*. "If well his suit has sped."

ROBIN Hold your tongues, will you!

HANNAH Robin, too shy to have revealed his love, is more than a little upset at seeing Rose embrace Dick. Disappointed, his shyness is forgotten, and he admits to her that she was the girl of his choice. Dick justifies his own action by saying he acted according to the dictates of his heart. Whereupon, Rose takes this as a text acceptable to her philosophy, and follows her true feelings by abandoning Dick in favour of Robin.

V.S. No.10. *Trio*. "In sailing o'er life's ocean wide."

V.S. No. 11. *Recit and Song*. "Cheerily carols the lark."

HANNAH Poor girl. Mad Margaret they call her. Like me she's a victim of the Ruddigore Curse. She was in love with Sir Despard, but when he succeeded my Roderic as baronet, it affected her mind. Look, she's off now, because Sir Despard and his evil crew, as she calls them, are approaching.

V.S. No. 12. *Full Chorus*. "Welcome, gentry."

V.S. No. 13. *Song and Chorus*. "Oh why am I moody and sad?"

HANNAH All girls flee from Sir Despard. And yet it's not his fault that he has to be bad. He gets his crime over first thing in the morning, and then does good for the rest of the day.

But see, Dick is approaching him. I'm afraid Dick has taken the loss of Rose to Robin very hard and he'll probably let the cat out of the bag. Yes, he's told Despard. (*Confidentially*) I can tell you that Despard had an elder brother Ruthven, who should have inherited the title — and the Curse. Despard believed he died. But I know for a fact that he didn't! He went into hiding — as Robin Oakapple.

Dick apologises for revealing Robin's secret — but protests he felt it was his duty. Despard has no regrets — he can now hand over his cares to Robin, and live a free and blameless life.

V.S. No. 14. *Duet*. "You understand."

V.S. No. 15. *Finale Act I*.

ACT II

HANNAH After a week as a bad Baronet, Robin is finding the task of committing crimes exceedingly difficult. In the Picture Gallery of Ruddigore Castle, he and his faithful retainer, Old Adam, are reviewing the state to which they have fallen, when to them come Dick and Rose (with the Bridesmaids, of course) seeking permission to be wed. Robin cannot steel his heart to refuse her touching plea.

V.S. No. 1. *Duet.* "I once was as meek."

V.S. No. 2. *Duet and Chorus of Bridesmaids.* "Happily coupled."

V.S. No. 3. *Solos and Chorus of Bridesmaids.* "In byegone days."

HANNAH Left alone in the gloomy Gallery, Robin addresses the portraits of his ancestors and begs for mercy. The room darkens, and then to his amazement, the figures come to life. Sir Roderic Murgatroyd, my Roddy, rebukes him for not carrying out his duty in a workmanlike fashion. He commands Robin to carry off a lady. Robin objects, but given a taste of the torture which he would be forced to undergo if he refused, consents unwillingly, and orders Old Adam to carry off a maiden from the village. The Ghosts, satisfied, change back to pictures again.

V.S. No. 4. *Chorus.* "Painted emblems of a race."

V.S. No. 5. *Song.* "When the night wind howls."

V.S. No. 6. *Chorus.* "He yields."

HANNAH As Robin lies exhausted, there enter Sir Despard, now completely reformed, and his newly wed wife — Margaret! She has more or less recovered her senses, although at times she reverts to her outlandish ways. Seeing the transformation in them, Robin realises his scruples prevent him from committing any other crime, and forgetting that he has ordered Adam to abduct a maiden, resolves to defy the Ghosts.

V.S. No. 7. *Duet.* "I once was a very abandoned person."

V.S. No. 8. *Trio.* "My eyes are fully open."

(*Exit Despard and Margaret. Adam here seizes Hannah bodily, and carries her struggling, to Robin*)

ADAM Master — the deed is done! I have carried off the maiden — but she fights like a tiger-cat.

ROBIN Hannah! This is not what I expected.

HANNAH You wretch! You have secured me, and I am your prisoner, but if you think I cannot take care of myself, you are mistaken. (*She pulls out a dagger*)

ROBIN (*Terrified*) Roderic! Uncle! Save me!

RODERIC What is the matter? (*Recognising Hannah*) Little Nannikin!

HANNAH Roddy!

RODERIC What do you mean by carrying off this lady? Are

you aware that once upon a time I was engaged to be married to her? I'm very angry indeed. Be off with you.

V.S. No. 10. *Duet*. "There grew a little flower."

ROBIN   Stop a bit — both of you.

RODERIC   This intrusion is unmannerly.

HANNAH   I'm surprised at you.

ROBIN   I can't stop to apologise — an idea has just occurred to me. A Baronet of Ruddigore can only die through refusing to commit a daily crime.

RODERIC   No doubt.

ROBIN   Therefore, to refuse to commit a daily crime is tantamount to suicide!

RODERIC   It would seem so.

ROBIN   But suicide is, itself, a crime — and so, by your own showing, you ought never to have died at all!

RODERIC   I see — I understand! Then I am practically alive!

ROBIN   Undoubtedly! (*Roderic embraces Hannah.*) Rose, when you believed I was a simple farmer, I believe you loved me?

ROSE   Madly, passionately!

ROBIN   But when I became a bad baronet, you very properly loved Richard instead?

ROSE   Passionately, madly!

ROBIN   But if I should turn out *not* to be a bad baronet after all, how would you love me then?

ROSE   Madly, passionately!

ROBIN   As before?

ROSE   Why, of course!

ROBIN   My darling! (*They embrace*)

DICK   Here, I say, belay!

ROSE   Oh sir, belay if it's absolutely necessary!

ROBIN   Belay? Certainly not!

V.S. No. 11. *Finale Act II.*

Basic Seating Plan

PROPS

Act I.   Stool, rocking-chair, riding crop.

Act II.   Rocking-chair, dagger.

NOTATION (see figure overleaf)

R — Robin	A — Adam	M — Margaret
Dk — Dick	Rd — Roderic	H — Hannah
D — Despard	r — Rose	Z — Zorah

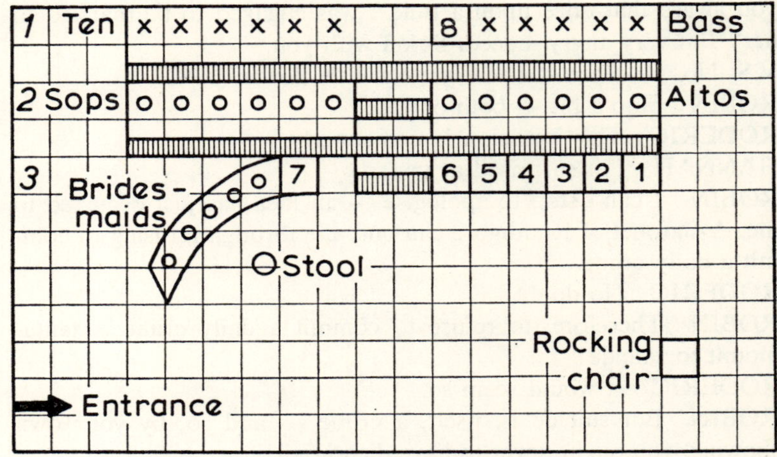

ROW 1 (Raised 2 double steps) ROW 2 (Raised 1 double step)
ROW 3 (Seated floor level)

Production for Script with Dame Hannah as Narrator

ACT I

1. Company enter in this order:

Row 1. Basses, Despard (to ⑧) { In twos — go up centre
        Tenors   { steps and divide.

Row 2. Altos }   In twos — go up centre steps
        Sopranos }   and divide.

Row 3. Adam, Robin, Zorah (to ④, ⑥, ⑦);

Bridesmaids, single file.
Rose to stool, Hannah to rocking-chair.
Remain standing till all on stage, then sit together, taking cue from Hannah.

2. *Overture.*

3. *Hannah's Solo.* She remains seated throughout.
   Introduction. All ladies stand except Rose.

Standing
Kneeling
Sitting

Bridesmaids move across to Hannah to listen to her story, grouping round her chair. Two stand behind chair, two kneel at either side, two sit on floor.

"And thus with sinning cloyed." Soberly, bridesmaids rise and walk slowly, thoughtfully, with downcast eyes, back to their seats, to sit on "-troyd."

4. *Narrative.* For this and all narrative, Hannah remains seated.

5. "Fair is Rose." Bridesmaids rise. Zorah steps forward for solo, level with Rose, indicating her. Rose sits with head bowed modestly.

   Postlude. Bridesmaids sit.

6. "If somebody there chanced to be." Rose stands and sings at stool, remains standing at the end.

7. "I know a youth." Robin comes straight forward, level with Rose. As number proceeds, both come closer gradually, to sing Verse 3 side by side.

   Postlude. Bow to each other, then return to seats.

8. "From the briny sea." Bridesmaids run single file R. Four stand in straight line R, while Zorah and one girl go off to fetch Dick, returning arm-in-arm with him (a). The trio passes in front of line slowly, and as it passes, girls singly, follow on from R (b), to form a procession. (c).

   Wheel when centre (d), to take position (e) for Dick's solo.

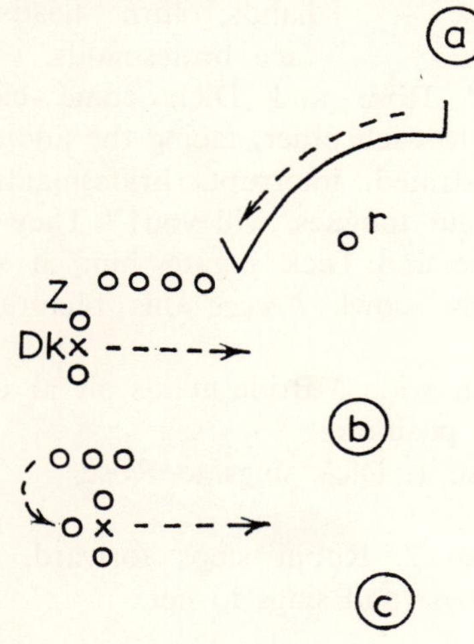

9. *Hornpipe.* Bridesmaids dance with Dick.

   End of music. Girls, laughing, run quickly back to their seats, and sit.

10. "My boy, you may take it from me." Robin comes forward

to Dick, centre, and shakes him by the hand warmly.

End of number. Robin goes immediately to his seat. Dick turns right, sees Rose, who catches his eye. He takes two steps towards her, then both, looking at each other, *freeze* for Hannah's narrative.

11. "The battle's roar" (*Introduction*). Dick crosses to kneel at Rose's side.

12. *Entrance of Bridesmaids.*
    (a) Rose and Dick stand and embrace.
    (b) Bridesmaids rise.
    (c) Robin stands then takes three paces towards couple.
    The above occupies the *Introduction.* As girls start to sing

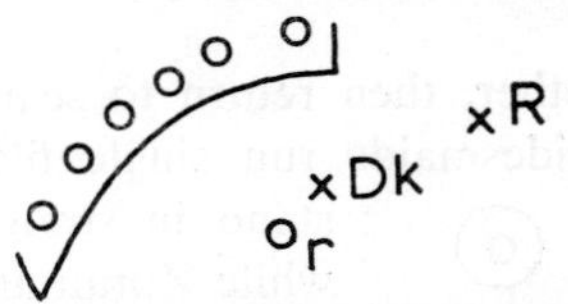

Rose and Dick break embrace, part slightly, but still holding upstage hands, turn heads to face bridesmaids.

"Hail the bridegroom." Rose and Dick come closer, holding hands and smiling to each other, facing the audience. At this point, Robin, frustrated, interrupts bridesmaids by saying petulantly, "Hold your tongues, will you!" They stop singing, pout at him. Rose and Dick regard him in some amazement, while he holds scowl. *Freeze* this picture for narrative.

13. "In sailing o'er life's ocean wide." Bridesmaids sit at once.

Initial position:

Verse 1. Dick sings to Rose.

Verse 2. Robin steps forward, level with Rose and sings to her.

Verse 3. Rose moves between men.

Trio. Dick moves forward.

Postlude. Robin offers his arm to Rose, and both sit ⑥, ⑤. Dick, disconsolate follows to sit ③.

14. Margaret enters, singing, R. She may use stage as she pleases for recit, but song should be sung motionless centre, finishing on her knees, with bowed head.

146

15. *Narrative*. Margaret holds pose for beginning of Hannah's narrative.

"She was in love with Sir Despard." Chorus (not bridesmaids) rises, and Margaret looks round fearfully to rise herself at "Look now," and cross to sit ②.

16. "Welcome gentry." Sung static, as choral item.

17. "Oh why am I moody and sad?" Despard comes down centre, cracking riding crop. He can make use of stage for melodramatic gesture — women always shrinking from him as he approaches. He should finish centre, feet apart, arms crossed. *Freeze* in that position for narrative. Chorus sits.

18. *Narrative*. Some miming as Hannah tells the story. Dick knuckles his forehead to Despard who treats him haughtily; then reacts to Dick's telling him about Robin. They 'chat' confidentially, and Despard claps Dick on the shoulder just before the duet "You understand." After duet, both men sit — Dick ③, Despard ①.

19. "Hail the bride." Full ladies' chorus rises. Zorah crosses to Rose and raises her. Both cross to Hannah and curtsey to her. Hannah rises and the three women take position RC, separated.

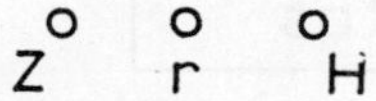

```
      o     o     o
  Z         r         H
```

"Hail the bridegroom." Men's chorus rises. Robin walks forward with Dick and Adam behind. They join the ladies thus: These six dance the *Gavotte*.

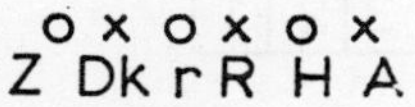

```
   o x o x o x
 Z Dk r R H A
```

"Hold, Bride and Bridegroom." Despard steps forward in line, apart LC.

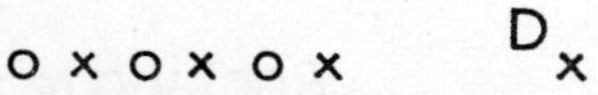

```
   o x o x o x        D
                        x
```

"'Twas I." Dick steps forward.

"Farewell, thou hadst my heart." Rose steps forward and sings to Robin.

"Take me." Rose crosses L to Despard.

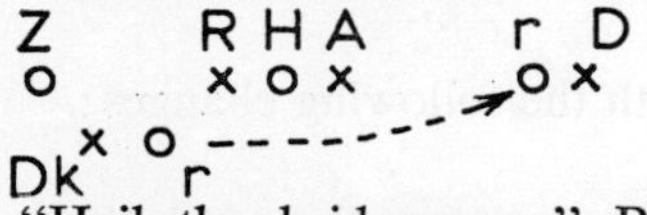

```
 Z      R H A      r D
 o      x o x      o x
   Dk x  o  r
```

"Hail the bridegroom." Bridesmaids step forward in arc R of principals. During this, Margaret creeps forward to be on Despard's left, slightly behind him.

```
    o o o o o
  o o        R H A        o M
   Z o        x o x      o x
     x                   r   D
      Dk
```

147

"Have I misread you?" Margaret steps in line with Despard.

<pre>
      Z   R H A   "So I am thine."
       o   x o x   Rose crosses to Dick.
        x o   x o   " Oh, happy the blos-
      Dk   r   D   M
</pre>
som." Zorah, Hannah, Adam join the line.

<pre>
                                        "Oh, wretched the
      o x o x o x   x o   debtor." Robin joins the
      Z Dk r R H A   D M   line.
</pre>

20. *End of Act*. No dance to be performed, but as music is being played, company exit.
Principals, led by Zorah.
Bridesmaids, ladies in twos, men in twos.

ACT II

Revised Seating Plan

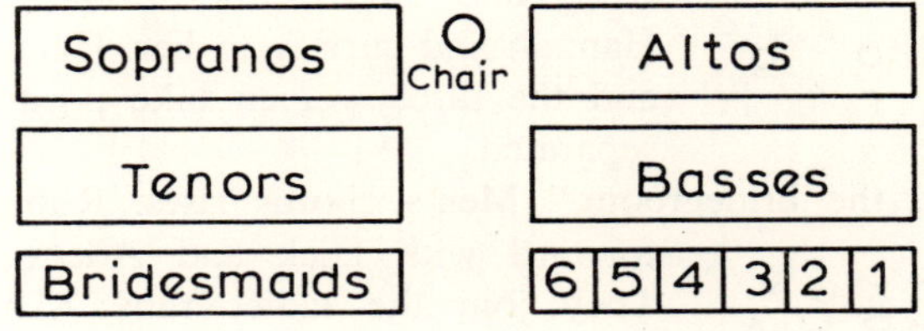

Note. The basic set is retained with the following changes:

1. Sopranos and altos will now occupy Row 1, tenors and basses, Row 2.
2. In middle of Row 1 is placed a chair for Roderic.
3. Stool removed.
4. Bridesmaids' seats now placed in Row 3.

1. Company enter in this order.

    Row 1.   Altos   ⎫   In twos — go up centre steps

              Sopranos ⎭   and divide.

              Roderic to new seat.

    Row 2.   Basses   ⎫   In twos — go up centre steps

              Tenors   ⎭   and divide.

    Row 3.   Margaret and Despard, to seats ④, ⑤.

Hannah to rocking-chair.

Remain standing till all on stage. Taking cue from Hannah, Despard, Margaret and ladies sit.

Men remain standing, but as ladies sit, they assume poses as for portraits. They must remain motionless and expressionless thereafter.

2. *Narrative.* Hannah seated (*speaking through introductory music if desired*).

3. "I once was as meek." Robin, followed by Adam, enters, and both creep melodramatically to sing LC.

    End of duet. Adam bows in servant's fashion to Robin and goes to sit ③. Robin remains LC.

4. "Happily coupled are we." Rose and Dick enter, arm in arm, skipping, followed by bridesmaids, in twos. Rose and Dick sing RC, bridesmaids form two diagonal lines behind them.

5. "In byegone days." Rose crosses to Robin and kneels. Bridesmaids kneel.

    "I yield." Rose runs back to Dick, and bridesmaids, rising on "O rapture" skip in twos to form two lines behind Robin.

    "For she is such a smart little craft." Movement must be fast and precise. Back row of girls, followed by front row, skip, single file, across in front of Rose and Dick, then to their seats. They should be in position there for Rose and Dick's first E♭. Then they sit one by one (starting at the right) on first and second beats of last four bars, *i.e.*, on "bright," "tight," "slight," "light," "trim," "prim." Singing the unison duet, Dick and Rose, still arm in arm move to their seats ②, ①, and arrive there to sit on final "craft," thus completing the bobbing movement of sitting on consecutive beats across the stage.

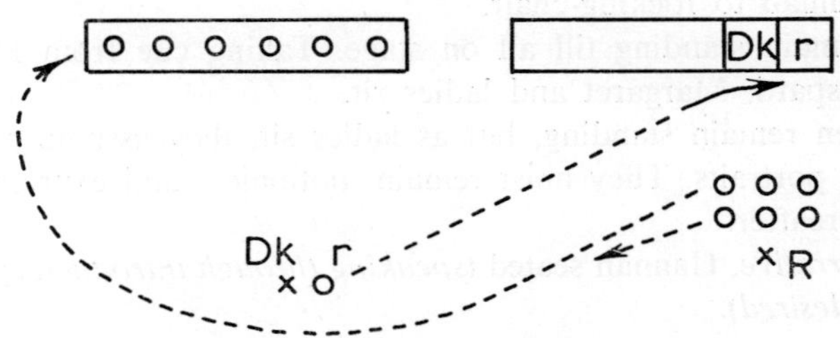

6. *Narrative.* As Hannah speaks, Robin crosses centre, and kneels, facing men.
   (While it is assumed there is no stage lighting, if it is possible to reduce some of the existing illumination, it would prove most effective.)

7. "Painted emblems." As music starts, men break their portrait posture. They remain in position until "Each from his accustomed place," when they move down in two columns starting from centre. Their steps should be slow and menacing before "Baronet of Rudigore," by which time they should have

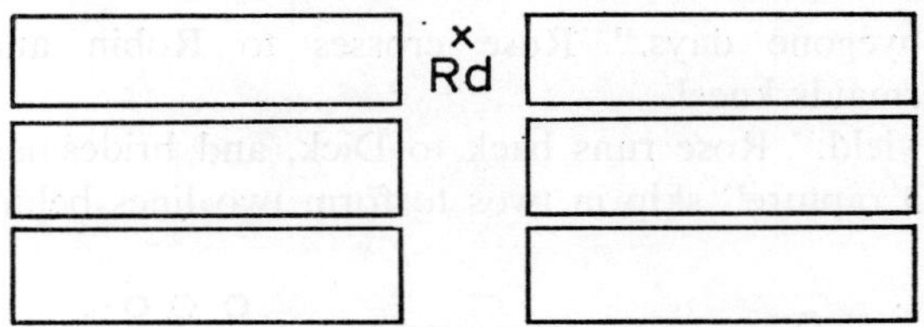

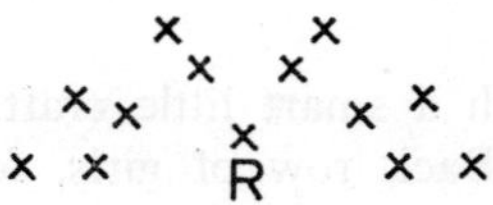

formed a double semi-circle round Robin, who has risen in

amazement. (*N.B.* Roderic still in original position.) By their forceful gestures, Robin is forced to kneel, when at "Blockhead," men pace round him in a single circle.

x
Rd

"Lest the King of Spectreland." By this time, they have divided again, into two double diagonal lines, pointing upstage to Roderic.

"Beware, beware, beware." Delivered from top row. Roderic descends slowly at "I am the spectre," to stand beside Robin by "Alas, poor ghost."

```
  x      x
 x x    x x
x x    x x
x  x   x  x
     R
```

8. "When the night wind howls." During applause for this number, mime takes place. (*See Script for Narrative.*) Roderic points an arm at the still kneeling Robin, who throws up his hands and shakes his head. All ghosts point an arm at him in unison, when Robin puts his arms across his face and writhes in agony. Then with bowed head he lifts one hand in submission, and nods his head. Immediately, play introductory bar of "He yields."

"I pardon you." Robin raises his head to sing, almost in a whisper, then collapses, face downwards.

"He pardons us." Ghosts sing to each other; then resume their impressive attitude, and with measured stride at "Painted emblems," move to their places on Row 2; Roderic last, to Row 1. All sit on final chord of music (*Bring up lighting at once.*)

9. "I once was a very abandoned person." Margaret and Despard come forward and sing and dance (with traditional moves) LC, not noticing Robin, who continues to lie in same position, centre, for Verse 1 of duet. Shaking his head to gather his wits, he begins to notice them in Verse 2; sits up at introduction to Verse 3, and pays particular attention to "I've given up all my wild proceedings."

10. *Patter Trio.* All three together centre. Traditional actions

x o x   Verses 1, 2.

R M D   Verse 3 chorus. As voices sing together, Margaret and Despard, singing, return to their seats. Robin moves RC at the end, shaking his head.

11. During applause, Hannah rises, apparently to continue

narrative. Adam comes forward stealth-
ily, and seizes her bodily, carrying her,
screaming, to LC, level with Robin.
"Roderic." Roderic comes down steps, speaking first to
Robin, then recognising Hannah.
"Be off with you." Robin and Adam
shrink back to their seats, Robin crossing behind Roderic.

12. "There grew a little flower." Roderic and Hannah walk slowly
to RC to sing duet.

13. After duet, quick movement as follows:
(a) Robin crosses to Hannah and Roderic, followed by Rose
and Dick.

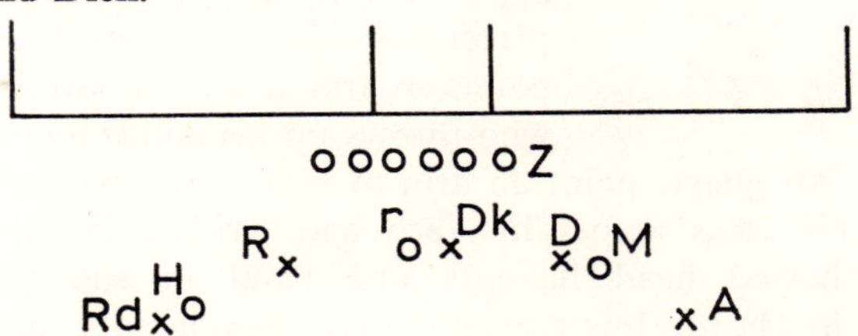

(b) Margaret and Despard come forward, leaving a gap beside
Dick.
(c) Adam follows to be on end of line, L.
(d) Bridesmaids form a line behind principals.
Then follows *libretto*.
"My darling." Rose joins Robin.
Dick looks disconsolate, but as soon as music for *Finale*
starts Zorah comes up on his left and curtseys coquettishly.
Dick partners her joyfully.

14. *Finale Act II.* All rise.

15. *End of Opera.* If written in vocal score, dance should not be
performed. As music of dance is played, all take one bow
then exit: Roderic and Hannah, Robin and Rose, Dick and
Zorah, Margaret and Despard — all arm in arm in pairs;
Adam, bridesmaids in single file.
Ladies in twos, men in twos.
If no dance in V.S., above exit takes place as soon as music
stops.

Suggestions for Costuming

PRINCIPLES	ACT I	ACT II
ROBIN OAKAPPLE	Smart sports suit or sports jacket with cravat.	Dark slacks, black polo-neck sweater, black shoes and socks.
DICK DAUNTLESS	Light-coloured slacks, white sports shirt, blue and white spotted neckerchief.	Same.
OLD ADAM	Trousers and waistcoat of dark suit, white shirt, black tie, black shoes and socks.	Same.
SIR DESPARD	Tweed suit, check shirt, brown shoes.	Dinner jacket (black).
SIR RODERIC	—	Evening dress, with opera cloak essential.
ROSE MAYBUD	Tailored dress, Puritan style, with high neck.	Short white dress, figure revealing.
MAD MARGARET	Tattered dress, torn and laddered tights, no shoes.	Demure black cocktail dress.
DAME HANNAH	Old-fashioned and matronly dress, shawl, thick stockings, lace-up shoes.	Same.
ZORAH	As for Bridesmaids.	Same.

CHORUS	ACTS I, II
MALE	Dinner jackets (black).
FEMALE	Short summer dresses.
BRIDESMAIDS	Short dresses, white or pastel colour, preferably identical.

11

THE YEOMAN OF THE GUARD

Note on Production

The Yeoman of the Guard is the nearest approach to Grand Opera in the whole series of G and S works. Its historical background and moving plot were influential in Sullivan's decision to keep writing in collaboration with Gilbert — for after the modified success of *Ruddigore,* he had, not for the first time, lost enthusiasm. But he responded magnificently to Gilbert's dramatic libretto, producing in particular a *Finale* to Act I not unworthy of Verdi. The work is thus deserving of special treatment for a concert version presentation.

The production provided is at once more elaborate in construction than the others; and yet at the same time is simpler — in that there is no chorus movement plotted. No increase in stage provision from that of the other productions is demanded: and yet, as a first example of how a producer can develop the basic plan, it is suggested that if performance in a medieval church is possible (and more opportunity of this is occurring with closures of historic buildings) the intensity can be heightened considerably.

The production is based on a series of tableaux, linked by narrative; with static chorus isolated from the action as in many stage productions of Handel operas and oratorios. The Narrator, for once, appears not as a character, but as one external entirely to the plot. He examines with a twentieth-century eye a tale of the past — unfolding it, interpreting it, and showing the relevance of its human situations to today's mode of living. He is thus not merely a story-teller, but a commentator. He should be played as a tutor delivering a lecture, making play with his lecture notes, and using the players as 'visual aids' to illustrate his talk.

It is stressed again that, with the exception of two large draught screens and a lectern (*see seating plan*), no additional material for staging is requested beyond that suggested for other works. These screens should be draped with curtain material, tapestry if possible, to create a Renaissance period atmosphere. Unessential, but an improving refinement, is to place a railing some 30 inches high in front of each front row of chorus (two male one female) from which tapestries can be suspended to the floor. This has the effect of further separating the principals, making the chorus appear as onlookers, commentators or judges (as in a medieval court).

Just these two examples should be sufficient stimulus for an inventive producer — given a talented company, financial opportunity to dress the stage well, and possibly some lighting effects — to elaborate this basic presentation to one with a dramatic impact, different from, but equal to a full stage production.

Basic Seating Plan

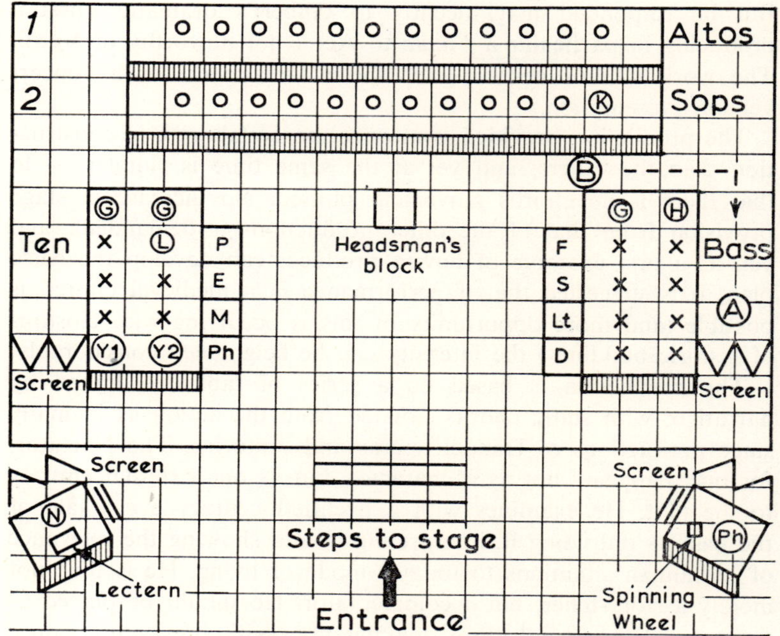

(Through centre aisle of auditorium)

ROW 1 (Raised 2 single steps) ROW 2 (Raised 1 single step)
ROSTRA (Raised 1 single step)

1. Ⓐ Changing area.
   Ⓑ Used as EXIT for stage only.
2. Rostra for narrator and Phoebe should be about a foot below stage level.
3. Headsman dressed initially as Guard (*see Production and Costuming*).
4. In Act I, the Guards should neither rise, nor sing with the Yeoman. They may, however, sing in the crowd scenes (*V.S. No. 2, V.S. No. 6*) and of course in the *Finale, Act I*.
   In Act II they can appear as Yeomen.
5. Assumed no stage lighting, but presumed that some lights over stage can be switched off to create a dim effect.
6. Narrator to have a reading lamp with operating switch.

PROPS

Act I. Headsman's block and axe, spinning wheel, bag of coins, keys.

NOTATION

Lt — Lieutenant	S — Shadbolt	E — Elsie
F — Fairfax	Y_1 — 1st Yeoman	Ph — Phoebe
M — Meryll	Y_2 — 2nd Yeoman	D — Dame
L — Leonard	G — Guard	K — Kate
P — Point	H — Headsman	N — Narrator

Script/Production

ACT I

Lighting — Stage area, dim; spinning wheel area, lit; narrator area, dim.

1. *Overture.* At repeat of *Tower motif* (*last 2 pages of V.S.*), company enter in twos, through centre aisle of auditorium. Altos, sopranos, Kate proceed almost to headsman's block then divide L and R to fill rows from side into centre. Altos, back row; sopranos, front row. Tenors and basses (paired). Tenors on R. Guards, headsman at appropriate intervals. Divide at Block L and R to fill back columns first.

Principals (paired as shown) divide at block L and R. Dame not partnered, so walks centre, but divides L.
Narrator and Phoebe. They do not enter stage area, but divide before it.

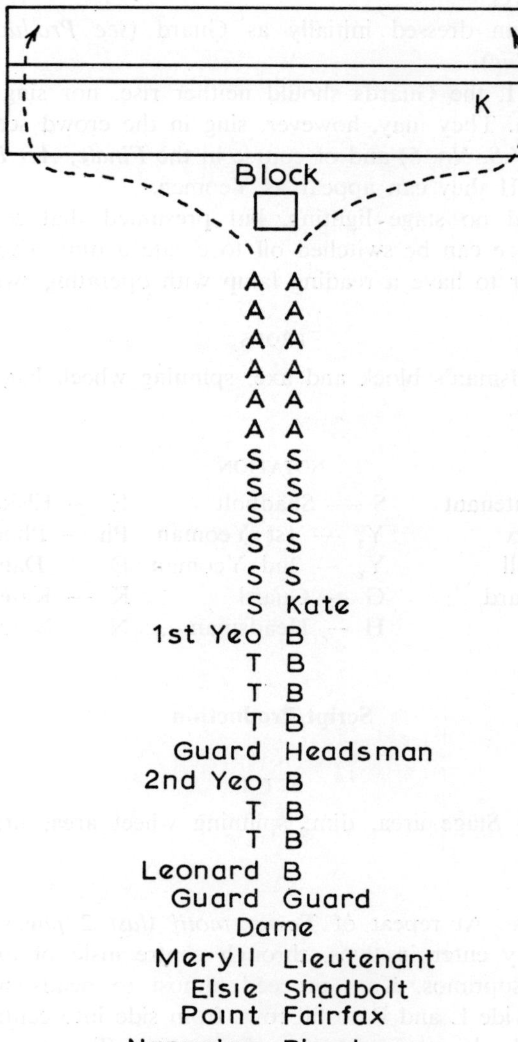

This movement to be completed before end of Overture.
All remain standing in position, to sit in unison on final bar.

2. V.S. No. 1. *Song.* "When maiden loves."
Verse 1. Sung sitting at spinning wheel.
Verse 2. Phoebe *after Introduction* stands, moves to centre front during three-and-a-half blank bars.
   "Ah me, ah me." Crosses slowly to her seat, to sit pensively at the end of song.

3. NARRATOR (*Switches on reading lamp.*) Ladies and gentlemen, that timeless love-song of a young maiden, Phoebe Meryll, transports us back through the centuries to the poetic days of Tudor England — a time when the ideas of Humanism and the Renaissance were seeping into this country from the Continent: to the days when existence was hard yet colourful, crude yet full of ceremonial dignity; when life was cheap, yet romantic; when a man could write a piece of music or a sonnet one moment, and the next could sign a death warrant. It was the age of the scholar gentleman, the man of parts — soldier, diplomat, alchemist, poet, musician, lover. One such was Colonel Fairfax, falsely imprisoned for sorcery in the Tower of London, and condemned to death so that his rich estate might be acquired by a knavish kinsman. With all the rich panoply of late medievalism, his tale unfolds on Tower Green, under the shadow of the grim, ancient Tower itself, guardian of the Nation's history.

4. V.S. No. 2. *Chorus.* "Tower warders." *Full lighting on stage.*
Chorus stand, men facing diagonally forward.
   At the end, ladies sit, Yeomen remain standing.

5. NARRATOR   Phoebe displays the single-minded romanticism of youth. Despite the fact that her father is Sergeant of the Yeomen of the Guard, she hardly shares the Yeomen's feelings of dedication to duty as carried out in the Tower — for although she has never spoken to him, she is already in love with the handsome Colonel Fairfax. Her views thus coloured, she sees the Tower as the cruel giant in a fairy tale, who must be fed with blood. But she is rebuked by Dame Carruthers, Housekeeper of the Tower, a matron who has grown grey in its service. Filled with a deeper sense of history than Phoebe, she regards the ancient building as an impartial guardian of Justice, and Watch-Dog of the City of London.

6. V.S. No. 3. *Song and Chorus.* "When our gallant Norman foes." Dame sings centre.

Postlude. She returns to her seat, and with the Yeomen, sits as the last chord is played.

7. NARRATOR Strange as it may seem, Phoebe turns to her father to find a more sympathetic ear. Meryll had fought under Fairfax in the past, and the Colonel had twice saved his life. So the honest Sergeant is prepared to go to any lengths to repay the debt. His son, Leonard, having been abroad for some years, has just returned to be appointed a Yeoman on account of his valour on the field of battle. Meryll resolves to send Leonard away before his arrival has been observed, and to substitute Fairfax (shorn of his beard) as his son.
Thus commences the medieval plotting.

8. V.S. No. 4. *Trio.* "Alas, I waver to and fro."

9. NARRATOR As Leonard departs, Fairfax, guarded, appears — being transferred to the condemned cell.

Recognising Sergeant Meryll, he greets him warmly.
Phoebe, admiring such bravery in the face of death, is much distressed. Fairfax bids her be comforted, philosophising on life and death in a manner befitting a scholar of the Age.

10. V.S. No. 5. *Song.* "Is life a boon?"

Production

Phoebe and Meryll rise to stand RC.
Leonard comes centre.

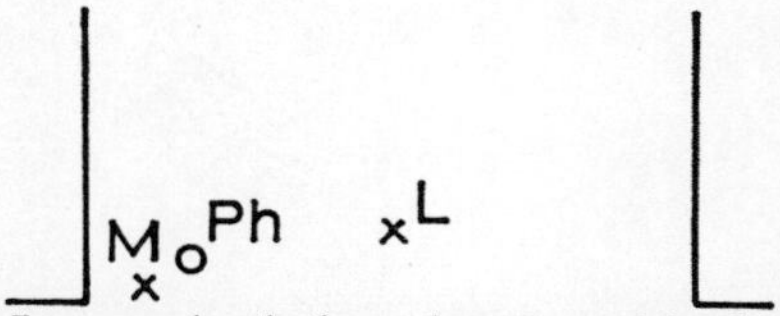

M o Ph   x L

On "farewell," Leonard shakes hands with his father, kisses
Phoebe on the cheek, and returns to his seat. Having watched him
depart, Phoebe leans for comfort on Meryll's shoulder.

Guards, L, step forward with Fairfax behind them. Guards, R,
come behind him, so that he stands in a square, centre back.

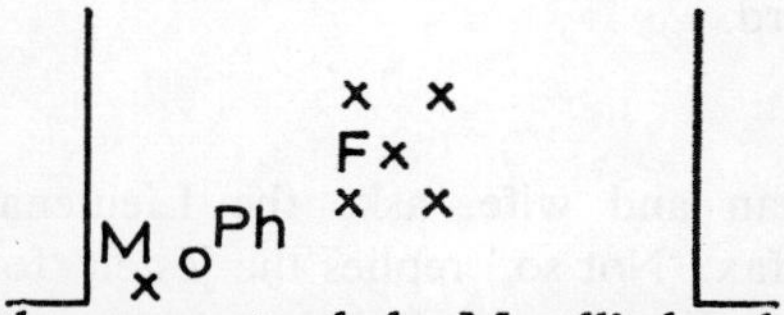

x x
F x
x x

M o Ph

He steps out of the square to shake Meryll's hand.
Phoebe covers her face with her hands, weeping.
Fairfax pats her gently on the head, before moving centre for
his solo.
Postlude. Fairfax steps back into the square, and Phoebe, weeping,
is led back to her seat by Meryll.

11. NARRATOR   Before Fairfax is led off, the Lieutenant of the Tower steps forth to ascertain if he has any last wishes. As an old friend, Fairfax makes one request. His false kinsman will succeed to his estate only if Fairfax dies unmarried. Could the Lieutenant find him a girl who, for a hundred crowns, would be prepared to marry him: she would, after all, be widowed within an hour?

Thus a second plot is set into operation. The Lieutenant promises to do his best to find a bride. As it transpires, he has not far to seek.

12. V.S. No. 6. *Chorus*. "Here's a man of jollity."

(Note. The last three staves of orchestral music in V.S. should be cut.)

13. V.S. No. 7. *Duet*. "I have a song to sing, O."

14. NARRATOR   Jack Point, the Strolling Jester, and his partner, Elsie Maynard.

Are they man and wife, asks the Lieutenant, thinking of Colonel Fairfax. 'Not so,' replies the jester, 'for though I am a fool, there is a limit to my folly.'
Furthermore, Elsie is a virtuous girl, and her mother travels with them. But, alas, she is desperately ill; and the hundred crowns offered by the Lieutenant is a sore temptation.

Guards do 'about turn' to face backstage.
Lieutenant comes forward with outstretched hand and Fairfax again comes forward.
The two 'converse' during narrative, guards holding position facing backstage — out of earshot as it were.

Guards, back, return to seats R.
Fairfax exits, L, front guards following him to resume their seats. (Fairfax goes to Ⓐ to remove his beard and don red cassock. He remains there.) Lieutenant retires to front, extreme L, to watch next scene without taking part in it.
Chorus rises.
Elsie and Point, during singing, move in a flurry about stage, miming fear and agitation.

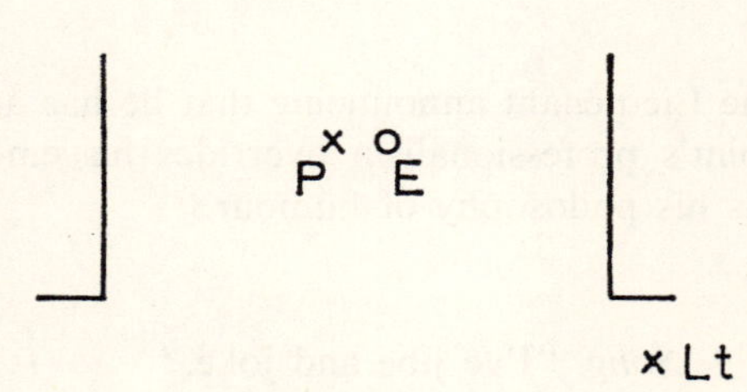

Traditional action and dance from principals.
Lieutenant, still standing, observes, unnoticed by Point and Elsie.

Lieutenant steps towards them, and all mime to suit narrative, with Point mannered in his repartee, as in stage productions.

Lieutenant dangles a bag of coins before Elsie.
She betrays anguish.

15. V.S. No. 8. *Trio*. "How say you maiden."

16. NARRATOR   Point sighs as he watches Elsie led away by Wilfred Shadbolt, the Head Jailer, for despite his expressed indifference, he is more than a little in love with her.

But on the Lieutenant announcing that he has a vacancy for a jester, Point's professionalism overrides his emotions, and he propounds his philosophy of humour.

17. V.S. No. 9. *Song*. "I've jibe and joke."

18. V.S. No. 10. *Song*. " 'Tis done, I am a bride."

Production

Positions:

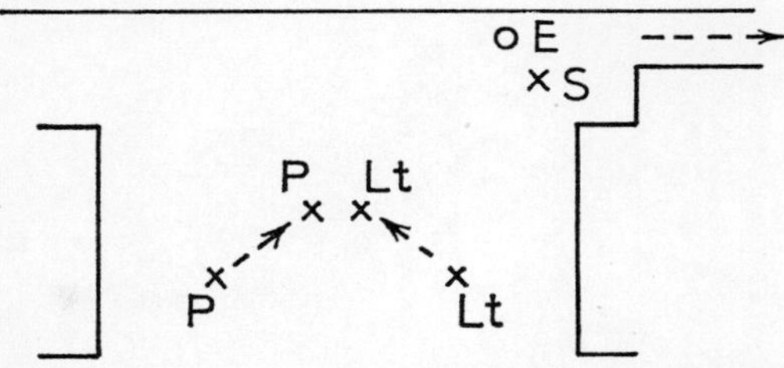

Postlude. Lieutenant beckons to Shadbolt, who lurches forward and binds Elsie's eyes with a handkerchief, then roughly leads her off by Ⓑ to concealment in Ⓐ.

Point starts to follow Elsie, but is halted by the Lieutenant.

Point switches quickly to exaggerated gestures of bowing and pirouetting, before commencing song.

Lieutenant returns to his seat at end of Verse 1. Point sings Verse 2 to audience, dancing to his seat on *Postlude*, to sit on final chord. Elsie, still blindfolded, is brought on at Ⓑ by Shadbolt, who undoes her handkerchief and pushes her forward, roughly. She staggers and moves centre, still in a daze, for her solo. Shadbolt remains at Ⓑ, arms folded, looking front.

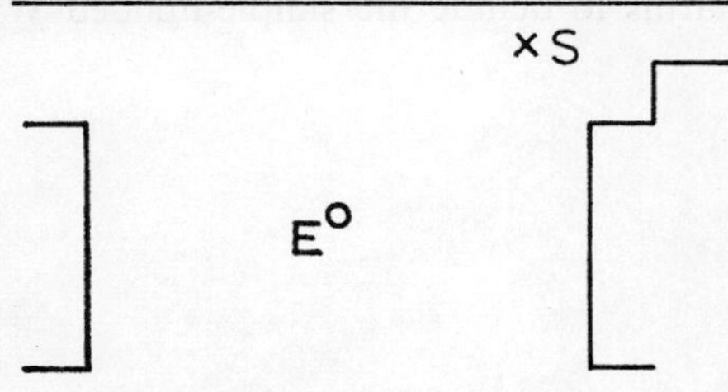

Postlude. Elsie returns to her original seat.

19. NARRATOR   With Fairfax now wed to Elsie, his kinsman's financial machinations are set at nought—but he is still condemned to death. Sergeant Meryll's substitution scheme can be put into practice only if the Colonel can be freed from his cell.

This is the task allotted to Phoebe — to win the key of the cell from the boorish, loutish Shadbolt.

In the past she had repulsed with disgust his eager invitations to become his mistress. Now with her beloved's life at stake, she finds an inward womanly strength to disguise her feelings of repugnance, as she uses her not inconsiderable feminine charms to delude the simple-minded Wilfred.

Production

Meryll and Phoebe rise and stand L, front, in earnest 'conversation'.

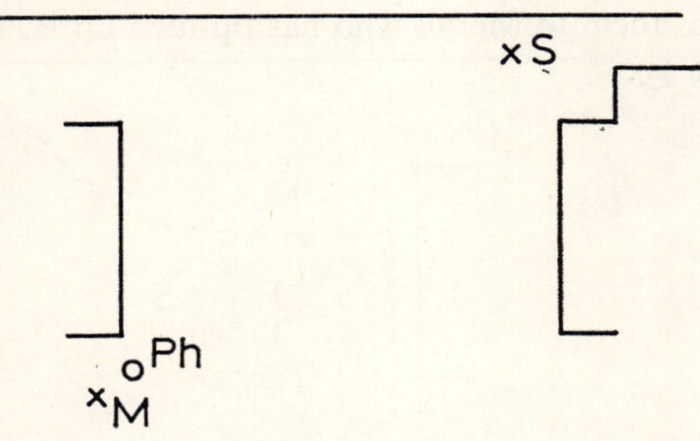

Meryll turns Phoebe to point out Shadbolt (still in same position, not seeing them).
Phoebe looks horrified, then pulls herself together. She steps forward along diagonal line to Wilfred, obviously calling him. He is surprised and lumbers forward, to meet her, centre, for her solo.

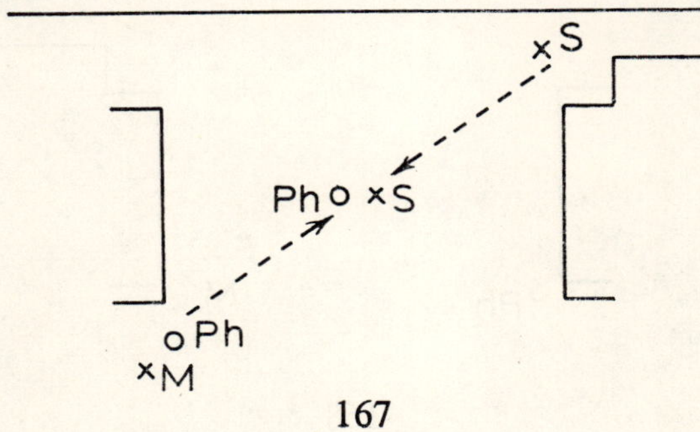

167

20. V.S. No. 11. *Song.* "Were I thy bride."

"And all day long." Phoebe takes keys from Shadbolt's belt and gives them to Meryll who has tip-toed up R. He then exits at Ⓑ, to Ⓐ.

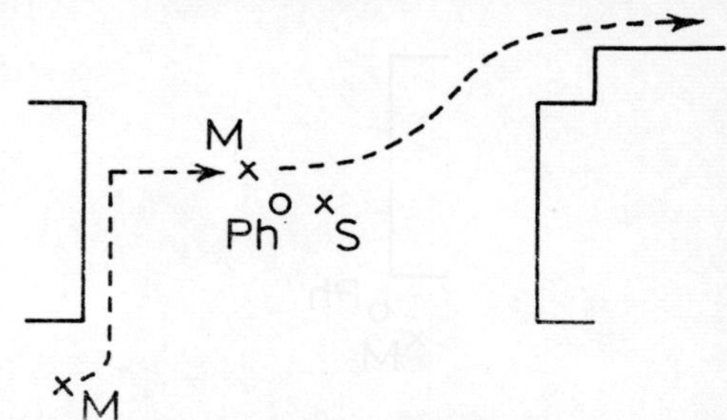

"The skylark's trill." Meryll returns the key to Phoebe who replaces it in Shadbolt's belt. Meryll exits again, to return with Fairfax (minus beard and wearing red cassock), and both stand at Ⓑ.

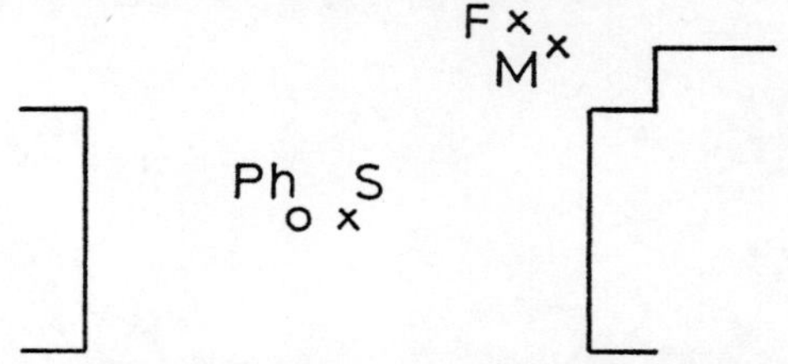

"I'm not thy bride." Phoebe skips to R. Shadbolt looks stupefied and returns to his seat.

21. V.S. *Finale Act I.*

Yeomen rise immediately music starts. Fairfax and Meryll walk slowly down to front, L, and turn to receive salutations of chorus. Meryll sings his solo from here.

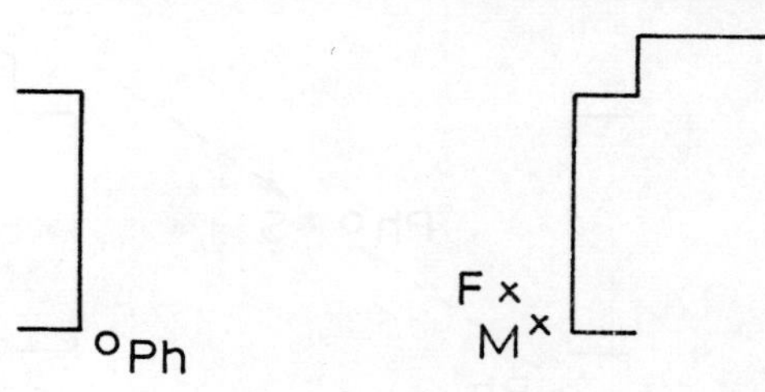

"Forbear, my friends." Fairfax crosses to centre, mid-stage. Final "Scarce a word of them is true." Fairfax, modestly dismissing tributes, goes RC.

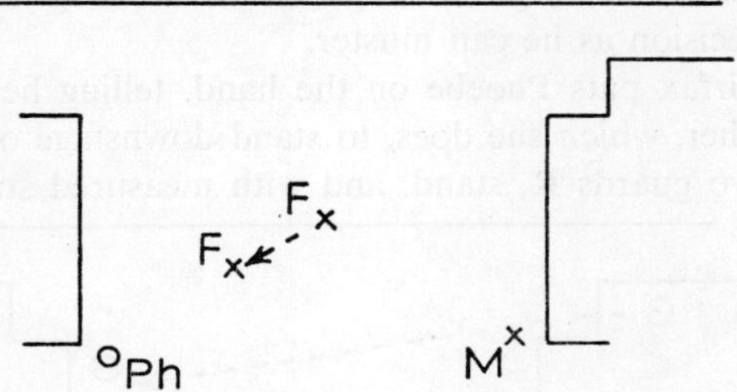

"Leonard." Phoebe runs to Fairfax.
"Oh brother, oh sister" (*together*)
Shadbolt rises, and lumbers centre for "Aye, hug him girl."

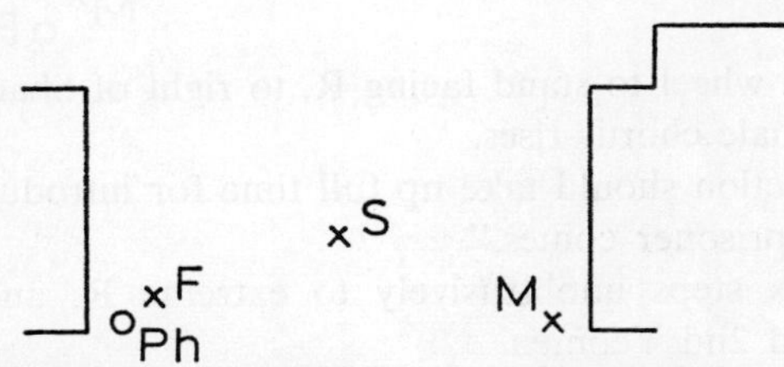

22. "The prisoner comes" (*orchestral introduction*).
The problem is to create an atmosphere of a dramatic procession in this lengthy piece, which normally on stage would be done by full chorus. So the order of movement to fill this page of music should be:

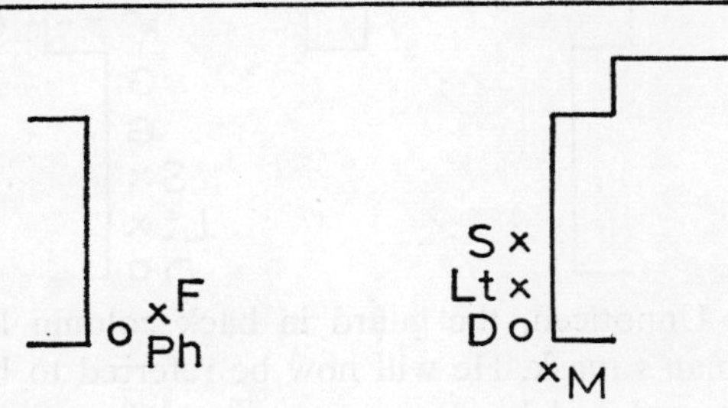

a) Phoebe clings to Fairfax.

b) Lieutenant and Dame stand, facing R.

c) Shadbolt collects his wits, and moves L to stand on Lieutenant's right, facing R, and showing as much military precision as he can muster.

d) Fairfax pats Phoebe on the hand, telling her to run to her father, which she does, to stand downstage of Meryll.

e) Two guards R, stand, and with measured stride cross stage

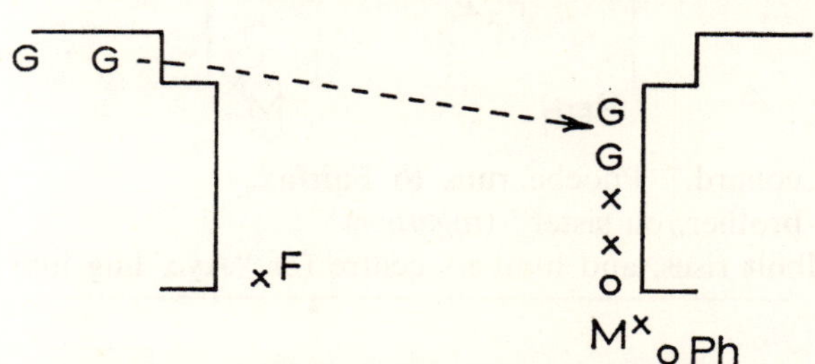

and wheel to stand facing R, to right of Shadbolt.

f) Female chorus rises.

This action should take up full time for introduction.

23. "The prisoner comes."

Fairfax steps unobtrusively to extreme R, and confers with 1st and 2nd Yeomen.

Two guards, Shadbolt, Lieutenant, Meryll, Dame do military right turn to face backstage.

Two guards L, rise and march forward parallel with front of stage.

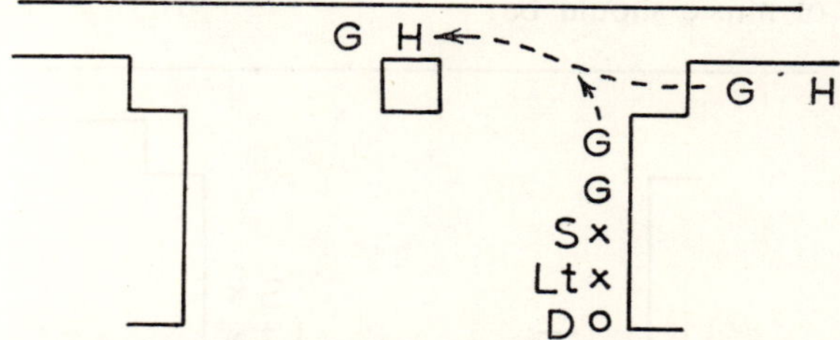

(Note. Unnoticed, the guard in back column has donned the headsman's mask. He will now be referred to by (H).)

As guard and headsman enter, guards and three principals join this procession.

Final "May heav'n have mercy."
Elsie comes forward and kneels RC for her solo.

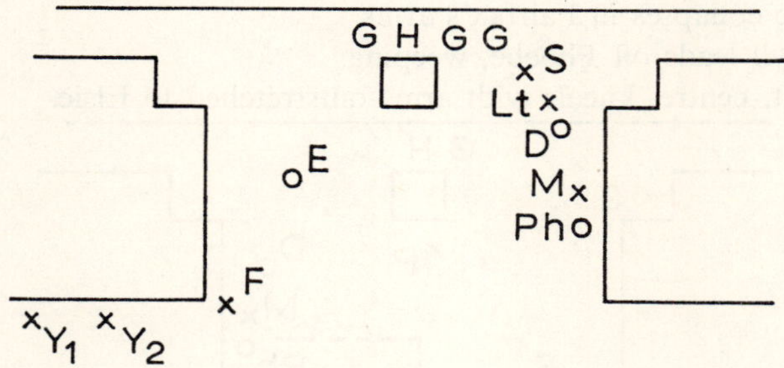

24. "My lord, my lord." Fairfax, and later 1st and 2nd Yeomen sing from extreme R.

25. "Astounding news." Lieutenant turns on Shadbolt. On his second "Thy life shall forfeit be," the two guards step forward, one on either side of Shadbolt and grasp his arms.

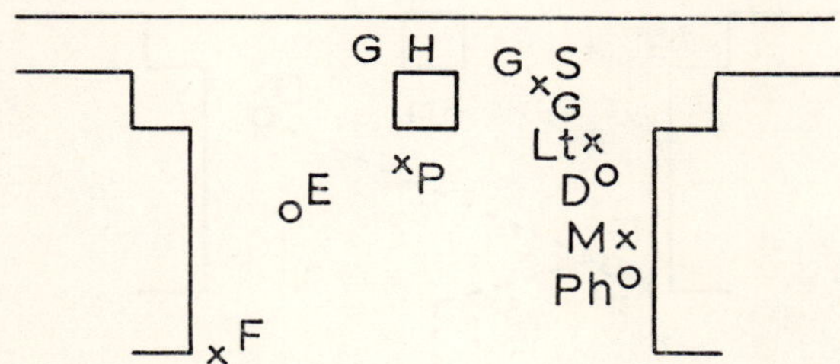

"Oh woe is you." Point runs forward and sings to Elsie.

26. "Let search be made throughout the land."

This is the point where company start to move off stage. Exit is made through centre aisle of auditorium, in procession, singing — but no one leaves auditorium till singing ends.

Order:

Back column of Yeomen, L and R come down LC and RC, meeting beyond Jack Point, and march off paired. Front column of Yeomen follow.

Sopranos, starting from sides; then altos, same.

Lieutenant.

Two guards and Shadbolt (row of three).
All these should be clear of stage as singing ends.
Then:
Elsie collapses in Fairfax's arms.
Meryll leads off Phoebe, weeping.
Point, centre, kneels with arms outstretched to Elsie.

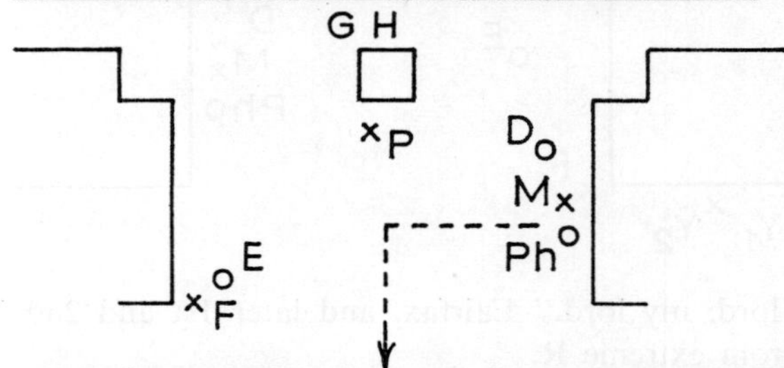

Dame marches stonily across in front of Point, takes Elsie from Fairfax and leads her off in state of collapse.
Fairfax follows alone.

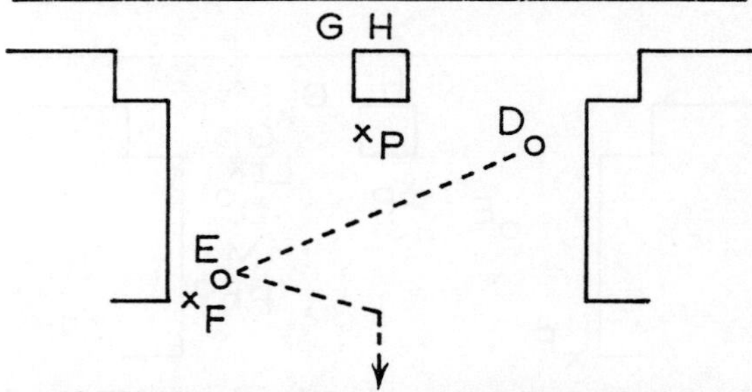

Guard and Headsman pass on either side of Point, who, still kneeling, has watched all this in bewildered anguish.
Point staggers off stage last, woebegone, dejected.

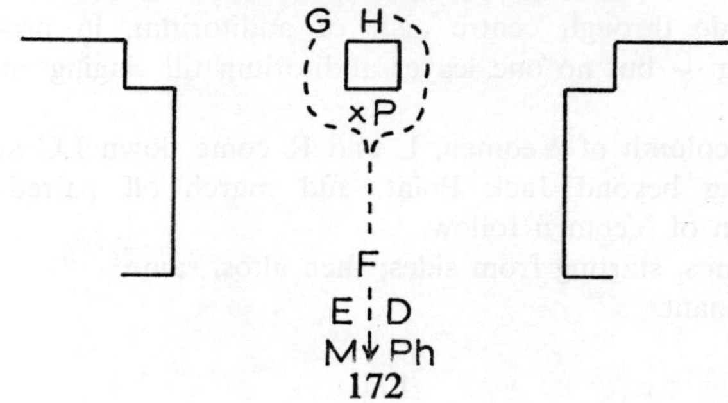

Narrator switches off his desk-lamp, collects his 'lecture notes' ostentatiously, and follows Point off.

ACT II

Basic seating plan as for Act I, except that headsman's block is removed. Full 'stage' lighting, Narrator's reading lamp off.

Company enter in order as before (not to music this time). Phoebe sits in her place on stage. All sit together, taking cue from Narrator.

Script

1. V.S. No. 1. *Chorus and solo.* "Night has spread her pall."
   Trills before last four bars of introduction. Chorus rises. Dame stands at her seat for solo and sits in disgust immediately it is ended.
   End of chorus. All sit.

2. NARRATOR   (*Switches on reading lamp*). Two days having elapsed since the escape, the affair brings together two strange bed-fellows — mercurial Jack Point, and the dull, lugubrious Wilfred Shadbolt. They have a common bond — they have both become love-lorn — and through the same cause — the escape of Colonel Fairfax. Elsie has been lost to Point by wedding the Colonel; and Phoebe, after her extraordinary flirtation with Wilfred, has turned completely indifferent to him since the escape.
   The atmosphere is ripe for the springing of a third plot. It is hatched thus.
   Wilfred wants to become a jester, and Point informs him that it is no easy task. However, they form a pact. Point will instruct Wilfred in the art of jesting, provided Wilfred says he saw Fairfax try to escape by swimming the river, shot at, and killed him.

3. V.S. No. 2. *Song.* "Oh a private buffoon."
4. V.S. No. 3. *Duet.* "Hereupon were both agreed."

5. V.S. No. 4. *Song.* "Freed from his fetters grim."

174

Point and Shadbolt rise from their seats, and walk, heads bowed,
hands behind back, directly across stage.
They bump into each other.
Recognising each other they start to 'chat'.

Heads together, conspiratorially.
They walk forward slowly to centre front, Point gesticulating and
obviously 'priming' Shadbolt.

Traditional 'business' for song and duet.
At the end. Point dances back to his seat.
Wilfred, much less agile, lumbers back to his.

Fairfax comes forward centre for his solo.

6. NARRATOR   Fairfax is not left long in doubt as to the identity of his bride. Dame Carruthers and her niece, Kate, have been caring for Elsie since her collapse on learning of her unknown husband's escape. From her semi-conscious ramblings, they have their suspicions that she has wed Fairfax.

Involved in duplicity as they are, up to this stage neither Fairfax nor Meryll is aware of whom had been the chosen girl. They receive the Dame's information differently. Fairfax is elated — for he has been captivated by the charm of the singing girl. And Sergeant Meryll? Despondent. He fears that Dame Carruthers will come to realize his complicity in the plot.

Each member of the quartet broods over a typically medieval situation — of romanticism fraught with fearsome portents of ill omen.

7. V.S. No. 5. *Quartet*. "Strange adventure."

8. V.S. No. 6. *Scene*. "Hark! What was that, sir?"
Six bars orchestra after "What can it mean?"

Production

Kate and Dame come forward on a diagonal to Fairfax, Meryll approaches from the other end of diagonal.

Fairfax bows courteously to the ladies, but Dame Carruthers scarcely acknowledges it. She remains very erect, looking Fairfax, then Meryll, directly in the eye.

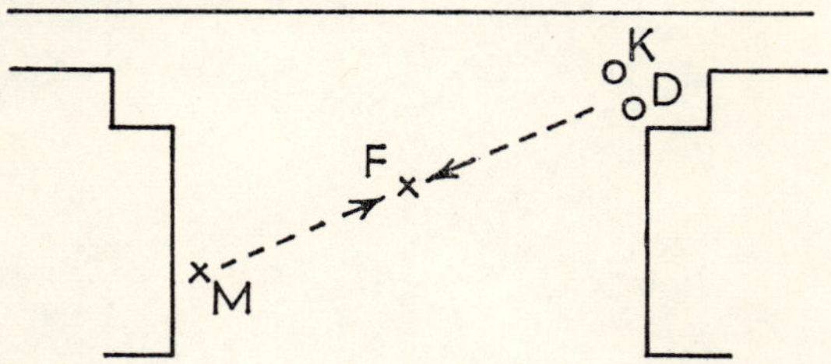

Fairfax exchanges a quick glance with Meryll.

Fairfax allows his happiness to show in his face for a moment, but Meryll, sick at heart, averts his head.

x	x	o	o
M	F	D	K

All assume serious expressions and form a straight line for the quartet

At the end Meryll and Fairfax bow to the ladies. Kate returns to her seat. Dame takes Fairfax's seat on Shadbolt's right.

Sound of shot is heard (behind Narrator's screen) then music.

Meryll runs R, front, followed more slowly by Fairfax.

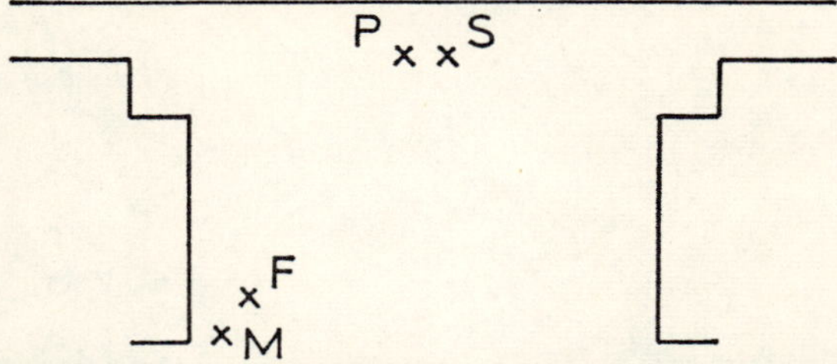

Point and Shadbolt run together, centre back, and confer furtively. Yeomen rise.

Bar before "Are the foemen in the land?"

Bar before "Who fired that shot?"
"My lord, 'twas I"

"Hail the gallant fellow"

Women rise.
Phoebe rises from her seat to stand anxiously on Meryll's right.

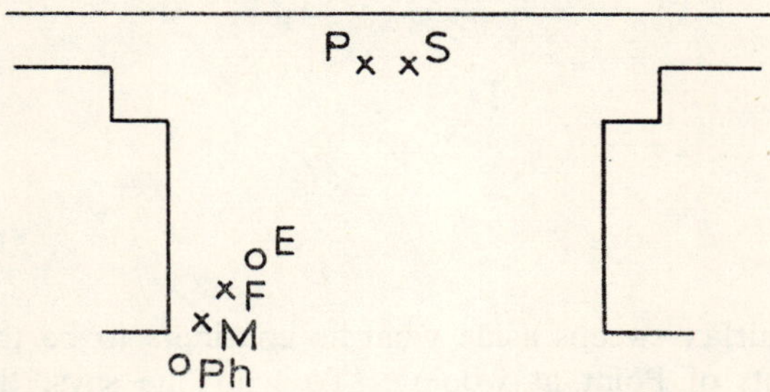

Elsie runs forward to Fairfax's left.
Lieutenant rises.
Shadbolt and Point start to come forward to sing duet LC.

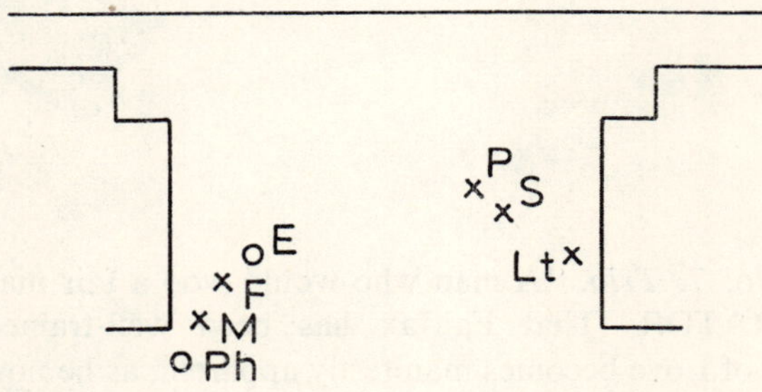

Point leads Shadbolt round crowd to acknowledge applause; he
leaves Shadbolt at his seat and returns centre as music is ending.
Chorus, Lieutenant and Meryll sit.

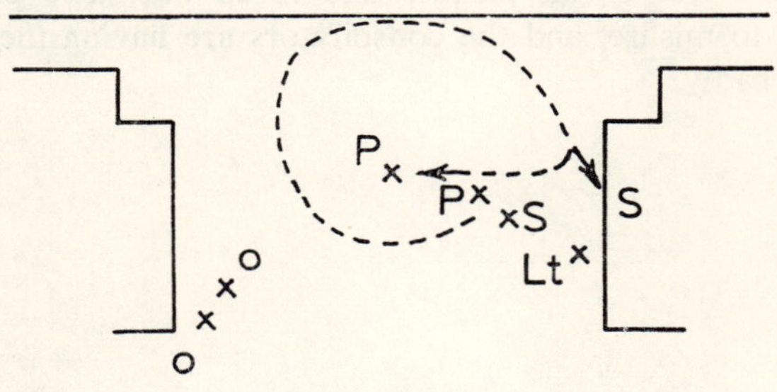

9. NARRATOR   Elsie weeps for the sake of her dead husband. Point tries to comfort her, saying, hopeful for himself, that she has the chance to choose again.

But Fairfax sweeps aside what he considers to be the clumsy attempts of Point at wooing. 'To woo', he says, 'is an Art in itself, and must be studied gravely and conscientiously.'

10. V.S. No. 7. *Trio.* "A man who would woo a fair maid."
11. NARRATOR   That Fairfax has been well-trained in the Courts of Love becomes manifestly apparent, as he now pursues the piquant pleasure of wooing his own wife. Elsie, believing herself widowed, succumbs to his charms. Phoebe is left in despair at losing the man whose life she had helped to save, and Point is heart-broken and inconsolable at the now irretrievable loss of his partner and loved one. The plots have begun to misfire, and the conspirators are having their fingers burnt badly.

Point moves R towards trio.

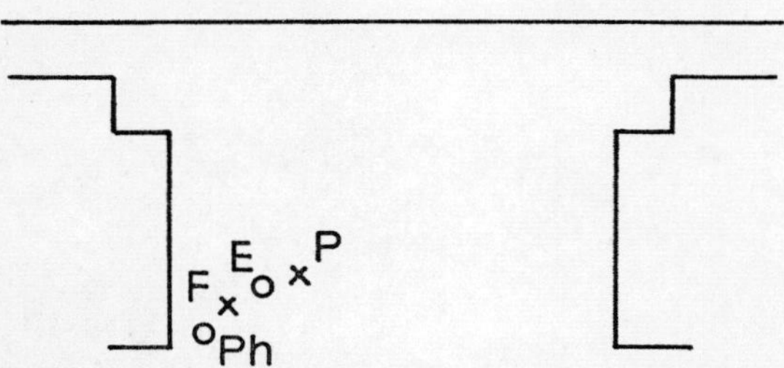

Fairfax takes both ladies by the hand and leads them across Point, to centre, for the *Trio*.
Point takes position RC.

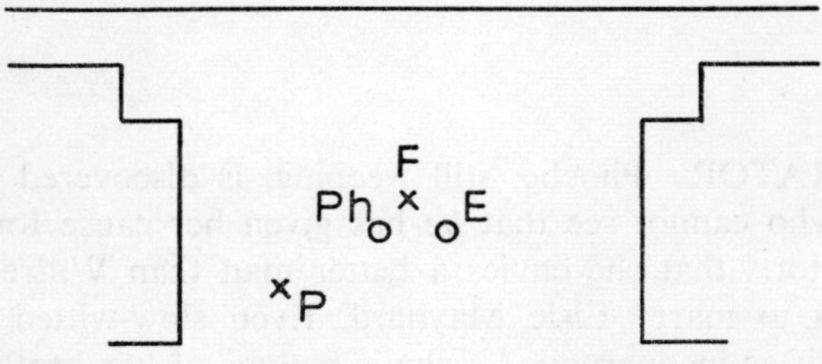

Traditional actions.
Fairfax leads Elsie LC, and whispers amorously in her ear. She begins to respond.

Phoebe and Point watch, first in disbelief, then in dismay.

12. V.S. No. 8. *Quartet*. "When a wooer goes a-wooing."

13. NARRATOR   Phoebe, still weeping, is discovered by Shad-bolt, who cannot see that *he* has given her cause for anxiety. She retorts that she envies a better man than Wilfred — one who is to marry Elsie Maynard. Even slow-witted Shadbolt sees this as incongruous — she is jealous of her brother? (*said slowly*) or (*with mounting anger*) can it be that it is Fairfax in disguise? Phoebe, realising that she has let slip the secret, buys Shadbolt's silence by agreeing to marry him.

When to them, comes the real Leonard, hasting back with a reprieve for Fairfax. Shadbolt is beside himself with rage at seeing Phoebe kiss yet another 'brother'. But again she quietens him by coquetry, saying that in a year — or two — or three — they themselves will be married. And today, they must rejoice at the wedding of Fairfax and Elsie.

Traditional actions.

Postlude. Fairfax and Elsie turn and move backstage. Point tries to follow, crossing Phoebe on diagonal, but Fairfax turns at exit

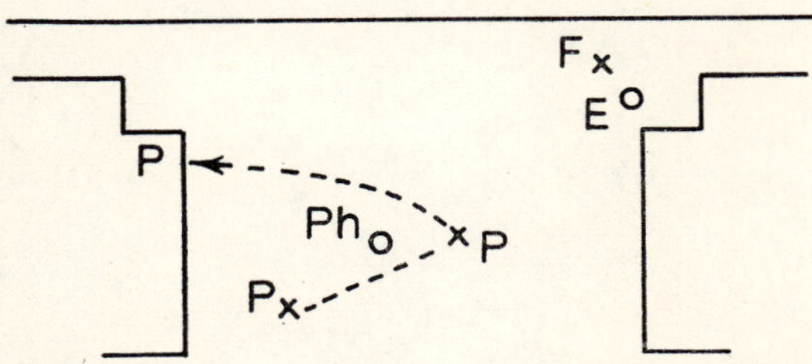

and, holding pose, repels him. Point staggers back behind Elsie to his seat. Fairfax and Elsie exit at Ⓑ to Ⓐ to change for wedding scene.

Shadbolt comes centre. Phoebe, RC, vents her temper on him.

Shadbolt mimes what the Narrator describes.

Phoebe runs to him, puts a finger to his lips, and allows herself to be caressed.

Leonard comes down extreme R. Phoebe runs to him, jumping into his arms and kissing him.

Shadbolt, centre, is furious.

Thus Phoebe, whose first song spoke of the yearnings of a woman of any era, accepts her lot with the fatalism of the age in which she lives — albeit giving sufficient hint that ageless feminine stratagems may yet save her.

The play within the play, so admired by Tudor dramatists, brings fiction to reality to conclude the opera. For Point and Elsie's dance duet, "The Merryman and his Maid," has turned from folk fable into the true tale of the Jester, his partner and her noble lord — Colonel Fairfax.

Phoebe beckons him, playing the coquette. Shadbolt comes to her side, and she takes his hand, grimacing to Leonard in the process.

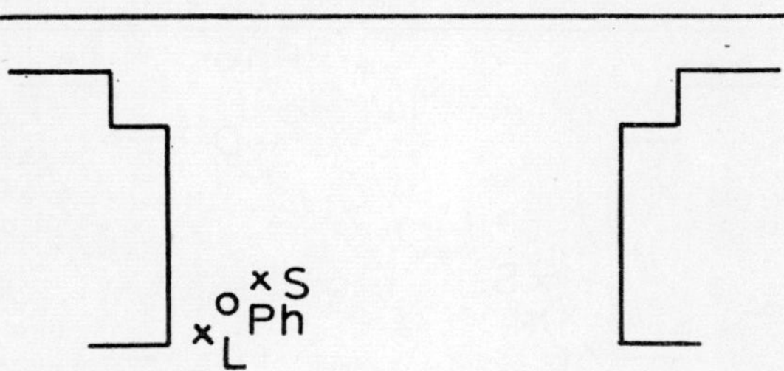

Now *freeze* positions for Narrator's summary.

14. V.S. No. 10. *Finale Act II.*

All rise. Phoebe crosses to Ⓑ, joined by Dame, to await Elsie. Meryll takes Phoebe's place. Elsie, now in bridal costume

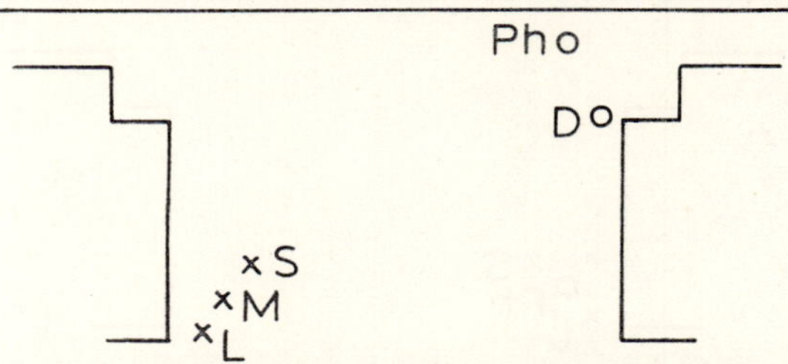

comes between Phoebe and Dame, and they proceed to mid-centre. Kate follows Elsie as 'train-bearer'.

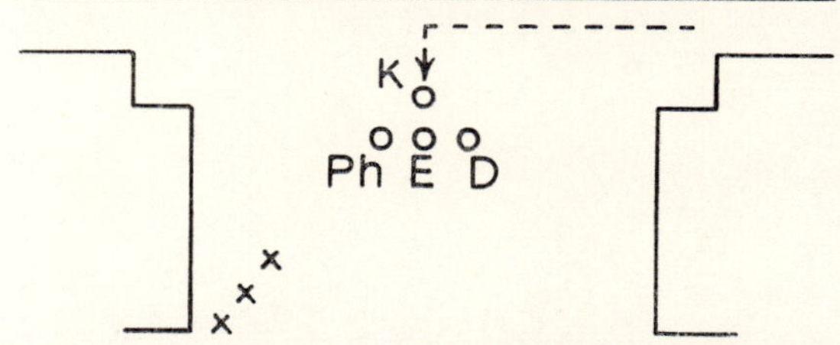

"'Tis said that joy in full perfection." Sung from above positions.

"With happiness her soul is cloyed" (*Chorus*). Lieutenant goes to Ⓑ to greet Fairfax, now in wedding costume.

Five bars orchestra. Fairfax and Lieutenant come down LC, Fairfax keeping his face front, away from Elsie.

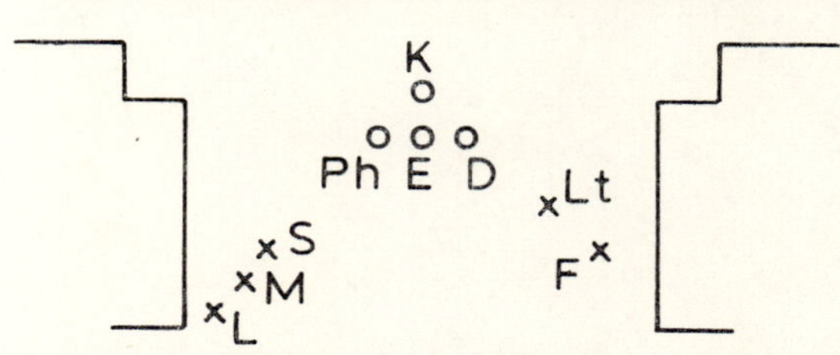

"A suppliant at thy feet." Elsie comes to kneel beside Fairfax, but slightly behind him.

"With happiness my soul is cloyed" (*Duet*). Fairfax and Elsie, LC, in each other's arms.

"O thoughtless crew." Point stumbles to centre. There follows traditional 'business', with Point eventually collapsing centre, hand outstretched to Elsie.

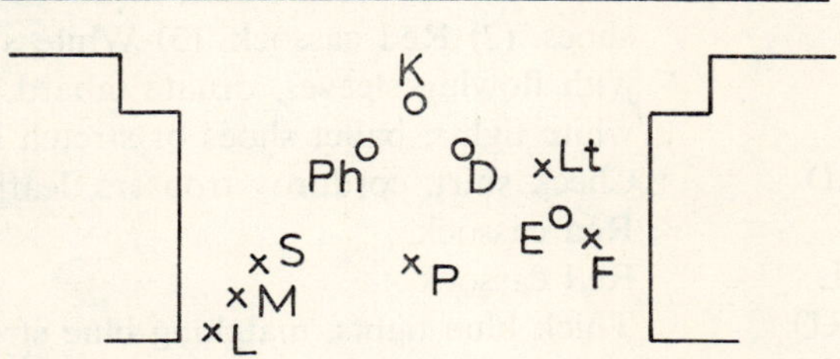

15. *End of opera.*
In above positions, whole company, except Narrator, take one bow.
Point crosses RC to bring Narrator on stage to take his bow. Then exeunt in this order: Narrator, Point, Fairfax and Elsie, Shadbolt and Phoebe, Meryll and Dame Carruthers, Kate and Lieutenant, Leonard, chorus (women) in twos as before, chorus (men) in twos as before.

Suggestions for Costuming

PRINCIPALS	ACTS I, II
LIEUTENANT FAIRFAX	Magenta cassock. (1) White open-neck shirt with flowing sleeves, thick black tights, black ballet shoes. (2) Red cassock. (3) White shirt with flowing sleeves, ornate tabard, thick white tights, ballet shoes or stretch slippers.
WILFRED	Check shirt, corduroy trousers, leather apron.
KATE	Red cassock.
MERYLL	Red cassock.
LEONARD	Thick blue tights, matching blue stretch-nylon crew-neck sweater, yellow balaclava, yellow stretch slippers.
POINT	
ELSIE	(1) White draw-string blouse, lattice-effect bodice/waistcoat, peasant skirt (below knee), white tights. (2) Tabard over (identical to Fairfax).
	Grey cassock.
PHOEBE	As for Female Chorus.
DAME	As for Elsie (1).
NARRATOR	Dark suit, white shirt, graduate (club) tie, black shoes, black graduate gown.

CHORUS	ACTS I, II
YEOMEN	Red cassocks.
GUARDS	Act I. Thick black tights, black stretch-nylon crew-neck sweater, black stretch slippers, black tabards. In addition, Headsman has a black mask.
FEMALE	Act II. Red cassocks.
	Purple cassocks.

12

THE GONDOLIERS

Note on Narrators

There are four possibilities of principals as narrator:
(a) Don Alhambra
(b) Giuseppe
(c) Marco and Giuseppe
(d) Duke and Duchess of Plaza-Toro

Of these, (c) is least likely. The 'link-man' must fill a double role of narrator and character, which calls for an additionally extrovert histrionic quality rarely noted in tenors, whose prowess lies more in the vocal field. (d) has possibilities, but the temptation would be to over-play both parts as husband and wife indulge in back-biting — which would lead to a distortion of the plot. Certainly, were Duke and Duchess to act as narrators, the ordered sequence of vocal numbers should be broken to give: *Overture*, "From the sunny Spanish shore," *Narrative, Opening Scene*.

Alternatives (c) and (d) are very much dependent on acting strengths within a company. Scripts would require to be written to suit known particular individual talents, so are not supplied here.

The likeable, breezy Giuseppe would make a good narrator. With his appealing common touch, he could make immediate contact with an audience. A script for him is offered. But there is no doubt that provided the actor has the authority to sustain the part, Don Alhambra is the character best suited for linkage. He is the master who manipulates the puppets.

Script for Don Alhambra as Narrator

Note. It must be repeated that the Don should see himself as the manipulator of, to him, the 'puppets.' Pompous, overbearing, condescending, he should appear as the diplomat and administrator par excellence, accustomed to handling important matters of state, well-versed in the political machinations of the eighteenth century. Not above making error (he did, after all, lose, or misplace an infant prince) he is not a man ever to admit his own failings or shortcomings — he always presents himself as omnipotent.

189

Overture.

DON Good evening, ladies and gentlemen. May I introduce myself? Don Alhambra bel Bolero, the Grand Inquisitor of Spain. As you may imagine, my high office calls for the solution of many weighty matters of state. One such may, I believe, hold your attention — the finding of a lost heir to the throne of Barataria. An impossible task? To some, perhaps. But to me merely an interesting exercise in my day to day functioning.

The story starts one fine morning on the Piazetta in Venice, where, posed against the background of the sparkling waters of the Grand Canal, are gathered a group of contadine, or peasant girls. They are singing happily, for they await the arrival of the two most handsome gondoliers in Venice — Marco and Giuseppe Palmieri — who are about to select their brides from the assembled maidens.

V.S. No. 1. *Opening Scene.*

V.S. No. 2. *Quartet.* "From the sunny Spanish shore."

DON The arrival of the Ducal Party from Spain was, in effect, the first indication to me of the task ahead. The Duke of Plaza-Toro was claiming his beautiful daughter, Casilda, to have been married in infancy to the son of the King of Barataria, and had come to seek my aid. Unfortunately, that unhappy monarch had been killed in an insurrection, and his son had been stolen in infancy.

Now the Duke was an impoverished adventurer, and a henpecked husband to boot — but, whenever he had the opportunity he compensated by stressing his ancestry, and his ability to lead men and fashion. So he indulged himself in outlining his qualities of leadership to his daughter, before departing with the Duchess to seek me out — leaving behind him Casilda, and their one and only attendant — the young man, Luiz.

V.S. No. 3. *Song.* "In enterprise of martial kind."

V.S. No. 4. *Recit and Duet.* "O rapture."

V.S. No. 5. *Duet.* "There was a time."

DON On my appearance with her father and mother, Casilda quizzed me in haughty tones as to her husband's whereabouts. Whereupon I informed her that there were some momentary complications as to his exact identity. Alas, with the perverse dissatisfaction of young women, she expressed disapproval of this state of affairs. I am happy to think I contented her by advising a philosophical approach to the whole business.

V.S. No. 6. *Song*. "I stole the prince."
V.S. No. 7. *Recit*. "But bless my heart."
V.S. No. 8. *Quintet*. "Try we life-long."
V.S. No. 9. *Chorus and Song*. "Bridegroom and bride"/"When a merry maiden marries."
DON I now considered it an appropriate time to inform the two gondoliers that one of them was a king, and that both should take up joint office as Ruler of Barataria until such time as the true king's identity was established. Unfortunately, as staunch Republicans, they did not take kindly to the idea of Monarchy, and indeed, being somewhat crude fellows, scarcely treated me with the deference due to my position. However, I was able to convince them of the undoubted benefits of royalty, and all would have been well, had it not transpired that they had been sufficiently ill-advised to have become bound by matrimonial ties. When I announced that women were not permitted to accompany their husbands in the initial stages of the period of joint monarchy, the statement led to an emotional female outburst.
V.S. No. 10. *Finale Act I* (starts with "Kind sir, you cannot have the heart").

ACT II

DON Some three months later, having placed all their gondolier friends in important positions, Marco and Giuseppe were well ensconced in Barataria, holding doubtful control over their plebian Court. Giuseppe expressed his views on the functions of Royalty as seen in Republican terms, but Marco seemed concerned less with the duties of office than with the lack of female company, voicing his thoughts in what he called a 'recipe for perfect happiness'.
V.S. No. 1. *Chorus*. "Of happiness the very pith."
V.S. No. 2. *Song*. "Rising early in the morning."
V.S. No. 3. *Song*. "Take a pair of sparkling eyes."
DON Marco's desires were soon to be satisfied, for unknown to their husbands, and to me, all the gondoliers' wives had contrived to hire a boat and make the journey to Barataria. They were received with great rejoicing, which led to the inevitable banquet — and a dance.
V.S. No. 4. *Scena*. "Here we are at the risk of our lives."
V.S. No. 5. *Chorus*. "Dance a cachucha."
DON My arrival at these junketings terminated the proceedings abruptly, for I had to advise the two monarchs against their ming-

ling with the lower orders. To prove my point, I gave an example of how democratic and egalitarian principles could be carried too far. Thereafter the two gondoliers received a further rebuke from their wives, who had just learnt that one of the husbands had been married in infancy — making one wife an unintentional bigamist!

V.S. No. 6. *Song*. "There lived a king."

V.S. No. 7. *Quartet*. "In a contemplative fashion."

V.S. No. 8. *Chorus*. "With ducal pomp."

DON   Thus did the Duke of Plaza-Toro, 'blazing in the lustre of unaccustomed pocket-money' as he put it, make his entry to the court of Barataria. His intention was to ingratiate himself with the rulers; instead he found it necessary to give them lessons in deportment. But even before this instruction in court etiquette, Casilda was to receive enlightenment (a) on the quality of love among the nobility and (b) on how the nobility acquired their financial substance.

V.S. No. 9. *Song*. "On the day when I was wedded."

V.S. No. 10. *Recit and Duet*. "To help unhappy commoners"/ "Small titles and orders."

V.S. No. 11. *Gavotte*.

DON   Casilda's parents departed to leave her to get to know her husband (whoever it was) better. But the arrival of the king's wives led once again to a mathematical-cum-philosophical wrangling. Happily, I was then in the position whereby I could present the solution to the problem — to everyone's satisfaction, I am gratified to think.

V.S. No. 12. *Quintet and Finale Act II*. "Here is a case unprecedented."

Script for Giuseppe as Narrator

Note.

There are four particular personality traits in Giuseppe's character which could well be stressed in his performance as Narrator.

(a) He is a 'hail-fellow-well-met' type — witness his slapping Don Alhambra on the back and calling him 'my man.' This cheerful, 'easy-to-get-on-with' manner should be communicated to, and receive a ready response from the audience, who should see Giuseppe as a 'good chap.'

(b) He has no pretentions to being anything other than the

'man-in-the-street.' Most of the audience should therefore identify themselves with him.

(c) With an eye for the ladies, he has a rugged sex-appeal to them, too. This attribute should be played upon to the ladies of the audience!

(d) There is a bit of the 'soap-box orator' in Giuseppe — witness his speech to the Don — "We are Venetian gondoliers. Republicans, heart and soul . . . ." So a flamboyant approach with, at times, exaggerated gesture, is appropriate to a forceful rendering of the narrative.

ACT I

Overture

GIUSEPPE Good evening, ladies and gentlemen. My name is Giuseppe Palmieri. (*Forcefully*) I am a Venetian gondolier, the son of Baptisto Palmieri, who led the last revolution. (*With conviction and exaggerated gesture*) A Republican, heart and soul, I hold all men to be equal. As I abhor oppression, I abhor kings: as I detest vain-glory, I detest rank: as I despise effeminacy, I despise wealth. (*Recollecting himself, and a little shame-faced*) At least, I held these views until recently, when a most unexpected thing happened to my brother Marco and myself. It changed our outlook quite a bit! Let me tell you about it. One fine morning on the Piazetta, beside the sparkling waters of our lovely Grand Canal, a crowd of pretty contadine, the peasant girls, had gathered together. They were eagerly awaiting the arrival of the two most handsome gondoliers in Venice — (*with a grin*) that's Marco and me — for we had agreed to choose our brides from them that very day!

V.S. No. 1 *Opening scene.*

GIUSEPPE As we all set off to get married, a hired gondola arrived at the Piazetta steps — carrying foreign nobility, a ducal party from Spain. It transpired that the Duke of Plaza-Toro's daughter, Casilda (quite an attractive bit of skirt really) had been married when a baby, to the son of the King of Barataria, and the family had come to see Don Alhambre del Bolero, the Grand Inquisitor of Spain about it. Actually, even I could have told them that the King had been killed in an insurrection and his son stolen in infancy.

Now the Duke was an impoverished adventurer — and he was also hen-pecked by his wife. He tried to make up for this whenever he could, by boasting of his ancestry and his ability to lead men and fashion. So, to give himself Dutch courage before his interview with Don Alhambra, he sang his little 'party-piece' to Casilda. Then the parents went off — leaving behind them Casilda and their one attendant — (*with a knowing look*) the young man, Luiz.

V.S. No. 2. *Quartet.* "From the sunny Spanish shore."

V.S. No. 3. *Song.* "In enterprise of martial kind."

V.S. No. 4. *Recit. and Duet.* "O rapture."

V.S. No. 5. *Duet.* "There was a time."

GIUSEPPE Just as things were getting interesting, the Duke and Duchess returned with the Don. Casilda, probably a bit confused, turned on the haughty air, and demanded information as to her husband's whereabouts. Don Alhambra told her there had been a bit of a mix-up, and he couldn't say exactly who her husband was. Casilda, naturally, was rather peeved, so Don Alhambra tried to smooth her feelings by suggesting a philosophical approach to the whole business.

V.S. No. 6. *Song.* "I stole the prince."

V.S. No. 7. *Recit.* "But bless my heart."

V.S. No. 8. *Quintet.* "Try we life-long."

V.S. No. 9. *Chorus and Song.* "Bridegroom and bride"/"When a merry maiden marries."

GIUSEPPE Having serenaded us at our wedding, our friends courteously left Marco and me alone to enjoy the company of our wives. When who should come along to disturb us but a pompous individual dressed all in black. I thought he was an undertaker and told him to clear off! This was a blunder, for he turned out to be Don Alhambra and he had come to tell Marco and me that one of us was a king! And that we should have to go to Barataria to act as joint rulers until it was decided which of us actually was the real king. Well now, here was a thought! We were Republicans and objected to the ideas of kingship. However, the Don pointed out various benefits, which included giving our friends important places at court. So we agreed to go.

Then he dropped a bombshell. At first we were not to be allowed to take our wives — and we'd just got married. Poor Tessa and Gianetta were very upset.

V.S. No. 10. *Finale Act I* (starts with "Kind sir, you cannot have the heart.")

GIUSEPPE   After three months in Barataria, Marco and I were finding it rather hard to combine Republican ideals with the duties of monarchy — our fellow gondoliers had turned into very demanding courtiers! I presented them with a list of our daily tasks, and at least it satisfied them sufficiently to provide double rations to sustain the joint rulers.

Marco, however, always a romantic, was pining not for food but for female company, and confessed as much to me by giving me what he called 'a recipe for perfect happiness.'

V.S. No. 1. *Chorus*. "Of happiness the very pith."

V.S. No. 2. *Song*. "Rising early in the morning."

V.S. No. 3. *Song*. "Take a pair of sparkling eyes."

GIUSEPPE   We were soon all to be made happy on this point, for, unknown to us, our wives had hired a boat and made the journey to Barataria. We were so pleased to see them, that immediately we offered them a banquet — and a dance.

V.S. No. 4. *Scena*, "Here we are at the risk of our lives."

V.S. No. 5. *Chorus*, "Dance a cachucha."

GIUSEPPE   Just as this merriment had reached its peak, who should come along to stop it but Don Alhambra? He gave Marco and me a ticking off for mingling with the lower orders. We had to listen to an example of what he thought was democracy carried too far. Then while we were still talking to him, we got into trouble from our wives! They came in just as the Don was telling us that we should soon meet Casilda, wife of the King, whichever of us he was. Hearing this Tessa and Gianetta realised that one of them was an unintentional bigamist! As tempers became frayed, Marco suggested we deal with the matter calmly.

V.S. No. 6. *Song*. "There lived a king."

V.S. No. 7. *Quartet*. "In a contemplative fashion."

GIUSEPPE   Still wrangling, we left the Throne Room, which gave the Duke of Plaza-Toro his chance to make a suitably impressive entrance — now well-attended and, as he put it 'Blazing in the lustre of unaccustomed pocket money.' I've no doubt he had hopes of ingratiating himself with us, his future sons-in-law. But he was cut down to size by the Duchess, he had to explain to Casilda how the nobility acquired their ill-gotten gains; and then, poor chap, when he met Marco and me, he wasn't very happy about our deportment, so felt it necessary to give us a dancing lesson!

V.S. No. 8. *Chorus*. "With Ducal pomp."

V.S. No. 9. *Song*. "On the day when I was wedded."

V.S. No. 10. *Recit and Duet*. "To help unhappy commoners" / "Small titles and orders."

V.S. No. 11. *Gavotte*.

GIUSEPPE After this, the 'young chickens', Casilda, Marco and I were left together, (*knowingly*) to get to know each other better. Just as we were in love with our wives and not her, she confessed she was head-over-heels in love with someone else. Gianetta and Tessa joined us in trying once again to solve the problem of three wives — two husbands. Not being mathematically minded, we didn't get very far.

But fortunately, Don Alhambra arrived, summoning the whole court together, to announce that he had found the solution.

After initial surprise, and perhaps some disappointments, everyone lived happily ever after!

V.S. No. 12. *Quintet and Finale Act II* "Here is a case unprecedented."

Basic Seating Plan

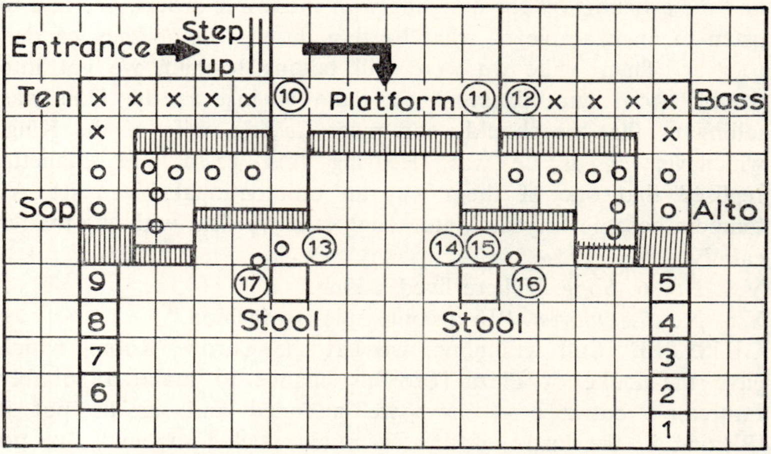

L-SHAPED ROSTRA (back)	Raised 2 single steps
L-SHAPED ROSTRA (front)	Raised 1 single step
PLATFORM	Raised 1 single step
STOOLS and PRINCIPALS ① to ⑨	Floor level

1. Tenors, two sopranos; basses, two altos — raised two single steps. Chairs for each.
2. Most sopranos, most altos. Principals ⑩, ⑪ on same level as platform. *i.e.*, raised a single step. Chairs for each.
3. Two sopranos, Fiametta ⑬, Gianetta ⑰; one alto, Vittoria ⑭, Giulia ⑮, Tessa ⑯ — stand at stools RC, LC, respectively. No chairs for them. When not acting, they sit on first step at feet of sopranos or altos as case may be.
4. Principals ① to ⑨ seated on floor level.
5. With a set of this design, most traditional action and dancing in musical numbers can be achieved.

PROPS

Act. I.   Baskets of roses for Fiametta, Gianetta and two sopranos, and for Vittoria, Giulia, Tessa and one alto only. Two mandolins.

NOTATION

Dk — Duke	A — Antonio	d — Duchess
L — Luiz	Fr — Francesco	C — Casilda
D — Don Alhambra	Gi — Giorgio	g — Gianetta
M — Marco	F — Fiametta	T — Tessa
G — Giuseppe	V — Vittoria	I — Inez
	Ga — Giulia	

Production for Script with Don Alhambra as Narrator

ACT I

1. Girls enter in twos led by Fiametta and Vittoria, Gianetta and Tessa, soprano and alto, soprano and Giulia, then sopranos R, altos L.

   Fiametta, two sopranos and Gianetta go to stool RC; Vittoria, Giulia, alto and Tessa to stool LC; sopranos to positions R, altos L. All sit together, taking cue from Fiametta and Vittoria. Fiametta sits on stool RC, two sopranos and Gianetta on floor either side of her;

Sop ∘ [F] ∘ Sop Ga ∘ [V] ∘ Alto
g ∘   ∘ T

Vittoria sits on stool LC, Giulia, alto and Tessa on floor either side of her.

2. *Overture.*

3. *Narrative.* Don Alhambra enters to come down stage from platform in dignified fashion to deliver narrative to audience from centre front. At the end he crosses to sit ①.

4. *Opening Chorus* (*Introduction*). Chorus rises. Soprano on Fiametta's left, rises to stand on diagonal behind her. Soprano on her right kneels. Gianetta keeps seated.

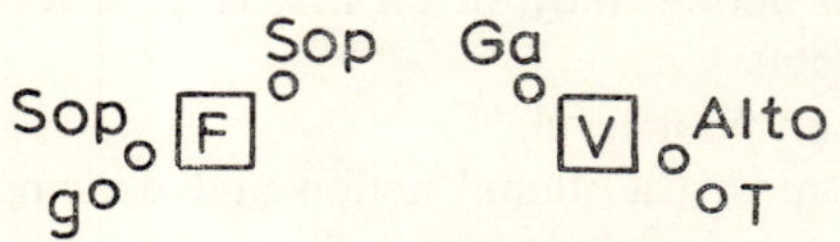

Similar grouping round Vittoria. These eight start to bind posies.

"Two there are for whom." Fiametta rises to sing her solo centre, then returns to sit for remainder of chorus.

5. "Good morrow, pretty maids" (*Introduction*). Men enter in twos, led by Francesco, Antonio and Giorgio; tenors R, basses L. Antonio and Giorgio remain on centre of platform.

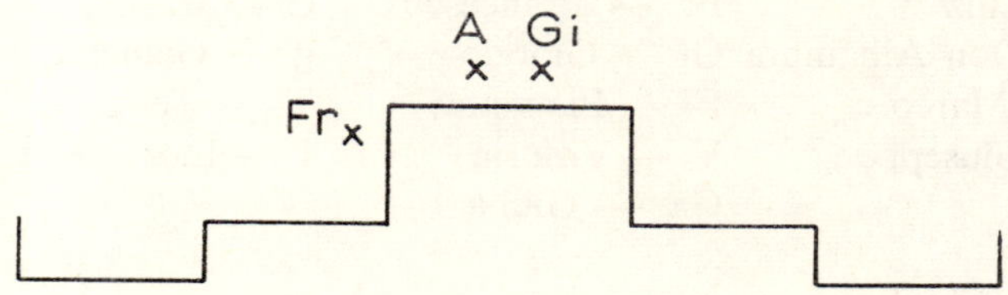

Francesco goes immediately to right of sopranos. Men file into their places.

" But what of us." Giorgio goes L to position similar to Francesco.

"With pleasure." Antonio sings from platform, then skips down centre front for his solo.

6. "For the merriest fellows are we." Fiametta and other five girls rise. Antonio sings and dances centre front.

Second Chorus. Antonio, singing and dancing, goes back to platform, joined by Francesco and Giorgio, who stand at ⑩, ⑫.

As soon as singing ends, Antonio moves to stand at ⑪.

7. "See, see" (*Introduction*). Fiametta runs on to platform beside Antonio, looking R in time to sing "See, see."

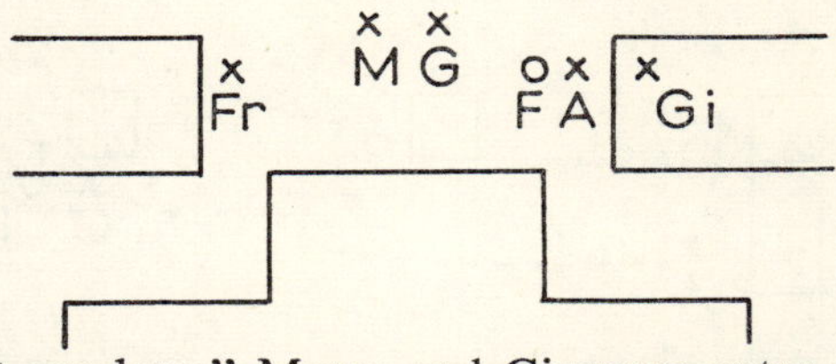

" Accept our love." Marco and Giuseppe enter and stand on platform to receive salutations.

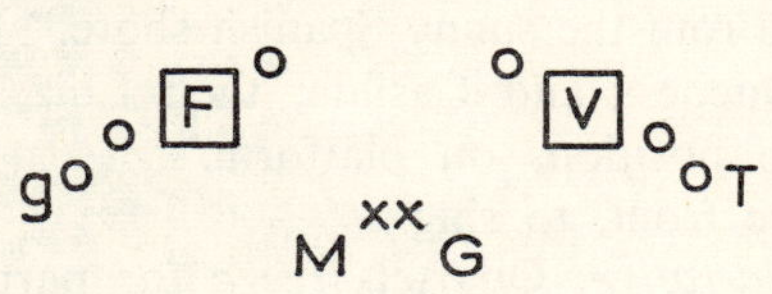

8. "Buon' giorno." Marco and Giuseppe step down slowly, acknowledging greetings, to stand together, just in front of line of stools. Fiametta follows later, unobtrusively, to stand at stool RC as before.

"Per voi." Fiametta and seven girls present roses to gondoliers.

"Servitori, umilissimi" (*Marco*). Marco and Giuseppe, as traditional, throw up roses. While Marco and men's chorus are singing, the eight girls collect the flowers from the stage.

9. "We're called gondolieri." Traditional actions.
10. "And now to choose our brides." Blindfolding done by Fiametta and Vittoria.

"My Papa, he keeps three horses."

1st time. Eight girls dance in a circle round the gondoliers.
2nd time. Marco and Giuseppe play blindman's buff.
3rd time. Marco and Giuseppe catch Gianetta and Tessa. Other six girls move back immediately in arcs in front of chorus (stage level).

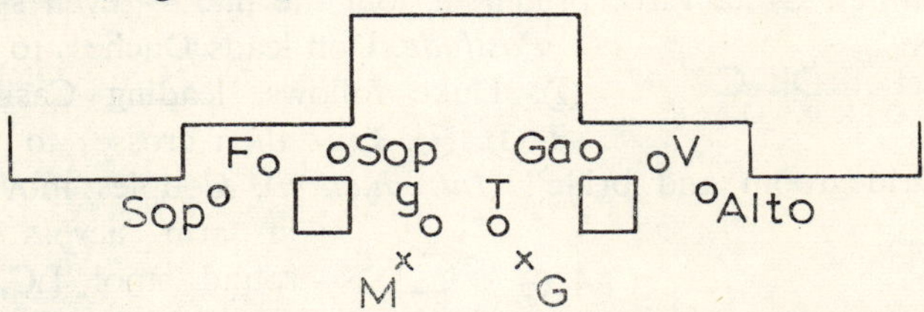

After "Well, I never." Couples move to stools, girls to sit on men's knees. Traditional 'business' thereafter.

"Fate in this has put his finger." Both couples rise, go arm in arm L, then back across stage in front of stools to positions at seats — Marco ⑥, Gianetta ⑦, Tessa ⑧, Giuseppe ⑨.

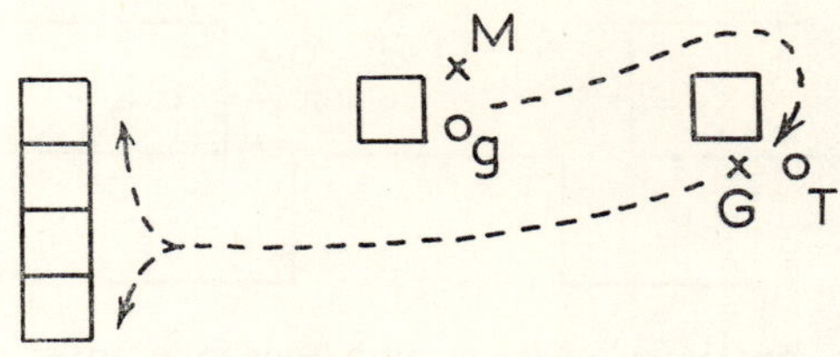

Final bar of music. Company sits.

11. "From the sunny Spanish shore." Duke, Duchess and Casilda, then Luiz, enter to positions on platform.

Then come down centre front, to sing.

12. *Narrative.* Quartet *freeze* for narrative, delivered by Don standing at his seat.

13. "In enterprise of martial kind" (*Postlude*). Duke offers Duchess his arm and they sweep L, in front of Casilda, to sit ③, ②.

14. *Duets.* Casilda and Luiz rush together centre.

15. *Narrative.* Immediately second duet ends, Don, Duke and Duchess rise; Luiz and Casilda break hurriedly to their original positions. Then Don leads Duchess to left of Luiz. Duke, following, goes to right of Casilda. Don then steps forward, centre, to deliver his narrative, during which time quartet *freeze.*

16. "I stole the prince." Sung from above positions.

17. *Recit.* Casilda steps forward in line with Don.

18. *Quintet.* Other three principals join the line — even spacing.

Postlude. Don leads Duchess to sit ①, ②. Duke follows, leading Casilda to sit ③, ④. Luiz then crosses to sit ⑤.

19. "Bridegroom and bride" (*Introduction*). Couples move arm in arm across stage, round stool LC, back to centre, *facing* chorus, to receive their good wishes. To be in position as singing commences.

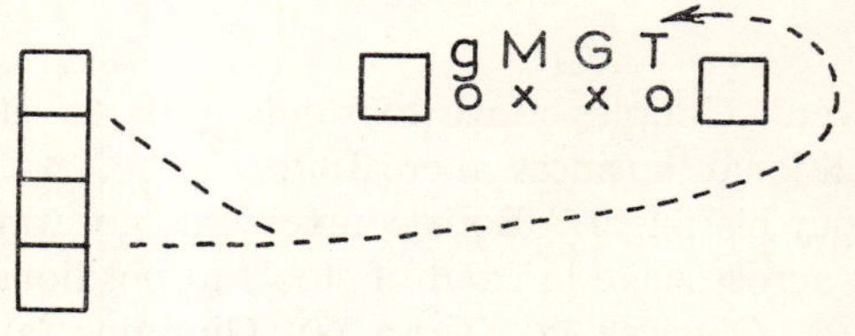

"We in sincerity." Couples break stance, offer congratulations to each other as at a wedding. Girls kiss each other on the cheek, men shake hands, opposite partners embrace, then couples go to sit on stools — each girl on her partner's knee. Marco and Gianetta sit RC, Giuseppe and Tessa LC.

20. "When a merry maiden marries." May be sung standing centre, or seated, on Giuseppe's knee, but at conclusion Tessa must return to his knee.

At the end. Chorus sits.

21. *Narrative.* Don comes centre stage for narrative; couples *freeze.*

22. "Kind sir, you cannot have the heart." Gianetta rises, and approaches Don, slightly behind him.

23. "Her former nursling." Marco joins Gianetta, Tessa and Giuseppe rise to take balancing position on other side of Don.

End of Recit. Don returns to his seat.

24. Opera now proceeds with traditional actions for principals.

"Sing high, sing low" (*Chorus*). Six girls dance with principals.

"Then hail, O King" (*Postlude*). Chorus sits on last bar.

"Now Marco, dear." Couples sit on stools.

"Away we go to an island fair." During first chorus, quartet move slowly to stand on front of platform L.

Marco's solo and quartet. Sung from above positions. Then principals must move quickly. Giuseppe embraces Tessa, then breaks fast to extreme R of platform, back, then looks back. Marco and Gianetta are still bidding each other farewell.

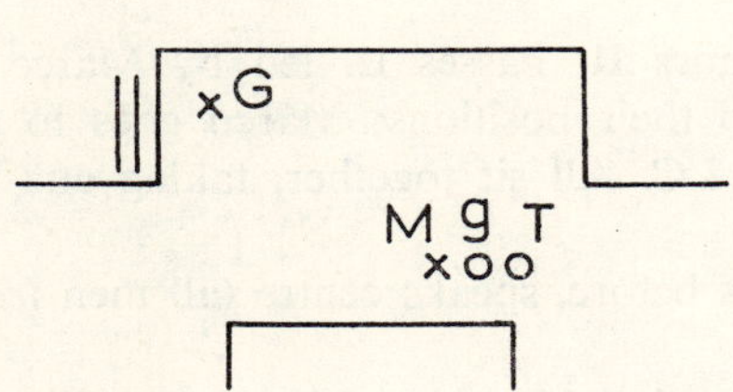

Tessa and Giuseppe, the passionate pair, feel they must embrace again, and rush into each other's arms, RC platform. As chorus sopranos and tenors reach final top A, Marco breaks from Gianetta, passes behind

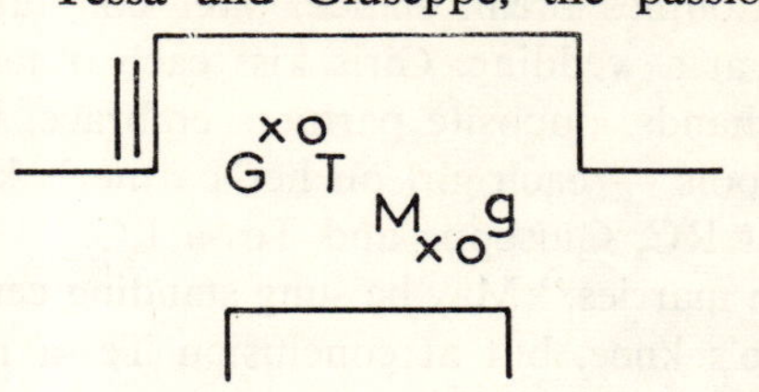

Giuseppe, and exits, to be followed immediately by Giuseppe. Tessa holds out her arms appealingly to him, then, holding hands to her face, she turns to collapse, weeping, on the shoulder of

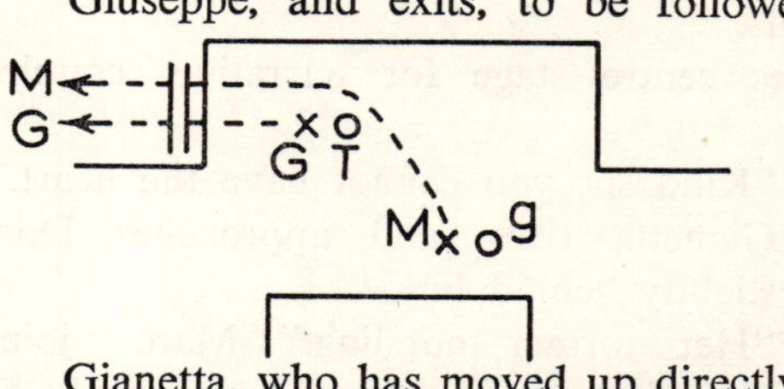

Gianetta, who has moved up directly beside her.

Postlude. Men exit quickly in twos, basses passing behind Tessa and Gianetta.

Girls assume disconsolate attitudes similar to that of Tessa and Gia-

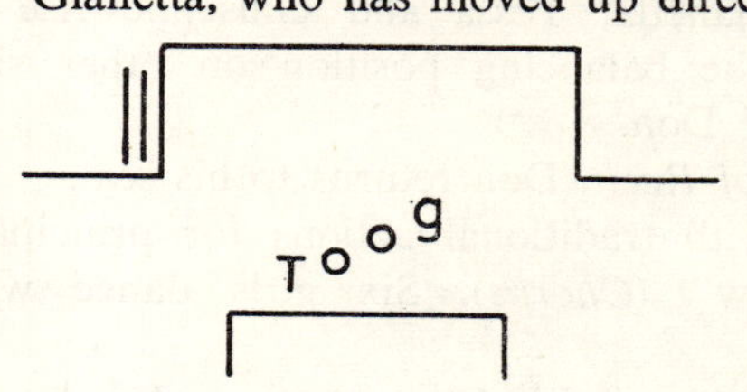

netta — and all hold pose till end of music.

After music exeunt: Tessa and Gianetta, girls' chorus in twos, Don with Duchess, Duke with Casilda, Luiz.

ACT II

Basic seating plan as for Act I. The stools remain in same positions, but as they are to serve as thrones (without backs), the crude Act I stools could well be replaced by more elegantly carved or tapestry-bound stools.

1. Men enter in twos, tenors R, basses L, led by Marco and Giuseppe. Men file into their positions; Marco goes to stool RC, Giuseppe to stool LC. All sit together, taking cue from Marco and Giuseppe.
2. *Narrative.* Don enters as before, speaks centre (all men *freeze*) then sits ①.
3. "Of happiness the very pith." Men rise, Marco and Giuseppe remain seated.

202

"Two kings of undue pride bereft." Marco and Giuseppe come together to sing centre, level with stools. Finished, they turn R and L and march back to their stools with mechanical precision, remaining standing for second chorus.

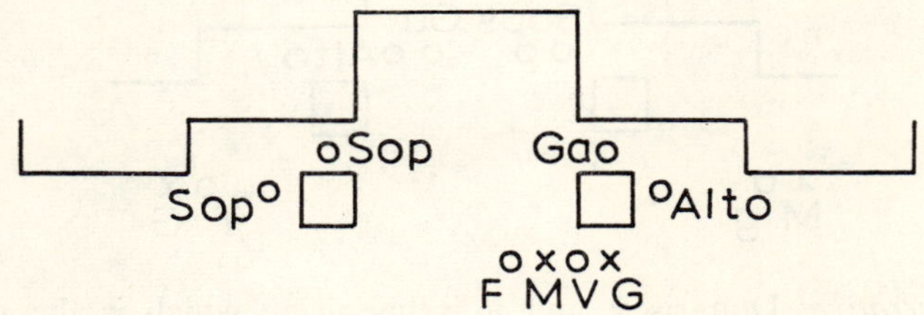

Postlude. Marco sits.

4. "Rising early in the morning." Giuseppe to use stage as he pleases, but must return to stool for end of song.

    Postlude. Giuseppe and chorus sit on last bar.

5. "Take a pair of sparkling eyes." Verse 1, Marco crosses to sing to Giuseppe. Verse 2, sung to audience. During applause, Giuseppe rises to congratulate Marco.

6. *Narrative.* Marco and Giuseppe *freeze.* Don rises to deliver narrative from his position ①.

7. "Here we are at the risk of our lives" (*Introduction*). Girls enter in twos, led by Fiametta and Vittoria, and file into their

positions. Fiametta and Vittorio are greeted enthusiastically by Marco and Giuseppe, and the girls sing their solos to the two gondoliers.

    "So here we are" (*Chorus — second time*). Fiametta and Vittoria lead Marco and Giuseppe to platform L, in time to greet their wives. Tessa enters first. Giuseppe runs to her LC, where they stand and sweeps her to stool

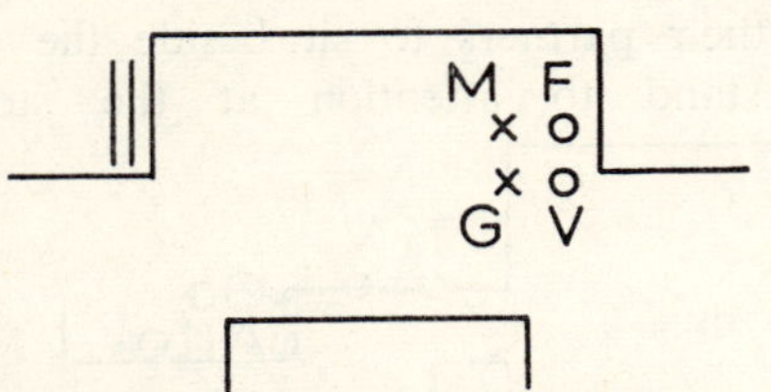

kissing or 'talking' excitedly. Marco sweeps Gianetta to stool RC. Fiametta and Vittoria move to centre of platform.

    "After sailing to this island." Positions.

8. "Cachucha." Dance provision dependent on dancing strength of company. Ideally for this set: Marco and Gianetta to

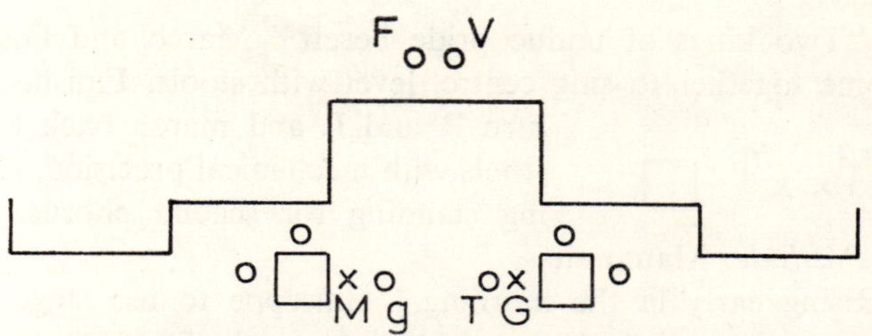

dance R front; Tessa and Giuseppe L front; Francesco and
Fiametta, Vittoria and Antonio on platform; two sopranos,
Giulia and alto in front of platform, between stools.

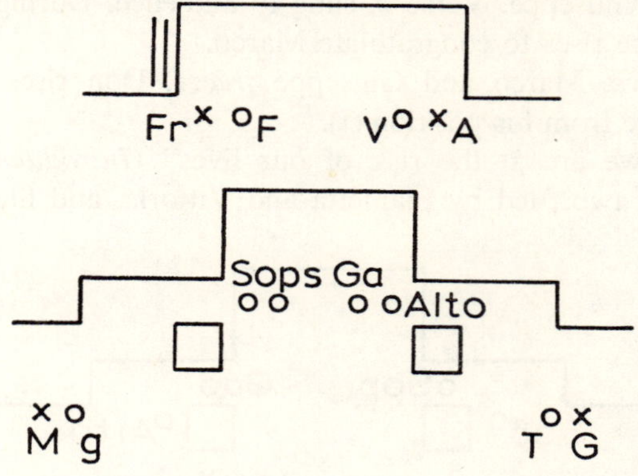

9. *Narrative.* Don rises; and it is his rising which is the signal
for chorus to sit after "Cachucha." He should make some
gesture of rebuke to wave them down — and for once, the
chorus should sit, not as a body, but go down in groups as
they observe him. Fiametta and Vittoria leave their partners
and run to sit on front step as before. Marco and Giuseppe,
rather put out, 'shoo' their partners to sit beside the girls
and they themselves stand to attention at the stools.

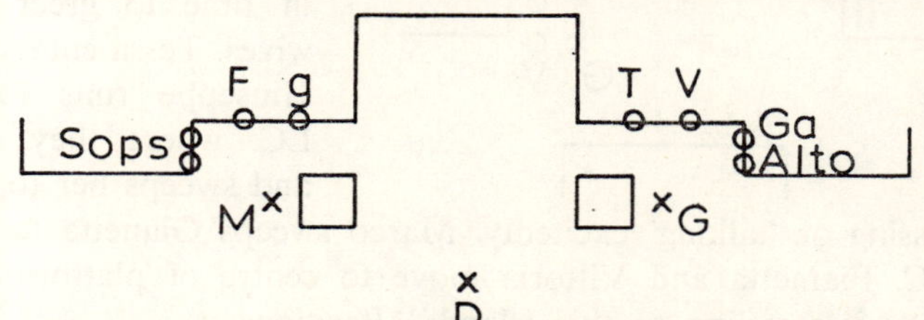

All this should happen very quickly, and all should *freeze*
as Don walks centre to deliver narrative.

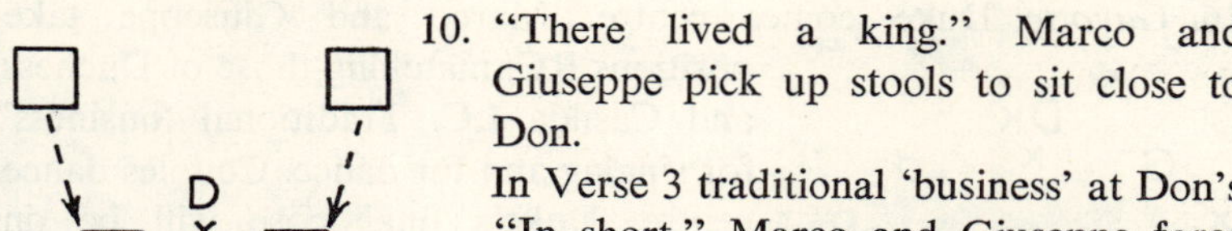

10. "There lived a king." Marco and Giuseppe pick up stools to sit close to Don.

In Verse 3 traditional 'business' at Don's "In short." Marco and Giuseppe force him to hold the note "In," while they return stools to original positions, before rejoining him, centre. After this lung stretching and the little dance steps at the end of the song, the Don is quite exhausted, so Marco and Giuseppe escort him to his seat ①.

11. "In a contemplative fashion." Gondoliers go back to centre to be joined by their wives.

"Quiet calm deliberation" (*last time*). After the argument the traditional march exit of the couples must be modified. All turn R and step towards seats ⑥ to ⑨, Tessa leading Giuseppe slightly upstage of the other two.

All should sit on final chord.

12. "With ducal pomp." Men rise. Duke enters and poses on centre of platform, then swaggers to centre front. Casilda and Duchess follow — Casilda to be ushered by Duke to RC, Duchess to LC.

Duke and Duchess sing from these positions.

Chorus repeat. Duke sweeps Casilda round stage R to show

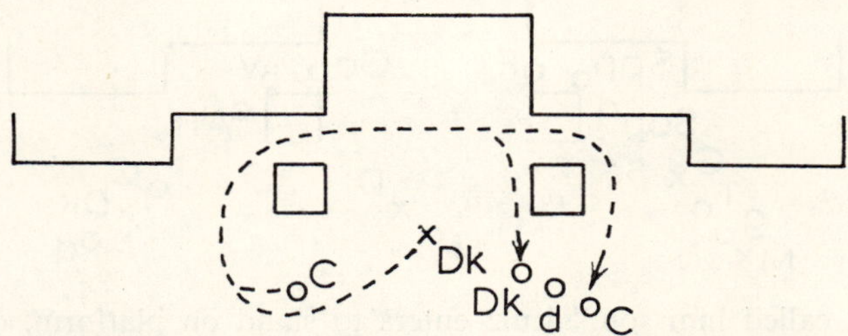

her to chorus; round stools, to bring her to Duchess's left at conclusion. Chorus sits and principals *freeze* for narrative.

13. *Narrative*. Don stands to speak at his seat.

14. *Duchess's Song*. Sung LC. Traditional 'business.'

15. *Duet*. Duke and Duchess may move about stage, but should end in original positions.

16. *Gavotte*. Duke comes centre. Marco and Giuseppe take positions RC, matching those of Duchess and Casilda LC. Traditional 'business' for singing and for dance. Couples dance centre, Duke's final pose will be on platform centre.

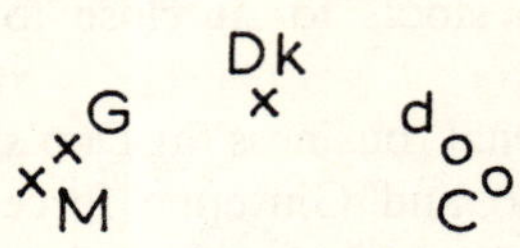

17. *Narrative*. Don stands at his seat. As he starts to speak, Duke leads Duchess to sit ③, ②. Casilda remains LC, while Marco and Giuseppe, having bowed to Duke and Duchess, fetch their wives to take above positions. This movement should be completed by the time Don reaches "a mathematical-cum-philosophical wrangling." Principals then *freeze* for remainder of narrative.

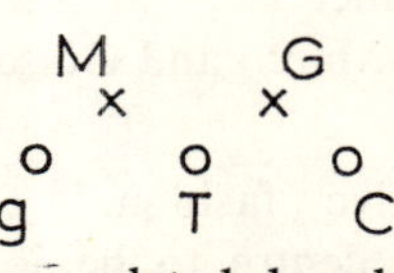

"Happily, I was then in the position." Don walks slightly R, then when finished speaking, exits, passing behind Casilda and Giuseppe.

18. *Quintet*. Traditional actions.

19. *Allegro vivace, Listesso tempo*. Gondoliers quartet move in a huddle R; Casilda moves L, to be joined by Duke and Duchess. Don arrives on platform with Inez (whereupon chorus rises) and sings "Now let the loyal lieges" from there.

"She will declare" (*Chorus*). Don brings Inez centre front; Principals form diagonal lines and six girls come closer in arcs.

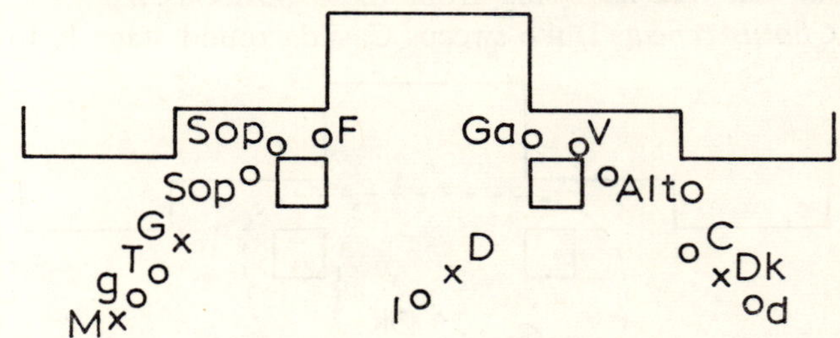

20. "I called him son." Luiz enters to stand on platform, centre, unobserved by any on stage.

"His name, Luiz." Inez gestures to Luiz, and Casilda rushes up to him.

21. "Then hail, O King." All on stage level kneel, extending upstage hands to Luiz and Casilda.

22. *Fanfare*. Appropriate, to cut this.

23. *Allegro con brio*. Principals on stage form a line across stage,

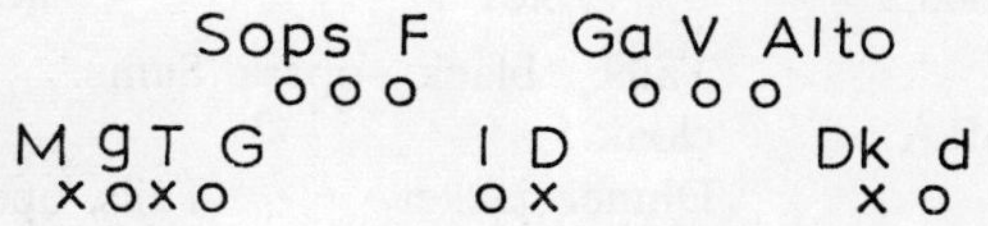

<pre>
        Sops F   Ga V Alto
        o o o   o o o
     M g T G   I D   Dk d
     x o x o   o x   x o
</pre>

and six girls form two lines in spaces between.
24. *End of Opera*. All take one bow, then exeunt:
Luiz and Casilda regally; Duke and Duchess very regally,
Duke fussily attentive to her; Inez; Don Alhambra with
Fiametta and Giulia on his arms, with two sopranos, Vittoria
and alto running behind; Marco and Gianetta; Giuseppe and
Tessa, who blows a kiss to audience.
Then girls in twos, men in twos.

Suggestions for Costuming

PRINCIPALS	ACT I	ACT II
DON ALHAMBRA	Tails, black opera cloak.	Same.
DUKE OF PLAZA-TORO	Dinner jacket (black), opera cloak.	Tails, opera cloak — different, more resplendent *e.g.* with red lining.
LUIZ	Linen jacket, dark trousers, white shirt.	Tails, opera cloak.
MARCO	Dinner jacket (black), cummerbund to match Giuseppe's.	Same, with opera cloak, lighter than Duke's to match Giuseppe's.
GIUSEPPE	As for Marco.	As for Marco.
FRANCESCO ANTONIO GIORGIO	As for Male Chorus.	As for Male Chorus.
DUCHESS OF PLAZA-TORO	Sombre, full-length evening dress.	Voluminous ball gown, dark colour.
CASILDA	As for Duchess.	Voluminous ball gown, light colour or white.
GIANETTA	Short dress, identical to Tessa's.	Same.
TESSA	As for Gianetta.	As for Gianetta.
FIAMETTA VITTORIA GIULIA	As for Female Chorus, preferably all three identical.	Same.
INEZ	—	long dark woollen dress, shawl.

CHORUS	ACTS I, II
MALE	Dinner jackets (black), either all with cummerbunds or none.
FEMALE	Short dresses, not formal, in light, bright colours.

13

UTOPIA LIMITED

Note on Production

Utopia Limited is the most costly opera of the series to costume for a full-stage production, the Act II drawing-room calling for sumptuous attire of the most regal Victorian style. In consequence, much care must be given to the choice of costumes for a concert version, and producer and wardrobe mistress must discuss and vet every member's costume, well in advance of presentation date, to allow for changes or alterations. (It is no use saying, "Bring bikinis for the Dress Rehearsal.")

The points to be borne in mind are to contrast Act I open-air simplicity of dress with occasion formality in Act II. The beach wear of Act I must be given great consideration. It should not be brash or sexy as in a gaudy modern musical. Innocent refinement is the watchword. The girls are not to flaunt themselves as 'pin-ups' nor the men as 'Mr. Universe'.

Note on King Paramount as Narrator

This is a particularly important part, as, the opera being generally unknown, the story must be put over with clarity. The King should be played as an easy-going individual, one not a lover of pomp and ceremony. He sees the humour of his situation, and is chatty and confidential to the audience.

It might appear that the Narrative he has to learn is lengthy — yet it is considerably less than that called for in the original Libretto.

NOTES

1. No seats for Row 3. When not standing, the ladies sit on step, in front of ladies of Row 2.
2. Seats ①, ⑫, ⑬, ⑭ should be substantial, carved (with arms), as they represent thrones.
3. Rostrum is raised a single step above Row 1, 2. It should be movable, as its position must be altered for Act II.

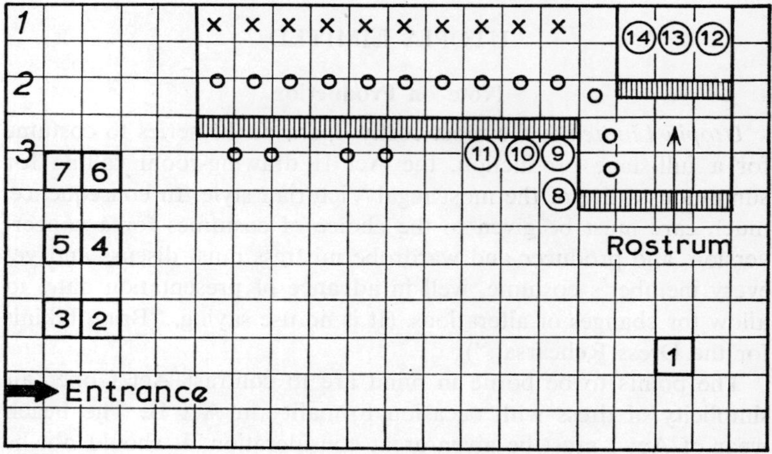

ROW 1 (Raised 1 single step) ROW 2 (Same level)
ROW 3 (Floor level — no seats)

Act I. Three copies of *The Palace Peeper*. (As this is a private newspaper, copies of a 'daily' should not be used. An obviously small circulation paper of the student magazine type should be provided.)
Crown for King.
Crackers for Tarara.
Manual for Fitzbattleaxe.
Lorgnette for Sophy.
A handbag and letter in envelope for Zara.

Act II. Two violins, two tambourines, two banjos for Flowers of Progress.

NOTATION

Kg — King	D — Dramaleigh	Z — Zara
Sc — Scaphio	F — Fitzbattleaxe	N — Nekaya
P — Phantis	C — Corcoran	K — Kalyba
T — Troopers	BB — Bailey Barre	S — Sophy
Ta — Tarara	B — Blushington	L_1 — Phylla
Ca — Calynx	L_2, L_3, L_4 — Ladies front row, who are dancers.	

211

Script/Production for King Paramount as Narrator

ACT I

1. Company enters thus:
   Men, single file to Row 1. Sit individually as soon as they reach their seats.
   Ladies, Row 2; ladies, Row 1, led by Phylla and L_2, L_3, L_4 who occupy positions ⑧ to ⑪.
   As the ladies reach their positions, they sit, recline, lie in picture groupings.
   Sophy, Kalyba and Nekaya to sit ⑬, ⑫, ⑭.
   Tarara and Calynx, dignified, to sit ②, ③.
   King to sit ①. (His crown is perched at a most informal angle on his head. Before he sits, he should take off his robe and hang it on the back of his throne. He then sits in relaxed attitude and starts to read *The Palace Peeper*.)
2. *Overture.*
3. V.S No. 1. *Chorus.* "In lazy langour — motionless."
4. KING 'Good news! Great news! His Majesty's eldest daughter, Princess Zara, who left our shores five years since to go to England — the greatest, the most powerful, the wisest country in the world — has taken a high degree at Girton, having achieved a complete mastery over all the elements that have tended to raise that glorious country to her present pre-eminent position among civilised nations!'
   So in a few months, Utopia may hope to be completely Anglicised. And what have we to gain?
   English institutions, English tastes and oh! (*change of tone*) English fashions. You'll find it all in *The Palace Peeper*. Oh, here are two of my courtiers — Calynx, my Vice-Chamberlain, and Tarara, my Public Exploder. (It's a new office, just created). You see, by our Constitution, we are governed by a Despot (me), who, although in theory absolute, is, in practice, nothing of the kind, being watched day and night by two Wise Men; whose duty it is, on his very first lapse from political or social propriety, to denounce him to the Public Exploder, and then it becomes his duty to blow up His Majesty with dynamite. Poor Tarara — he's highly nervous of his duties. Watch him — he's practising! But he needn't worry, he'll never need to blow me up. The *Wise* Men, Scaphio and Phantis, will never denounce me. This paper

212

ACT I

King reads from paper, sitting.

King rises.
Rhetorical question.

Walks centre, ruminating.
Slaps paper.
Looks R. Calynx looks up, stands to bow as his name is mentioned;
so for Tarara.
Calynx and Tarara 'converse' with each other.
King, centre, turns to confide in audience.

Tarara takes out cracker — offers it to Calynx fearfully.
Calynx pulls it — Tarara upset.
Calynx and Tarara sit.

(it's very well written) teems with circumstantially convincing details of my abominable immoralities! But the Wise Men merely wink at them — it suits their purpose.

Oh, here they are approaching — I'd best be off.

5. V.S. No. 2. *Chorus*. "O make way for the Wise Men."

6. V.S. No. 2a. *Duet*. "In every mental lore."

7. KING Now then, they're plotting. Phantis although he's 55, is desperately in love with me daughter, Zara. (He doesn't have much chance now she's been to Girton!) Still Scaphio, who is even older, and knows nothing about love, gives him every encouragement. I'm their slave, they think, and I shall have to give consent.

8. V.S. No. 3. *Duet*. "Let all your doubts take wing."

9. V.S. No. 4. *Chorus with solos*. "Quaff the nectar."
   First four bars Introduction.
   Second four bars Introduction.
   "La, la" — and *chorus*.

End of singing.

Postlude and *Introduction* to V.S. No. 4a.

10. V.S. No. 4a. *Song*. "A king of of autocratic power."
    "My subjects all."
    "Come hither, daughters." *Introduction bars 1 to 4.*
                                      Introduction bars 5 to 8.
                                      Introduction bars 9, 10
    "How fair! How modest!"

Looking R. Goes back to sit ①.
Chorus rise, keep standing for duet — then sit again.
Scaphio and Phantis enter and sing. RC. End of duet
they remain RC, heads together conspiratorially.
King, still seated, leans forward to address audience confidentially.
Phantis (hand to heart) mimes love.

Scaphio congratulates Phantis.

Sung RC. At the end, they go to sit ④, ⑤.
All ladies of chorus rise.
L_1, L_2 run to centre.
L_3, L_4 run to centre.
Four girls dance with garlands, centre, during which time King
lounges on throne.
Three girls go to diagonal RC. Phylla crosses to King.

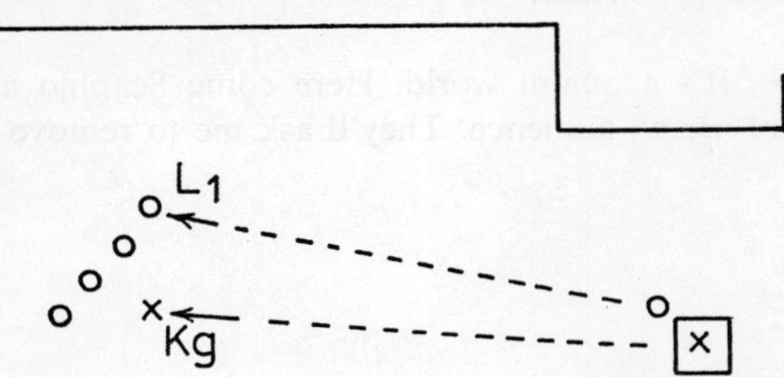

Phylla assists King to put on his robe, adjusts his crown. He pats
her head, then regally, marches to sing RC. Phylla joins diagonal.

King appeals to chorus.
Kalyba comes down step of Rostrum, and stops.
Same for Nekaya.
Sisters take hands and skip to top of next step, then stop and
assume demure appearance.
Girls stand posed.

"See how they blush."

"How English and how pure."
11. V.S. No. 4b. *Duet*. "Altho' of native maids the cream."
    End of singing, Introduction to Recit.

12. V.S. No. 4c. *Song*. "Bold-faced ranger."
    Last chorus.
    "The lecture's ended."

"Quaff the nectar."

13. KING It's a quaint world. Here come Scaphio and Phantis
    to grant *me* an audience. They'll ask me to remove my crown.

I cannot help looking at the humorous side of life — even
The Palace Peeper. See here — "Another Royal Scandal" by
Junius Junior. "How long is this to last?" by Senex Senior.
"Ribald Royalty" by Mercury Major. "Where is the Public
Exploder?" by Mephistopheles Minor. When I reflect that all
these outrageous attacks on my morality are written by me,
at your command —

Sisters step forward sedately to LC.

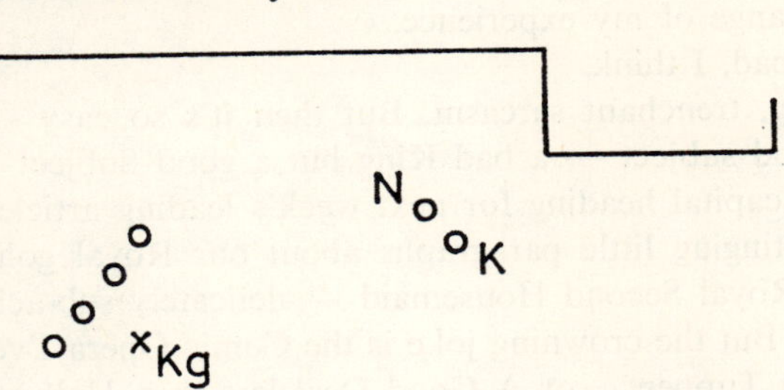

Pose.
Sisters sing LC.
Sophy descends steps regally, passes in front of sisters, who curtsey low, to centre. There she curtsies to King, who, eyeing her with admiration, gives a most courteous bow.
Sophy sings centre.
Sisters dance, then curtsey to Sophy.
Sophy sings centre, then curtsying to King, she sweeps L, up steps to her seat, followed by Kalyba and Nekaya (who first curtsey to King).
Dancers dance back to their seats.
Chorus sits on last bar of music.
King strolls centre. Scaphio and Phantis cross to take position on either side of him.

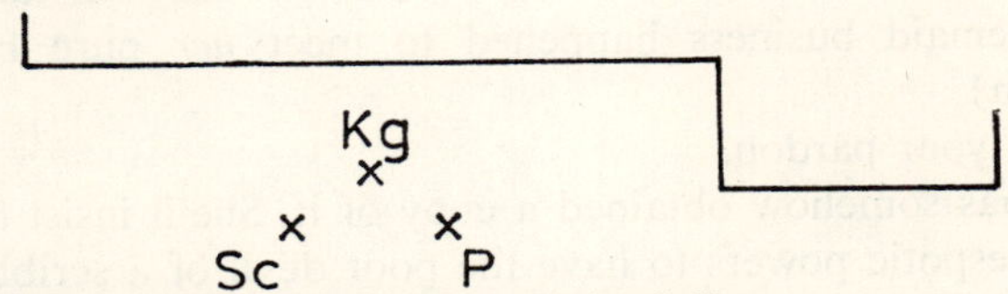

They cough and look at crown meaningfully.
King removes crown and shakes his head, then produces *The Palace Peeper.*

Scaphio and Phantis turn their heads away disdainfully.

King pauses and looks from one to the other.

— well, it's one of the funniest things that have come within the range of my experience.

Not bad, I think.

Biting, trenchant sarcasm. But then it's so easy — I'm such a good subject — a bad King but a good Subject — ha! ha! — a capital heading for next week's leading article. And then the stinging little paragraphs about our Royal goings-on with our Royal Second Housemaid — delicately sub-acid, are they not? But the crowning joke is the Comic Opera I've written — 'King Tuppence, or A Good Deal less than Half a Sovereign'. Humorous, quaint. Properly considered, what a farce life is.

14. V.S. No. 5. *Song*. "First you're born."

15. KING It's all very well. I always like to look on the humorous side of things; but I do *not* think I ought to be required to write libels on my own moral character. Naturally, I see the joke of it — anybody would — but Zara's coming home today; she's no longer a child, and I confess I should *not* like her to see my opera — though it's uncommonly well written; and I should be sorry if *The Palace Peeper* got into her hands — thought it's certainly smart — very smart indeed. It is almost a pity that I have to buy up the whole edition, because it's really too good to be lost.

And Lady Sophy — that blameless type of perfect womanhood! Great heavens, what would *she* say if the Second Housemaid business happened to meet *her* pure blue eye! Damn!

I beg your pardon.

She has somehow obtained a copy of it. She'll insist that I use my despotic powers to have the poor devil of a scribbler slain.

But I'll be cunning. I — I am waiting until a punishment is discovered that will meet the enormity of the case. I am in constant communication with the Mikado of Japan who is a leading authority on such points.

Oh, Lady Sophy, as you are powerful, be merciful!

16. V.S. No. 6. *Duet*. "Subjected to your heavenly gaze."

17. V.S. No. 7. *Chorus with Solos*. "Oh maiden,
          rich in Girton lore."

King reconsiders paper.
Looks at Scaphio.

To Phantis.

At the end, Scaphio and Phantis return to their seats.
King puts on crown again, lop-sided.
Rather rueful.

Sophy rises and descends steps, reading *The Palace Peeper*.

He catches sight of Sophy reading paper.

To audience.
Sophy now comes on stage, still reading.
Sophy approaches him flourishing paper furiously, demanding an explanation.
She holds her pose through this speech.

King kneels, with arms outflung in ostentatious gesture.
Sung centre. Dance of repudiation by Sophy at *Postlude*, when she retires to her seat. With a rueful gesture, King returns to the throne.
Full company rise except Sophy, Nekaya, Kalyba and King.

Introduction.

"Oh maiden, rich in Girton lore.

"Five years have flown."
"Knightsbridge nursemaids."

**

Four troopers, single file, march to centre, upstage; do right turn, and stand to attention.

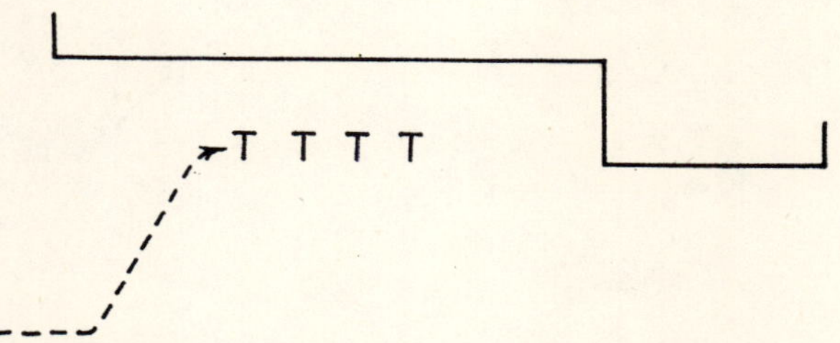

Enter Zara, on Fitzbattleaxe's left arm. She walks slowly and graciously, acknowledging singing, to centre.

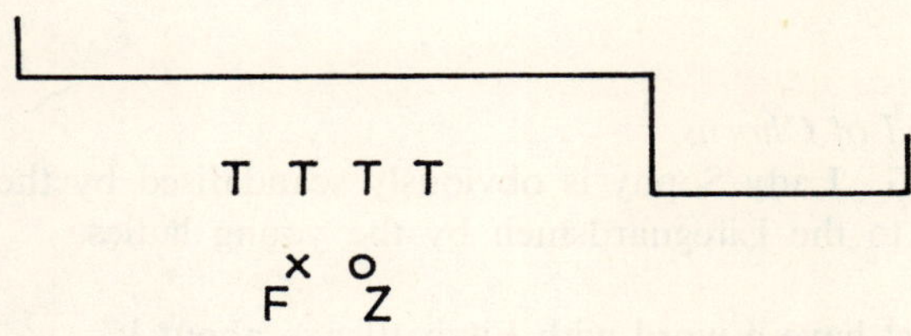

Zara drops Fitzbattleaxe's arm. He stands to attention.
Troopers — two right turn, two left turn; march to stand forming rectangle.

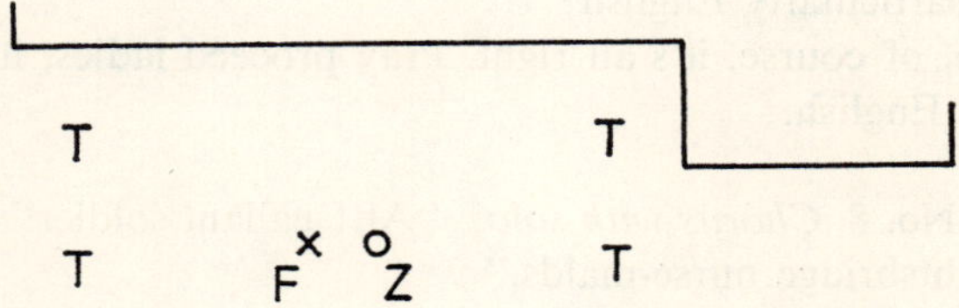

After troopers sing "We are the escort First Life Guards."

End of Chorus.

18. KING   Lady Sophy is obviously scandalised by the attention
    paid to the Lifeguardsmen by the young ladies.

    I must have a word with Fitzbattleaxe about it.

    They won't be offended?
    Oh? They are quite hardened to it? They get a good deal of
    that sort of thing standing sentry at the Horse Guards?
    It's particularly English?
    Then, of course, it's all right. Pray proceed ladies, it's particu-
    larly English.

19. V.S. No. 8. *Chorus with solos.* "Ah! gallant soldier"
    "Knightsbridge nurse-maids."

    After *Fitzbattleaxe's Solo.*
    "Oh the hours are gold."

Production

Eight ladies front row come forward to circle and inspect the troopers — four going round each pair — showing admiration. During chorus, King, followed by Sophy, Nekaya and Kalyba, enters and stands LC.

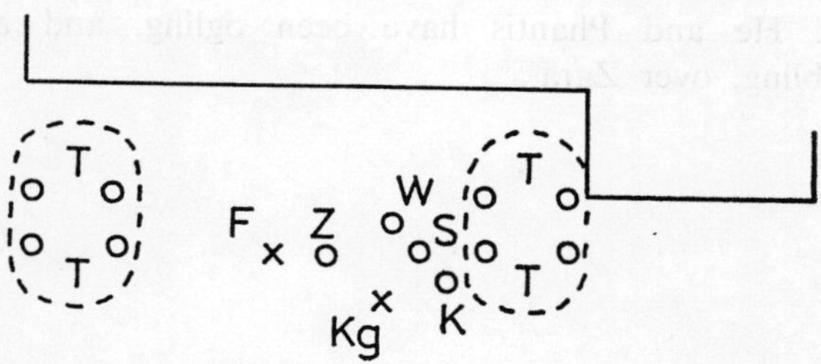

Sisters' eyes are wide open in amazement and Sophy is highly indignant at the women inspecting the troopers. She views them haughtily through her lorgnette.
All *freeze*.
To audience.

Crosses in front of Fitzbattleaxe and Zara to former's right. King whispers in his ear. Fitzbattleaxe whispers in King's ear.
Fitzbattleaxe whispers in King's ear in reply.

Fitzbattleaxe nods.
Fitzbattleaxe nods again.
King breaks from Fitzbattleaxe and makes pronouncement. On stage all come to life again, ladies becoming more amorous towards troopers.
Zara places a hand on Fitzbattleaxe's arm.
Ladies, two to each trooper, lay their heads on troopers' shoulders. Troopers still stand to attention. This is too much for Sophy, who gathers her charges, and with a curtsy and withering look at the King, departs to her seat.

King, beaming benignly, retires to sit on throne, to watch.
Scaphio and Phantis leave their seats to come RC, watching with obvious jealousy, Zara's interest in Fitzbattleaxe.

Last 4 bars.

20. **KING** I'm afraid this passionate attraction for the opposite sex is infectious. Even old Scaphio, the non-lover, is affected by it. He and Phantis have been ogling, and are now squabbling, over Zara.

But trust the English Lifeguardsman to find a solution — and one to suit his own designs.

'In England, when two gentlemen are in love with the same lady, and until it is settled which gentleman is to blow the other's brains out, it is provided by the Rival Admirers' Clauses Consolidation Act, that the lady shall be entrusted to an Officer of Household Cavalry as stakeholder, who is bound to hand her over to the survivor (on the Tontine principle) in a good condition of substantial and decorative repair.'

Troopers do right turn and march R, to stand in line behind ⑥,
⑦. Their girls, taken aback, make a movement to follow, but then
resignedly go back to their seats. Chorus sits.
King speaks from throne, seated. Scaphio and Phantis, nudging and
pushing for better position, fall on their knees, with outstretched
arms to Zara.

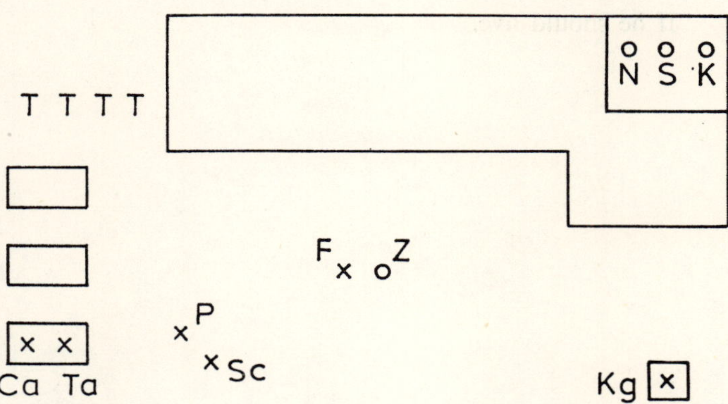

She, horrified, steps back a pace. Fitzbattleaxe steps forward on the
diagonal, pulling forth a manual and mimes quoting from it.

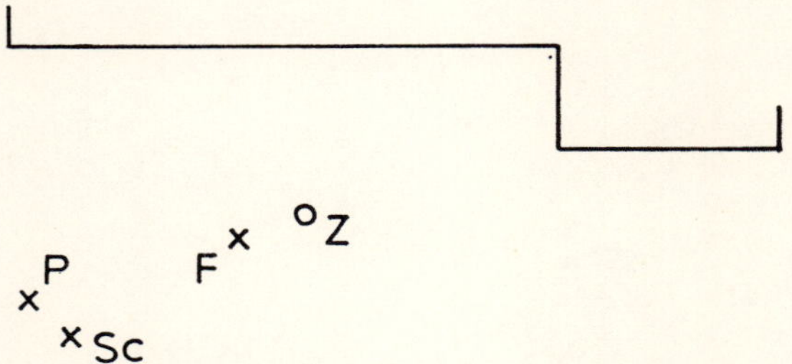

King rises and, from throne, delivers this speech in the flat tone of
one quoting an often delivered ruling.

I've read the Rules myself.
And, of course, the lady will be handed over to *this* worthy
officer of the Household Cavalry!
21. V.S. No. 9. *Quartet*. "It's understood."
  "I hold the lady."
  "If I should live."

  "If he should live."

Quartet.
Postlude.

Production

Change of tone.

King sits.
Scaphio and Phantis rise. ⓐ
Fitzbattleaxe takes Zara's hand through his arm.
Scaphio goes to Fitzbattleaxe, sings to him confidentially, then self-satisfied, moves round to Phantis' original position. ⓑ
Phantis, who has been moving up on "and all her predilections," does the same, returning to Scaphio's original position. ⓒ

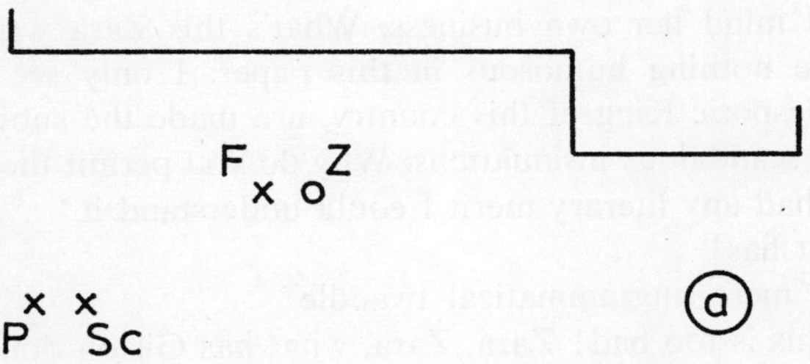

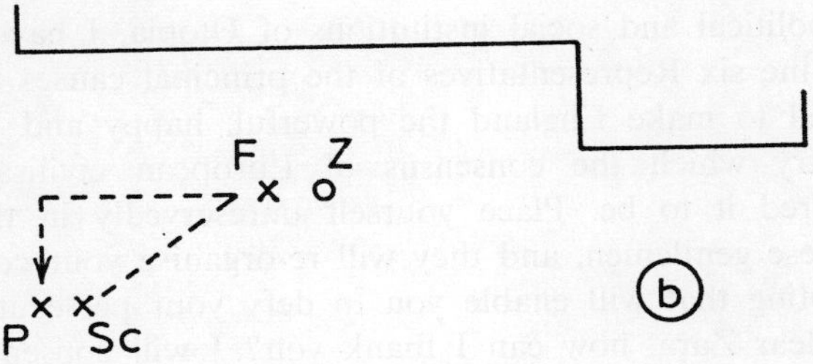

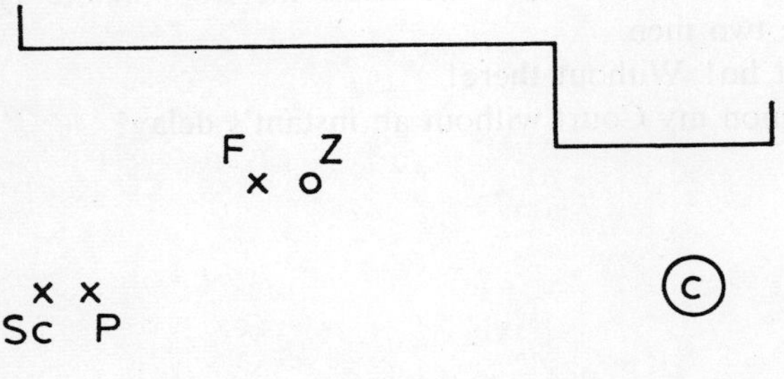

F Z
x o

P Sc
x x

ⓐ

F Z
x o

P Sc
x x

ⓑ

F Z
x o

Sc P
x x

ⓒ

Scaphio sings to Phantis, Fitzbattleaxe sings to Zara.
Scaphio and Phantis return to their seats.

22. V.S. No. 10. *Duet*. "Oh admirable art."
    Postlude.

23. KING   Zara!

Damn!
I beg your pardon.
Who gave her that paper?
Lady Sophy! Lady Sophy's an angel, but I do sometimes wish she'd mind her own business. What's this Zara writes?
'I see nothing humorous in this paper. I only see that you, the despotic King of this country, are made the subject of the most scandalous insinuations. Why do you permit these things? If it had any literary merit I could understand it.'
But it has!
'It is mere ungrammatical twaddle.'
Oh this is too bad! Zara, Zara, what has Girton done to you?
'My poor father! Attend to me. With a view to remodelling the political and social institutions of Utopia, I have brought with me six Representatives of the principal causes that have tended to make England the powerful, happy and blameless country which the consensus of European civilisation has declared it to be. Place yourself unreservedly in the hands of these gentlemen, and they will re-organise your country on a footing that will enable you to defy your persecutors.'
My dear Zara, how can I thank you? I will consent to anything that will release me from the abominable tyranny of these two men.
What ho! Without there!
Summon my Court without an instant's delay!

Fitzbattleaxe raises Zara's hand to his lips, bowing military fashion, then retires to sit ⑦.
King comes forward holding out his hands to Zara. She opens her handbag, pulls out a *Palace Peeper*, which she puts in his hands, then an envelope, which she places on top of paper.
Turning on her heel, she goes to sit ⑥.
To audience.
Opens letter and scans first lines.

Reading letter.

King becomes more and more excited.

With relief.

With new authority.
Strides LC front.

24. V.S. No. 11. *Finale Act I (Introduction).*

"Why, what does this mean?"
Allegro marziale.

"When Britain sounds the trump."
"Uhlahlica."

"A complicated gentleman."

"Uhlahlica."
25. V.S No. 11a (*4 bars Introduction*).

Production

All rise. Tarara, Scaphio, Phantis come forward R, on diagonal.
Sophy, Nekaya, Kalyba come from Rostrum to stand opposite, L.
Zara RC front, Calynx R front. (Calynx brings on each Flower
of Progress).

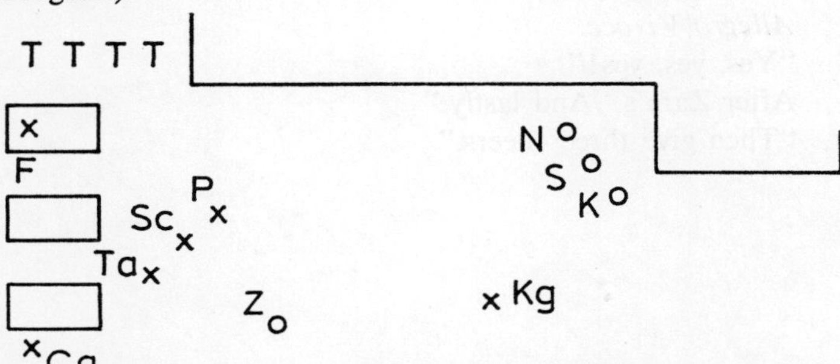

Scaphio, Phantis, Tarara in conspiratorial huddle.
Troopers march single file to centre back, do right turn and stand
to attention. Fitzbattleaxe follows, marching to RC left of Zara.

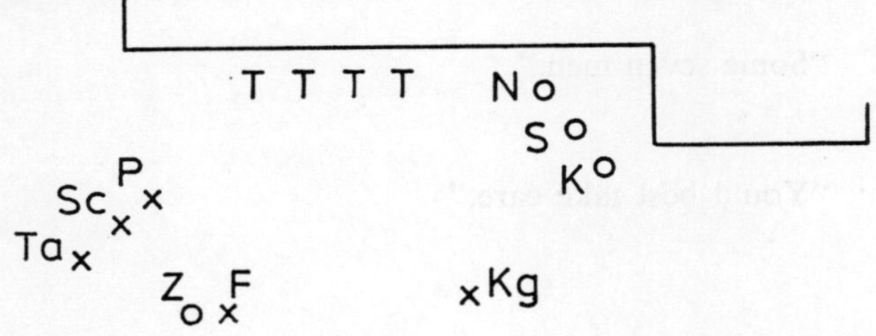

Zara presents Fitzbattleaxe.
Fitzbattleaxe does left turn, marches to King, who shakes hands.
Fitzbattleaxe then steps back one pace.

Calynx ushers on Sir Bailey Barre, who stands R of Zara.

Barre crosses to King, who shakes his hand.

Barre steps back one pace, R of Fitzbattleaxe. Calynx ushers in Lord Dramaleigh and Mr. Blushington, who stand R of Zara.

231

Postlude of Verse 1.
Postlude of Verse 2.

"Uhlahlica."
Allegro Vivace.
"Yes, yes, yes!"
After Zara's "And lastly."
"Then give three cheers."

"Some seven men."

"You'd best take care."

"Let's seal this mercantile pact."

Dramaleigh crosses to King, 'business' as for others.

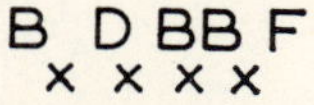

B   D BB F   Blushington crosses — same 'business'.
  x   x x x

Blushington startled — others stolidly indifferent.
Calynx ushers in Goldbury, who stands R of Zara.
Goldbury to King, 'business' as for others.
Calynx ushers in Corcoran, who stands R of Zara.
Corcoran to King, 'business' as for others.
Positions now:

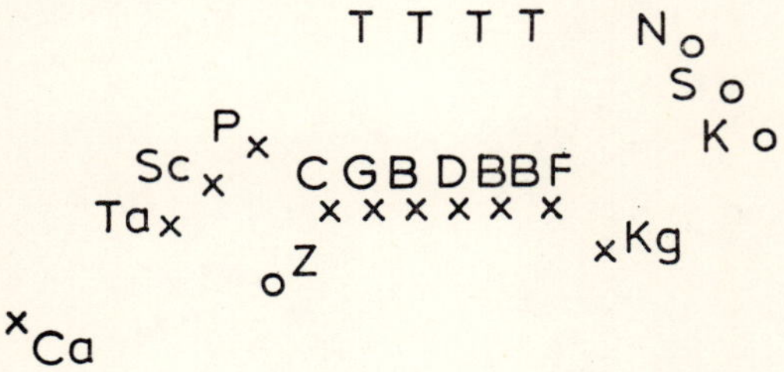

```
          T  T  T  T      N o
                            S o
           P                K o
        Sc  x
      Ta x     C G B D BB F
         x    x x x x x x      x Kg
              o Z
    x Ca
```

Goldbury one step forward for Solo. At the end, bows to King and
steps back in line. Zara crosses in front of line, shaking hands, to
join Fitzbattleaxe.

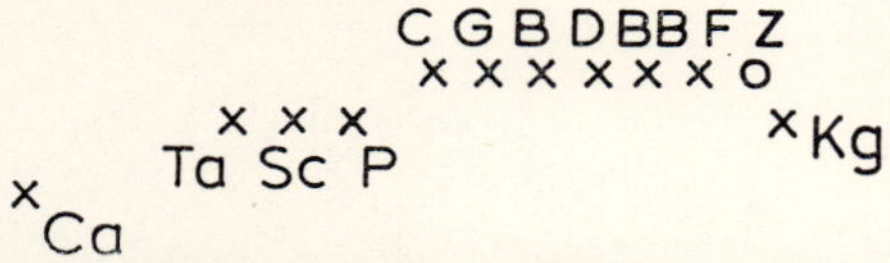

```
          C G B D BB F Z     Tarara,  Scaphio  Phantis
          x x x x x x o      come forward in a line, turn
      x x x              x Kg    left and face King.
      Ta Sc P
  x
   Ca
```

Principals start exit as Chorus starts to sing, in order. King; Sophy,
followed by Nekaya, Kalyba (all four crossing in front of other
principals). Calynx, Tarara, Scaphio, Phantis.
Remainder of chorus is sung static, and all remain in position until
music ends. Then exit: Fitzbattleaxe and Zara (crossing front);
Corcoran, Goldbury, Blushington, Dramaleigh, Bailey Barre (in
groups, talking). Troopers marching; ladies; gentlemen.

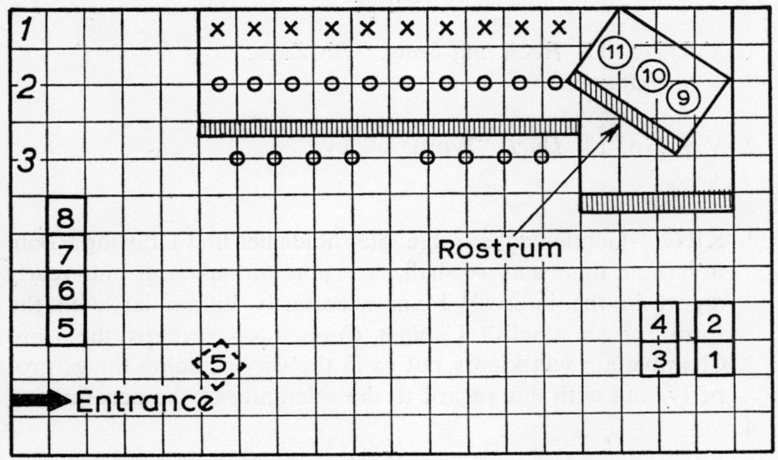

ROW 1 (Raised single step) ROW 2 (same level)
ROW 3 (floor level — no seats)

NOTES

1. Seat ⑤ placed RC initially — later moved in line with ⑥ to ⑧.
2. Instruments for Flower of Progress placed unobtrusively beneath seats **R**.

Script

1. V.S. No. 12. *Recit and Song*. "Oh Zara."
   Introduction.

2. V.S. No. 13. *Duet*. "Words of love."

3. KING   Gentlemen, our daughter holds her first Drawing Room in half an hour and we shall have time to make our half-yearly report in the interval. I am necessarily unfamiliar with the forms of an English Cabinet Council — perhaps the Lord Chamberlain will kindly put us in the way of doing things properly, and with due regard to the solemnity of the occasion.

   We take your word for it that this is all right.
   You are not making fun of us?
   This is in accordance with the practice at the Court of St. James's?
   Oh! It is in accordance with the practice at the Court of St. James's Hall? It seems odd, but never mind.

4. V.S. No. 14. *Septet*. "Society has quite forsaken."
   Introduction.

Production

Zara and Fitzbattleaxe stroll on arm in arm. He ushers her to seat RC before commencing to sing.

May be sung seated or standing. At the end Fitzbattleaxe kisses Zara's hand.

She exits R. Fitzbattleaxe remains standing at chair.

King enters with other Flowers of Progress, in groups, talking; some passing, others pausing to chat to Fitzbattleaxe.

King takes centre stage, and when he speaks, all give him courteous attention.

Dramaleigh bows. He and Goldbury fetch three chairs from L. Fitzbattleaxe places his chair centre for King; other three Flowers of Progress fetch chairs from R. Line of chairs in this order . . .

B F G Kg D C BB   Dramaleigh bows King to
x x x x   x x x   his seat, then all others sit
together.

King looks along both sides of line.

To Dramaleigh.

Dramaleigh whispers in his ear.

With a bow to King, Flowers of Progress fetch their instruments. Then traditional 'business'.

Postlude.

5. KING   Now then — for our first Drawing Room.
6. V.S. No. 15. *Entrance of Court.*

7. V.S. No. 16. *Drawing Room Music.*
   At the end.

All bow to King. Dramaleigh and Goldbury replace chairs L, then sit ①, ②. Others replace chairs R (Fitzbattleaxe taking King's) and sit, as shown. Seat ⑤ now in line. Instruments placed below chairs.

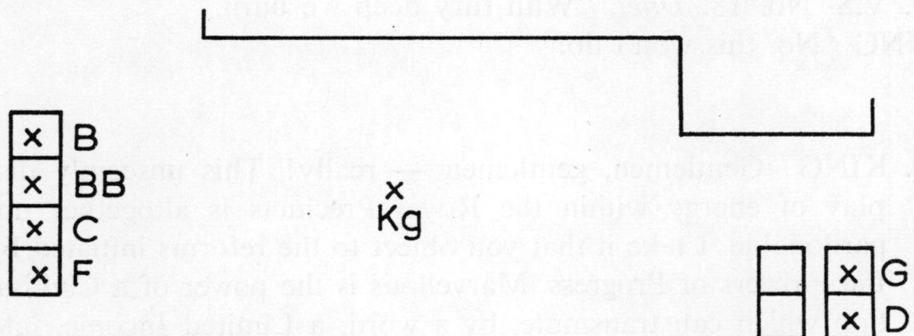

King speaks with some pride.
The whole to be played with the utmost formality, timed to finish as music ends.
Flowers of Progress stand. Then enter in order:
Zara, greeted by King who leads her to sit ⑪; he sits ⑩. Sophy to sit ⑨. Nekaya and Kalyba to stand ③, ④. Front row of ladies' chorus to form two squares for dance, centre. Row 2 ladies, partnered by men, take their places at seats. Troopers march single file to position back, R of chorus. All sit together (except dancers and troopers) on final bar.

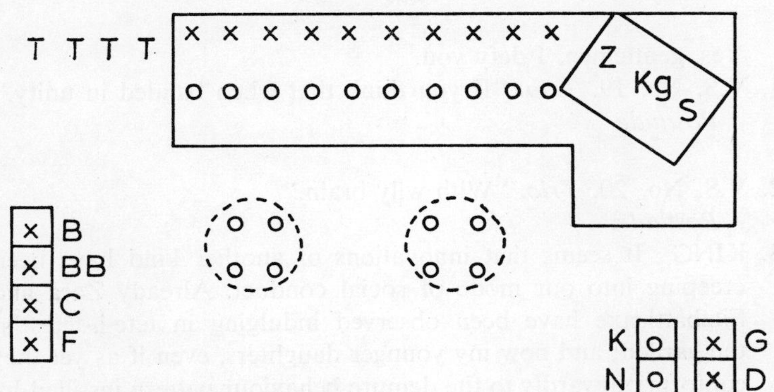

Eight ladies perform a courtly dance.
Dancers bow to King and sit on step in front of ladies, Row 2.

8. V.S. No. 17. *Recit and Chorus.* "This ceremonial"/"Eagle high."
    Recit.
    "Eagle High."
    (N.B.   Cut Postlude page of orchestral music.)
9. V.S. No. 18. *Duet.* "With fury deep we burn."
KING   No, this won't do.

10. KING   Gentlemen, gentlemen — really! This unseemly display of energy within the Royal Precincts is altogether unpardonable. I take it that you object to the reforms initiated by the Flowers of Progress. Marvellous is the power of a Civilisation which can transmute, by a word, a Limited Income, into an Income (Limited).

Of course, *you* don't like it. All your *harmless* schemes for making a provision for *your* old age are ruined. *Your* Matrimonial Agency is at a standstill, *your* Cheap Sherry business is in bankruptcy, *your* Army Clothing contracts are paralysed, and even *your* Society Paper, *The Palace Peeper*, is practically defunct. Really, gentlemen, your schemes were most irregular. However, if you will be so good as to formulate a detailed list of your grievances in writing, addressed to the Secretary of Utopia (Limited), they will be laid before the Board, in due course, at their next monthly meeting.

Yes, gentlemen, I defy you.
11. V.S. No. 19. *Trio.* "If you think that when banded in unity."
    Postlude.

12. V.S. No. 20. *Trio.* "With wily brain."
    Postlude.
13. KING   It seems that innovations of another kind have been creeping into our mode of social conduct. Already Zara and Fitzbattleaxe have been observed indulging in tête-à-têtes in the garden; and now my younger daughters, even if as yet they conform outwardly to the demure behaviour pattern instilled by Lady Sophy, have at least contrived to escape her eagle eye to keep an assignment with Mr. Goldbury and Lord Dramaleigh.

King rises.
Company rises and sing without action. All sit at the end.
Scaphio and Phantis enter melodramatically to centre. All company *freeze*, except King, who leans forward to listen.

King rises for this final line, then comes down from throne to LC.

P×   × Kg
Sc ×

King remonstrates gently.

With gravity.

With suave courtesy.

Scaphio and Phantis, beside themselves with rage, approach with shaking fists. King holds up an admonishing hand.
With quiet confidence.

King dances off L, to throne, placidly. Scaphio and Phantis remain centre, where they are joined by Tarara.
Trio performed with heads together.
All three exit R.
From throne, seated.

14. V.S. No. 21. *Song.* "A wonderful joy."
15. V.S. No. 22. *Quartet.* "Then I may sing and play."
    At the end, after dance.
16. V.S. No. 23. *Recit/Song.* "Oh would some demon power"/
    "When but a maid."
17. V.S. No. 24. *Recit.* "Ah, Lady Sophy."
18. V.S. No. 24a. *Duet.* "Oh rapture unrestrained."
    Dance.

    End of dance.
19. V.S. No. 24b. *Tarantella.*

    Last four bars.

20. V.S. No. 25. *Chorus.* "Upon our sea-girt land."
    Introduction.

    "And all is owing."
    "Down with them."

    At the end.

Goldbury and Dramaleigh lead Kalyba and Nekaya centre.

Quartet to RC back, 'talking' quietly, not observing next scene.
Sophy comes down to sing centre.

King comes down to Sophy.

Dance centre, during which Goldbury, Dramaleigh, Nekaya and Kalyba notice action and watch in amazement. Zara, having observed beginning of dance, rises in amazement and comes down to LC back, where she is joined by Fitzbattleaxe.
'Business' as in Libretto.

DN G K S Kg Z F
xo   xo   ox   ox

time for dance.

Three couples come forward to join King and Sophy in

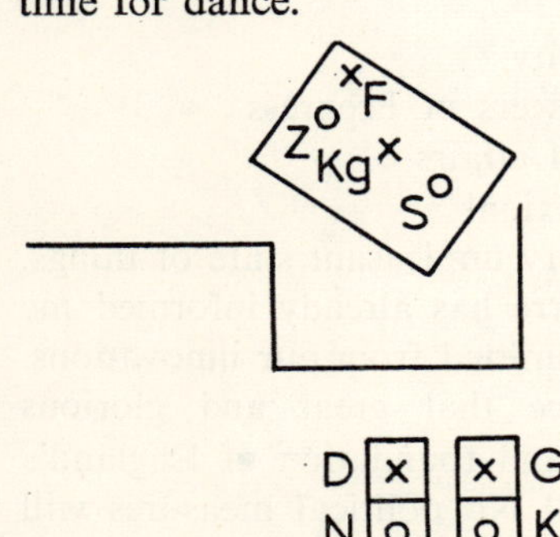

All sweep off L, fast — Zara to her seat, Fitzbattleaxe to stand behind her. King and Sophy to original seats. Kalyba and Goldbury to sit ①, ②. Nekaya and Dramaleigh to sit ③, ④.

Scaphio and Phantis and Tarara run on in great excitement, with oratorical and passion rousing gestures, going round and stirring up chorus. Male chorus rises.
Female chorus rises. Flowers of Progress rise.
Scaphio, Phantis, Tarara get yet more impassioned in their gestures. They point in time to Flowers of Progress.

Picture, with Tarara (pointing at Flowers of Progress R), Phantis (pointing at Flowers of Progress L), Scaphio (arm raised to heaven), centre stage.

x Sc
x   x
Ta   P

21. KING What means this most unmannerly irruption?
Is this your gratitude for boons conferred?
SCAPHIO Boons? Bah! A fico for such boons, say we!
These boons have brought Utopia to a standstill!
Our pride and boast — the Army and the Navy —
Have both been reconstructed and remodelled
Upon so irresistible a basis
That all the neighbouring nations have disarmed —
And War's impossible! Your County Councillor
Has passed such drastic Sanitary laws
That all the doctors dwindle, starve and die!
The laws, remodelled by Sir Bailey Barre,
Have quite extinguished crime and litigation:
The lawyers starve, and all the jails are let
As model lodgings for the working-classes!
In short —
Utopia, swamped by dull Prosperity,
Demands that these detested Flowers of Progress
Be sent about their Business, and affairs
Restored to their original complexion!
KING My daughter, this is a very unpleasant state of things.
But — all is well. Sir Bailey Barre has already informed me
of the essential element hitherto omitted from our innovations.
Government by Party! Introduce that great and glorious
element — at once the bulwark and foundation of England's
greatness — and all will be well! No political measures will
endure, because one Party will assuredly undo all that the other
Party has done; and while grouse is to be shot, and foxes
worried to death, the legislative action of the country will be
at a standstill. Then there will be sickness in plenty, endless
lawsuits, crowded jails, interminable confusion in the Army
and Navy, and, in short, general and unexampled prosperity!
ALL Ulahlica! Ulahlica!
KING Your hour has come.
Away with them, and let them wait my will.
From this moment Government by Party is adopted, with
all its attendant blessings; and henceforward Utopia will no
longer be a Monarchy Limited, but, what is a great deal better,
a Limited Monarchy!

All principals stand.
Scaphio, Phantis, Tarara turn to face King defiantly.
Scaphio delivers speech facing audience, Tarara and Phantis now both facing him (V formation).
Scaphio acts as an outraged orator, flamboyant of gesture.

Tarara and Phantis applaud him.
To Zara, quietly, but with intensity, thus quelling outburst.
Holds up an admonishing hand.

With sudden new authority to Scaphio, Phantis, Tarara.
The four Lifeguardsmen march forward and lead the three men off, R.

22. V.S. No. 26. *Finale Act II.*
    Verse 1.
    Verse 1 (chorus).
    Verse 2.

23. *End of opera.*

Kg S Z F
× o o ×

Zara sings from her position on rostrum. King leads Sophy down to centre, followed by Zara and Fitzbattleaxe.

King centre.

Full company take one bow.

Exeunt in this order: King and Sophy; Zara, Fitzbattleaxe; Dramaleigh, Nekaya; Goldbury, Kalyba; Corcoran, Bailey Barre, Blushington.

Front row ladies, single file; second row ladies partnered by men.

Suggestions for Costuming

PRINCIPALS	ACT I	ACT II
KING PARAMOUNT	Beach shorts, tee shirt, beach robe, sandals, crown.	Evening dress tails.
SCAPHIO PHANTIS *(Judges)*	Black cassocks.	Same.
TARARA *(Public Exploder)*	Red cassock.	Same.
CALYNX *(Vice-Chamberlain)*	Black cassock.	Dinner jacket (black).
DRAMALEIGH *(Lord Chamberlain)*	Formal dark suit, white shirt.	Evening dress tails.
FITZBATTLEAXE *(Army Captain)*	Dinner jacket (white), with medal ribbons.	Same.
CORCORAN *(Captain, R.N.)*	Dinner jacket (white), with medal ribbons.	Same.
GOLDBURY *(Company Promoter)*	Smart grey two-piece suit, white shirt.	Dinner jacket (black).
BAILEY BARRE *(Q.C.)*	Black jacket, pin-stripe trousers.	Evening dress tails.
BLUSHINGTON *(County Councillor)*	Cheap two-piece suit, badly matching shirt and pullover, bowler hat.	Dark two-piece suit, cheap and shiny tie.
PRINCESS ZARA	Garden party ensemble, large hat.	Ball gown (white).

PRINCESSES
  NEKAYA
  KALYBA
	Floral summer dresses.	Cocktail dresses.

LADY SOPHY	Formal tweed suit.	Dark, voluminous ball gown.

See Note on Production.
For Act I, the ladies costumes can be a mixture of short towelling beach dresses, one-piece bathing costumes and bikinis, with overlays of raffia for grass skirts, and floral garlands in a number of cases. The costumes over-layed should not be floral; the others should. Any costume with cut-outs, garish zig-zag stripes or rectangular patterns should be avoided.

CHORUS	ACT I	ACT II
MALE	Beach shorts, tee shirts, towelling shirts, sandals.	Dinner jackets (black).
TROOPERS	Dinner jackets (white).	Same.
FEMALE	See above.	Cocktail dresses.